W9-CNB-577

DISCARDED

The Chains of Interdependence

U.S. Policy Toward Central America 1945-1954

Michael L. Krenn

M.E. Sharpe
Armonk, New York
London, England

Library of Congress Cataloging-in-Publication Data

Krenn, Michael L., 1957–
The chains of interdependence : U.S. policy toward
Central America, 1945–1954 / Michael L. Krenn.
p.   cm. — (Perspectives on Latin America and the Caribbean)
Includes bibliographical references and index.
ISBN 1-56342-943-X (alk. paper)
1. Central America—Relations—United States.
2. United States—Relations—Central America.
3. United States—Foreign relations—1945–1953.
4. United States—Foreign relations 1953–1961.
5. Central America—Foreign relations. 6. Dependency.
I. Title. II. Series.
F1436.8.U6K74   1996
303.48′2730728—dc20   96-23389
CIP
Printed in the United States of America

The paper used in this publication meets the minimum requirements of
American National Standard for Information Sciences—
Permanence of Paper for Printed Library Materials,
ANSI Z 39.48-1984.

IBT (c) 10   9   8   7   6   5   4   3   2   1

Table of Contents

Acknowledgments

When I completed my first book, my colleagues glibly informed me that the second book would be easier. Now that this project is finished, those same colleagues are telling me that the *third* book will be even easier. I suppose I can take some solace in imagining that is true. At that rate, my fourth and fifth books should practically write themselves.

This book, however, did not write itself. It obstinately required a good deal of effort. Fortunately, I was aided in this project by a wide variety of colleagues, funding institutions, and archivists and librarians. I would like to take a few moments to thank those responsible for assisting in this work.

First and foremost, I wish to thank the University of Miami's Office of Research and Sponsored Programs for providing two successive summers' worth of research funding.

Second, I would like to offer my grateful thanks to the archivists and librarians at the Harry S. Truman Presidential Library, the Dwight D. Eisenhower Presidential Library, the Library of Congress Manuscript Division, the National Archives, the Council on Foreign Relations, and the Seeley G. Mudd Manuscript Library, Department of Rare Books and Special Collections.

I also need to acknowledge the input of a number of my colleagues who made the ultimate sacrifice: reading rough drafts of various parts of the manuscript and then, as tactfully as possible, making suggestions for revisions. I did not always take the suggestions, though in every case that I did, the manuscript benefited enormously. Mark Gilderhus and Robert McMahon provided extremely useful comments on early drafts of the introduction and early chapters. My doctoral advisor, Lloyd C. Gardner, found that old graduate students never fade away; they just keep asking for letters of recommendation and comments on rough drafts. Thomas Leonard read and commented on an early draft of the first chapters and listened to so many of my presentations at conferences dealing with the project that he probably *heard* more of the manuscript that anyone else. My old Rutgers mate, David Schmitz, took it upon himself to read some early writing and then read what I then considered to be a final draft. He convinced me to take one more shot at getting it right.

I would like to offer a posthumous thanks to Howard Schonberger. I met this extremely gifted scholar only once, when he served as a commentator on a panel of which I was a participant. Though the study of U.S.–Central

America relations was not his primary interest, I approached him after the session and asked if he could look over the first few chapters of the manuscript. He eagerly agreed and followed up with a meticulous review, replete with excellent suggestions and much needed words of encouragement. Just a short time later, he passed away. The profession lost not just a fine scholar, but a supreme gentleman.

Finally, I would like to thank Peter Coveney of M.E. Sharpe Inc. for fortuitously dropping by my office last year and suggesting that I might send this manuscript to Stephen Dalphin. Working with Steve and the M.E. Sharpe staff, particularly Esther L. Clark and Christine Florie, was a true pleasure.

I'm not sure that thanks are sufficient for my wife, Corinne Graff–Krenn, and my children, Annaleah, Madelinne, and Summer. After approximately four years of my being consumed by this project, however, it is about the best I can offer.

The Chains of Interdependence

Introduction

Challenges and Possibilities

In the last few years, the American people have been bombarded with descriptions of the "new" world in which they live. We now live in a "global village," in which goods, people, and ideas intermingle with little regard for national borders and identities. Interdependence is the new buzzword used by the pundits to explain this development. The end of the Cold War has called forth a new beginning for the world's people. In its most dramatic (and slightly ominous) characterization, it has been referred to as the "new world order."

It might surprise the American people (and perhaps even the pundits) to know that such talk is not new. Nearly fifty years ago, following World War II, Washington was abuzz with exactly the same term as it is today—interdependence. To better understand exactly what that term means in its historical sense, it behooves us to reexamine that tumultuous period in American history. What were the ideas behind interdependence? What was it supposed to accomplish? And, since the new calls for interdependence seem to indicate that it didn't succeed, why did it fail?

The world had dramatically changed. As World War II came to a close, U.S. policymakers were unanimous on that point. The changes went beyond those resulting from the death and destruction directly relating to the conflagration of war, although no one doubted that the level of mayhem had reached nearly unimaginable proportions. It went beyond the new technologies of annihilation, though there was no denying the awe and fear created by those mushroom clouds over Japan. The changes were of a more fundamental sort. The war had changed the *world*. It was now discussed in terms of its smallness; of how it had "shrunk," as though the war, through its very destructiveness, had literally blown vast chunks of it away. New methods of communication and transportation were partly responsible for the use of such terms. In more basic language, however, what they were referring to was that the complex intermeshing of economics, politics, and societies on a *world* level which had been taking place since at least the early twentieth century meant that *nations* could no longer see themselves as purely autonomous players. Trade—a vast marketplace of imports and exports—spanned the globe, involving all nations and people. Such trade had engendered more intensive political interchanges between nations, as alliances, defensive treaties, tariff agreements, and so forth were carefully put into place to cement the economic relationships. And the exchange of goods was resulting, more and more, in an exchange of people, as citizens of one nation more frequently visited another, sometimes to seek even more trading possibilities, sometimes simply to see how other peoples lived their lives.

World War II had demonstrated how fragile that developing system had been. Jealousy, fear, greed, lust for power, and national rivalries—some ancient, some of more recent vintage—had torn the prewar world to shreds. What would now replace it? It was to answering that monumental question that U.S. officials quickly turned their attention.

Adding a sense of urgency to such considerations was the developing Cold War. Fears of Soviet expansionism and worldwide meddling pervaded the high-level policy discussions among U.S. officials. The Soviet Union, after all, did pose a solution to the postwar world's problems, with its promises of a better future through communism. That the United States, with its long history of capitalist entrepreneurship and defense of private property, found little of value in such a system was not surprising. Yet, they worried that the sirens' song of communism might find receptive audiences in the war-torn countries of Europe, as well as among peoples in Asia, Africa, and Latin America who were slowly breaking free of years of colonialism and/or underdevelopment. Soviet adventurism would have to be contained.[1]

Though there is little doubt that U.S. policymakers faced formidable challenges after World War II, both in the form of the massive destruction caused by the conflict and the threat posed by the Soviet Union, it would be erroneous to conclude that those policymakers sought merely to rebuild the world or simply protect it once it was reconstructed. U.S. officials saw a world to be *remade*; U.S. policies, therefore, would be proactive rather than reactive. Their belief that this could be accomplished was understandable. The United States had not, of course, been immune to the destructive forces of the war. No one could deny, however, that in relative terms, it had been virtually unscathed. Its wartime casualties, while just as tragic, were slight when compared to those of any of the other major warring powers. Its civilian population had not suffered bombings, sieges, famine, or major disruption. The industrial base of the country, far from being laid to waste, had expanded during the war. The nation's government continued to run smoothly, even taking the death of its wartime leader—Franklin D. Roosevelt—in mournful stride. By almost any measurements possible, the United States had emerged from World War II as the strongest nation in the world, perhaps in history.

And from their position of incredible power and wealth, U.S. policy-makers makers looked to not simply rebuild the world; they would improve as they went. Their rhetoric reflected the ideals and goals they set—democracy for all peoples, an end to militarism and the repression and threat to peace it brought, economic advancement for every nation. It would be a world in which war and revolution would no longer be necessary (or tolerated). Freedom, peace, and prosperity—ideals the American people had lived with for years—would be brought to the peoples of the world, weary from decades of oppression, war, and want. Especially would this hold true for the population of the underdeveloped world.

The word most used to describe this grand notion of remaking the world was "interdependence." In the eyes of U.S. officials, the world (at least the noncommunist world) had been inextricably brought closer together. The war itself had not served so much as a catalyst for this closeness; more so, it had served as a symbol of its necessity. The world economy had become so intertwined that it was sometmes difficult to separate the individual national strands. Nations produced, sold, and bought their goods in a giant world marketplace. And in the period after the war, this was more necessary than ever. The industrialized nations needed the markets and raw materials of the underdeveloped world; the latter needed the consumer goods, investments, and technology that the former could provide. This interdependent world market meant progress and prosperity for all. For the United States, of course, it meant the securing of postwar markets for its enlarged industrial plant and sources of raw materials to feed its industrial engine. For the other industrialized nations, it was the pathway to redevelopment and a return to their former standards of living. And for the underdeveloped world, it offered the best hope for eventual economic development and more self-sufficiency. Taken as a whole (as it had to be), the system would also provide a solid bulwark against communism.

The same held true in the military and political fields. The second of the century's world wars might not be the last, and as it had shown, there was little room for neutrality in global conflicts. Even the United States, with its fantastic war machine, could not safeguard the entire planet or police every nation. Each country would have to shoulder some of the burden, in protecting both their borders from external aggression and their societies from internal subversion and disorder. The safety and stability provided by mutual defense agreements (an interdependent military system) would allow all nations to develop and prosper. Politically, the United States sensed a growing demand for social justice, freedom, and government responsibility among the world's people. For its policy-makers, this was evidence of a general acceptance of U.S. ideals of democracy and liberalism. The war had served as symbolic in this regard—the moral (as well as the military) might of the world's democracies had triumphed over fascism, totalitarianism, and repression. Such ideals, if allowed to flourish everywhere, would enable people to prosper, and would do away with the need for war and revolution as resolutions for international or national problems.

Economic, political, and military interdependence; a world of free trade prosperity, safety from war and revolt, and guided by the principles of democracy and freedom—these were the ideas that flowed forth in the rhetoric of U.S. officials. In a way, of course, this kind of thinking was hardly new to the United States. America as a "city upon a hill," fulfilling its Manifest Destiny, making the world "safe for democracy," and serving as the "arsenal of democracy"—all were images as old as the nation. In that image, the United States served as world benefactor, bringing its ideals—which had worked such miracles within its own borders—to all peoples. Of course, the history of American "beneficence" in this regard had not always been a happy one. A legacy of interventions and barely concealed imperialism existed prior to the war.

It also sounded a great deal like the rhetoric trumpeted after World War I. And in some ways, it was. Yet, the horror of World War II pushed many U.S. officials to realize that mere "cheerleading" for such a system of interdependence was not enough. The United States would now have to take a much more active role, and the system, once established, would have to be much more institutionalized and permanent.

There were, however, two major differences between those older references to the American "mission" and the new musings about interdependence after World War II.   First, interdependence—in its ideal form—meant nations truly working *together*. In other words, salvation for the world would not come from the United States simply imposing its will (as well intentioned as such imposition might be). Woodrow Wilson's approach to Latin American problems, for example—in which he would "teach" them to elect good men—was no longer applicable. Why this was so is found in the second difference: interdependence was a tacit acceptance by U.S. officials that their nation *needed* other nations. Certainly, the United States had something to give the other nations of the world, and it was hoped that those nations would recognize that fact. On the other hand, they had something to give the United States (whether in terms of raw materials and markets, alliances, and so forth). A more give-and-take relationship would have to come about if the United States was to assure their cooperation.

The theory of interdependence assumed economic, political, and military connections between all nations (excepting those behind the Iron Curtain, of course). But for many U.S. officials, its greatest contribution would be in terms of what it would mean for the nations in the underdeveloped world—Asia, Africa, and Latin America. The United States needed what these nations had to offer—their markets, resources, strategic positions, votes in the United Nations, and any other assistance they might provide. Yet, these nations so desperately needed what the United States had—capital, technology, military capacity for protection, and democratic ideals of freedom and justice. Here were regions where interdependence could really work wonders, with the greatest, richest, most powerful nation on earth working shoulder to shoulder with small, poor, powerless countries and peoples to build what more than one U.S. official referred to as a "better world."

By the mid-1950s, however, the reality of U.S. policies of interdependence for those underdeveloped regions seemed to make a mockery of such rhetoric. Promises of democracy and freedom, peace and anti-militarism, and economic development had degenerated into support of dictators, the supply and training of often brutal military forces, and economic programs that seemed to perpetuate exploitation and stagnation. What had happened? Was talk of interdependence merely rhetoric—words empty of conviction, put forth simply for the consumption of the U.S. and world public? Were the goals just too lofty; so idealistic as to be incapable of being reached? Or did other challenges—specifically the threat of the Soviet Union—force U.S. policymakers to contradict their goals in the interest of national survival? The answers to these questions are important, for on them hangs an understanding of exactly what U.S. foreign policy makers wanted to accomplish in the postwar world.

As this study will suggest, none of those explanations adequately explain why the U.S. talk of an ideal interdependence failed to result in a better world. Certainly, some of the U.S. foreign policy rhetoric was just that—words, often spoken off the cuff or in the heat of the moment. Nevertheless, one cannot read through the thousands upon thousands of pages of documents produced by policymakers during those years without coming to the conclusion that for the vast majority of them, the rhetoric was sincere (at least when first uttered). There was no conspiracy to conceal the "true" intent of U.S. policy from either the domestic or foreign audiences.

Nor did the rhetoric, at least in its generalized form, reflect goals so Olympian in nature as to be unattainable. The United States did not have the power to simply put the world together in any fashion it wished, like some global set of building blocks. Yet, in terms of aiding the development of the ideals which it espoused, it had significant powers of suggestion (and, sometimes, even more than that). The balance sheet of what the United States *did* accomplish during those hectic years—and one does not have to view those accomplishments positively to appreciate their magnitude—is surely testimony to this conclusion.

And finally, we cannot simply blame the extraordinary challenge posed by the Soviet Union for the apparent contradictions between U.S. words and deeds. Defenders of U.S. policy have argued that the nation's intentions were good, but the overriding need to combat the insidious spread of communism forced the United States to use methods which sometimes betrayed U.S. ideals. Critics charge that U.S. officials wholeheartedly embraced the ideology of anticommunism, believing that the policies used to support it would best protect U.S. interests. As we shall see, however, U.S. policymakers *knew* that there were other, and even more efficient methods than the support of anticommunist dictators, the supplying of repressive, pro–American militaries, and ineffective programs of economic development for battling the communist threat. Yet, their acceptance of the benefits and the necessity of interdependent economic, political, and military systems compelled them to ignore those alternatives. In short, interdependence was not a reaction to Soviet expansionism. Indeed, it may have hindered a more positive reaction.

This study will examine the development of the ideas behind the theory of interdependence during the first decade after World War II, specifically on how it would impact on U.S. relations with the underdeveloped world. By focusing on the specific application of the policies designed to construct interdependent economic, political, and military relations with the nations of Central America, we will see, first, how U.S. officials defined interdependence and what they wanted it to accomplish; second, how they went about trying to accomplish their goals; and third, why the high ideals behind interdependence were eroded and compromised.

Considering all of the excitement going on in other parts of the world during that time, this choice of focus may surprise some.[2] It is certainly true that in the frenzy of activity in that period some areas of the world tended to attract less attention than others. With Europe and the Far East to be reconstructed, and with the emerging nations of Africa and Asia to be watched and worried over, it is not shocking that Central America commanded relatively little interest among high-ranking U.S. officials. The papers of Harry S. Truman, Dean Acheson, Dwight Eisenhower, and John Foster Dulles do not dwell at length on the five nations of that region. Indeed, until the Guatemalan "crisis" of 1953–1954, Central America hardly existed for them at all.[3]

Exist it did, however, and the job of putting U.S. policies into practice there devolved upon the pertinent officials and staffs of the State, Commerce, Treasury, and War (later Defense) departments, the Central Intelligence Agency (CIA), and various interdepartmental committees, agencies, and programs devised during those years. The high idealism of U.S. statements concerning interdependence seemed superbly suited for the region. Believed to be brimming with natural resources and potential markets, strategically located, and—to varying degrees—supportive of many U.S. ideals, but also long prey to dictators and repression, politically unstable, pathetically underdeveloped, with a population largely illiterate, underfed, and undereducated, Central America provided U.S. officials with an excellent area in which to put interdependence into practice. And since the area was already so closely tied to the United States in economic, military, and political terms, the task would be that much easier. Yet, by 1954, it was here that the contradictions between U.S. rhetoric and actual policy became painfully, and almost immediately, apparent. United States support for dictators such as Nicaragua's Anastasio Somoza, its equipping and training of harshly repressive military forces such as in Honduras and El Salvador, and its seemingly exploitative economic policies belied the ideals that its officials often sprinkled through their speeches. And it was here that U.S. officials debated, discussed, analyzed, wrestled with, and, ultimately, failed to come to grips with the seemingly inherent contradictions posed by their concept of interdependence.

It may also surprise some that this work treats the period 1945–1954 as whole cloth, failing to address the "differences" between the policies of the Truman and Eisenhower administrations toward Latin American. Robert R. Bowie, who served as a major figure in State Department policy planning from 1953 to 1957, came to these conclusions concerning those differences:

> the strategy which was in fact adopted, the broad line of policy, was not greatly different from that under the Truman Administration. And I don't think it could be, because fundamentally, those basic lines of policy. . .were the product of the external conditions, as they were perceived, and the American sense of its interests, which really weren't partisan. . . . There really wasn't much room for great change.[4]

"Change," such as it was, was not due to dramatic differences in perceptions or modes of doing things between the two administrations, but rather to the dawning realization that interdependence—at least as it was first put forward—was not really working as planned in Central America. As U.S. officials came face to face with the contradictions between their rhetoric and U.S. actions, there were discernible shifts and reorderings. Yet, all of this began to occur in the last years of the Truman presidency; the contradictions had merely become more clear by the time Eisenhower came to office and the necessary readjustments became more institutionalized. Interdependence continued to be a key element in U.S. policy.

In the end, U.S. policymakers had to face the fact that the contradictions they encountered were largely self-imposed and were, ironically, direct results of their pursuit of interdependence. They quickly discovered that some of the goals of interdependence clashed with the interests of the United States. Other goals seemed to face challenges from the very people in the underdeveloped world they were designed to aid, and U.S. officials soon found themselves in the awkward position of "imposing" democracy or using repression to stifle popular movements. Finally, other goals were imprisoned by U.S. perceptions of the peoples of the underdeveloped world who were to be worked with; "exceptions" to the ideals of interdependence were explained in terms of cultural and racial qualifications.

And when all was said and done, U.S. officials also had to come to grips with a painful reality—they could not shape the changes affecting the world to fit their own views of interdependence. It was not that they were ignorant of such changes; indeed, they often keenly perceived them. The breakup of colonial empires, the growth of nationalism and the rising tide of expectation in the underdeveloped nations, and the development of new economic, social, and political forces in those countries were events grasped, if not entirely understood, by U.S. statesmen. In seeking to guide such changes down pathways cleared and defined by the U.S. ideal of interdependence, however, they instead found themselves increasingly bogged down in a dense jungle of contradictions; so dense, in fact, that by 1954 and the overthrow of the Guatemalan government, the idealistic foundation of interdependence had been all but lost in tough, cynical talk of "national security."

The world is again in the midst of great change. "Evil empires" have collapsed; previously impenetrable walls have come down; new and amazing improvements in communication and transportation seemingly bind the world together in ways never imagined. Scholarly debate on multiculturalism and diversity promises to break through old ethnic and racial barriers, bringing the world's peoples to new heights of understanding and acceptance. Of course, we are reminded, much remains to be done. Religious and ethnic conflicts still rage throughout the world. Old stereotypes and national hatreds simmer beneath the surface, often erupting. There is still much that the "haves" can do for the "have nots." The answer seems simple enough: in our "smaller" world (even smaller than the world of 1945) nations must work together. Interdependence; the global village; a new world order—the years immediately after World War II revealed the tremendous possibilities inherent in those images. Yet, as the United States finds itself once again hastening to proclaim a new interdependence and as U.S. troops attempt to physically enforce it in nations such as Haiti, Somalia, and Bosnia, it should be borne in mind that they also revealed that the problems facing the world—no matter how small it may get—are not often given to simple, all-encompassing answers.

Notes

1.   The literature on the beginnings of the Cold War is vast. The best over-view is Melvyn P. Leffler's, *A Preponderance of Power: National Security, the Truman Administration, and the Cold War, 1945–1952* (Stanford, 1992).

2.   The scholarly work on the topic of U.S. relations with Central America in the postwar decade is quite limited. Thomas M. Leonard, *The United States and Central America, 1944–1949: Perceptions of Political Dynamics* (University, AL, 1984) is the most useful starting place. Leonard provides a nation-by-nation discussion of U.S. views of political changes in the five Central American countries. He argues that the United States was merely an "observer" of Central America during those years and generally "ignored" the region. An appendix contains a valuable thumbnail sketches of the U.S. diplomats concerned with the region. Two monographs that cover the entire breadth of U.S.–Central American relations also need to be consulted. Walter LaFeber, *Inevitable Revolutions: The United States in Central America* (New York, 1984), is a marvel ous synthesis. In its desire to demonstrate continuity in U.S. policy toward Central America, however, it loses sight of some important differences in that policy following World War II. This must be supplemented, however, with Leonard's recent book, *Central America and the United States: The Search for Stability* (Athens, GA, 1991). Claiming that the "overriding consideration" in U.S. policy toward that region after World War II was the communist menace, he concludes that the United States "supported the old order" (xv). Most other works on U.S. relations with Latin America after the war treat Central America only peripherally: Stephen Rabe, *Eisenhower and Latin America: The Foreign Policy of Anticommunism* (Chapel Hill, NC, 1988); David Green, *The Containment of Latin America: A History of the Myths and Realities of the Good Neighbor Policy* (Chicago, 1971); Bryce Wood, *The Dismantling of the Good Neighbor Policy* (Austin, 1985); Gaddis Smith, *The Last Years of the Monroe Doctrine, 1945–1993* (New York, 1994), and F. Parkinson, *Latin America, the Cold War, and the World Powers, 1945–1973* (Beverly Hills, 1974), for example, concentrate on U.S. relations with the more powerful nations of that region—Brazil, Argentina, Mexico, and Chile—though all look, in varying detail, at the Guatemalan crisis.

3.   For the Guatemalan episode, see Richard Immerman, *The CIA in Guate-mala: The Foreign Policy of Intervention* (Austin, 1982); Stephen Kinzer and Stephen Schlesinger, *Bitter Fruit: The Untold Story of the American Coup in Guatemala* (Garden City, NY, 1983); Piero Gleijeses, *Shattered Hope: The Guatemalan Revolution and the United States, 1944–1954* (Princeton, 1991); and Blanche Wiesen Cook, *The Declassified Eisenhower: A Divided Legacy* (Garden City, NY, 1981), Chs. VI and VII.

4.   Robert R. Bowie, Oral History, 10 Aug. 1967, p. 29, Dwight D. Eisen-hower Library, Abilene, Kansas (hereafter DDEL).

1

The Chains of Interdependence

After World War II, the attention of U.S. policymakers was focused on the immediate problems caused by the conflict: the reconstruction of Europe and the rehabilitation and rebuilding of Japan.[1] Other areas of U.S. concern were the underdeveloped nations, specifically the colonial possessions of their wartime allies, where nationalist wars of liberation were either under way or beginning to flicker to life.[2] Compared with the often dramatic U.S. policy initiatives in these areas its diplomatic efforts in regards to Latin America appear slight. A number of historians have noted that Latin American issues were always secondary to those involving Europe and Asia.[3] This has often led to the assumption that U.S. policy toward Latin America in the first decade or so after the war was basically one of treading water. As Walter LaFeber has put it, the U.S. attitude, specifically in regard to Central America, was simply one of "maintaining the system," one based on the continued dependent political and economic status of Central America.[4]

Such analyses are misleading, for they suggest that U.S. policy toward Latin America after World War II was basically a continuation of earlier efforts. And since the region was relatively crisis-free, there seemed little reason to try new programs or announce new goals. In fact, however, U.S. policymakers were aware that the war had made any thoughts of simply "maintaining the system" obsolete. Since the late nineteenth century, the United States had taken a more and more commanding position in the hemisphere. The views of the Latin Americans were not often taken into consideration.

World War II changed that viewpoint. The United States still viewed itself as the commanding presence in the hemisphere, but its position was no longer unchallenged. The war had demonstrated that while oceans made good shields from attack, the advanced technology of warfare meant that no area of the world was entirely safe from predatory enemies. Another change had been in the very basis of the U.S. relation to Latin America. That relationship had usually been predicated on the assumption that the Latin Americans "needed" the United States—for protection, for capital, for "advancement." Yet the war had revealed the tremendous need the United States had for Latin America. For raw materials, for strategic air and military bases, for "cooperation," Latin America assumed a new value. It also acquired more of a voice in demanding different things from the United States. The leaders of that region made it clear that they expected reciprocal benefits after the war—more military and economic aid, more recognition of their viewpoint in hemispheric affairs. And the very fact that the nations of Argentina and, to a lesser extent, Chile had not given their full support to U.S. efforts indicated that the United States would have to either get a bigger stick or reevaluate its policies.   In this very different situation, many U.S. policymakers believed that their nation could not (and should not) be content with reestablishing the status quo antebellum. The changes brought about by the war indicated that revisions of the "system" were inevitable.[5]

All of this did not mean *radical* change. What it did mean was that U.S. policymakers would not be content to merely "maintain the system." They would reinforce what was beneficial, improve what was inefficient, remove what was inappropriate. The results, if U.S. initiatives were properly received, would be a hemisphere of political freedom, economic prosperity, and safety from the terror of war or the encroachments of communism.

In the following pages, the economic, political, and military goals of U.S. policymakers in terms of Latin America will be examined. The more specific goals in regards to Central America will be highlighted.

A Workable, Stable, and Productive Economic System

A 1949 report by the State Department's Policy Planning Staff (PPS) laid out the economic goals of the United States as being "to create a workable, stable and productive economic system among the free nations of the world," in which each could "sell abroad those goods and services which it can most efficiently produce and . . . purchase from other countries those goods and services which it can least efficiently produce."[6]

Although the United States emerged from the war as the most powerful economic force on earth, such power could not be maintained without strenuous effort. According to the Department of Commerce, the most immediate economic problem for the nation after 1945 was that of converting a wartime economy—"sustained by the overriding governmental demand for goods and services"—to one "again dependent upon the extent and character of private demand." Officials worried about the problems that might accompany this necessary redirection of the economy. Some of these, such as "paralyzing industrial disputes" and "damaging delays in production," were already evident by 1946 and would undoubtedly continue: "The continuing rise in prices, the probability of new wage demands, the uneven provision of the components of production were all elements of the economic problems which faced the business community and the Nation."[7] For some officials, such as economic advisor Lincoln Gordon, it was a situation reminiscent of an earlier time: "The problem was how to . . . avoid the kind of terrible postwar recession, or depression, which had followed World War I. . . . all of us . . . were very conscious of the great depression, very much worried about unemployment and about sliding back into the sort of situation that we had emerged from at the beginning of the war."[8]

In looking for solutions, U.S. policymakers were adamant about the necessity of reestablishing and enlarging the nation's foreign trade. Even before the end of the war, the Bureau of Foreign and Domestic Commerce (BFDC) had produced a report entitled "Industries Needing New Markets (Export) at the End of the War." Nearly twenty-five industries, including aircraft, car, and shipbuilding, chemicals, steel, lumber, drugs, and agricultural machinery, were mentioned as needing export markets to ease the transition to peacetime production.[9] Little had changed by the end of the conflict, as Commerce cited the need for foreign trade expansion in "establishing the markets for American products which shall supplement domestic demand and create the atmosphere for healthy economic development." Specifically, it noted that, "The postwar market requirement of business is for a volume of consumption half again as large in real terms as prewar sales."[10]

The problem, however, was not simply one of producing products for sale on the world market. Demand would most certainly be there; until national economies around the globe recovered, the United States would be the leading source of industrial production. The rub came in finding the means for those economies to purchase U.S. goods. Western Europe was in shambles. Its own industrial base had been leveled, and its links with profit-producing colonies in Asia and Africa, as well as its long-established trade with areas such as Latin America, had been strained to the breaking point.[11] One solution had been the Marshall Plan which, as explained by Assistant Secretary of Commerce Thomas C. Blaisdell, Jr., "was in part a substitute for the dollars which were formerly earned in the Far East by exports to the United States."[12]

As Blaisdell indicated, however, the Marshall Plan was simply a substitute. A more permanent answer lay in reconnecting Western Europe with its former markets, letting it earn money through trade with Asia, Africa, and Latin America. That money, in turn, could then purchase U.S. goods—certainly a "workable, stable and productive" system for all.[13]

Reviving Western Europe would not only help U.S. exports, but would also aid in rebuilding economies in the underdeveloped world. And those regions, even more so than Europe, were essential to the well-being of the U.S. economy. A Department of Agriculture study in 1950 pointed out that Europe was steadily declining as a U.S. market. From a high of 80 percent in the 1880s, by the postwar years Europe was taking just 35 percent of all U.S. exports (and that total was expected to fall during the 1950s). The slack would have to be taken up by the non-European world.[14]

The problem, once again, lay in insuring the purchasing power of the underdeveloped nations. While some areas, such as Latin America, had achieved sizeable dollar reserves during the war, those had declined rapidly after the conflict. The solution seemed a simple one: buy more products from the underdeveloped world so that it might in turn buy more products from the United States. As one report put it, "a large volume of imports, plus expanded travel abroad, provide the only enduring means of supplying the dollar exchange necessary for additional exports. . . . this is a new departure in United States trade promotion which heretofore was focused on exports."[15]

While not an entirely "new departure" (many U.S. policymakers were making the same point after World War I), it is evident that U.S. officials were acutely concerned over the question of imports of products, specifically raw materials, from the non-European nations.[16] Such imports were increasingly viewed as essential to the functioning of the U.S. domestic economy. The International Development Advisory Board

(IDAB) claimed that "we get from them [underdeveloped countries] 73% of the strategic and critical materials we import—tin, tungsten, chrome, manganese, lead, zinc, copper—without which many of our most vital industries could not operate." And as the President's Materials Policy Commission (PMPC) noted in 1951, U.S. demand for raw materials was increasing, and not just as a result of increased defense needs: "Even in the absence of large defense expenditures our material requirements will grow with the increase in our real national income."[17]

The U.S. purchase of raw materials from the underdeveloped nations would serve the interests of both. The United States would secure the vital natural resources essential to its industries; the producers of those resources would take in U.S. dollars with which to purchase U.S.-made consumer goods. But the benefits would not stop there. By encouraging the expansion of both the export and import capabilities of the non-European world, the United States would also be aiding its allies. A study of the President's Commission on Foreign Economic Policy (known as the Randall Commission) observed that, "Many of the nations of the North Atlantic Alliance, most conspicuously perhaps Great Britain and Western Germany, and in addition our potential political ally in the Orient, Japan, require expanding markets for their industrial output and expanding sources of their supplies of foodstuffs and industrial raw materials."[18]

In this way, U.S. economic policy overlapped with political and even military concerns. The system would also hold the free world together while staving off challenges from the communist threat. As described by President Truman, "economic development is the spearhead of the forces of freedom. The building of military strength is not enough to win the peace we seek. We must press the attack in the battle of raising the living standards and fulfilling the hopes of mankind for a better future." The Department of Defense stated that, "Mutual trade is, therefore, essential to attract and hold allies. Mutual trade can be channelled to make us and our allies strong, and, by helping to raise our allies' standard of living, expand the mass markets required for our own—as well as our allies'—economic growth. . . . a strong, vigorous and competitive U.S. economy is the foundation upon which the military and economic strength of the free world rest."[19]

Given the apparently interlocking nature of this mutual trade, it was not surprising to find many in the United States commenting on this new interdependence. A policy statement adopted by the National Foreign Trade Council in 1951 summed up the issue:

The development of rapid communication and transportation, and the increasing trend toward industrialization everywhere, have made all nations economically interdependent. The state of our domestic economy, with its vast and ever-expanding capacity to produce and consume, has become of tremendous importance to the economic well-being of the rest of the world. Our own economy, in turn, has become increasingly dependent upon raw materials produced in other lands, and the availability of these raw materials in adequate quantities is a vital factor in our own capacity to produce and consume. It is imperative that our foreign economic policy recognize the interdependence of the economies of the free nations.[20]

Not only was it imperative, it was also quite logical. John Stambaugh, who worked with the Foreign Operations Administration (FOA) during the Eisenhower administration, recalled that, "Basically the theory was this, that the world was becoming very interdependent and getting smaller every day, and that, in the long run, the law of comparative advantage was bound to work."[21] The comparative advantage idea Stambaugh was referring to was based on a simple premise: nations should turn out those materials or products they can most efficiently produce. Why should an underdeveloped nation, rich in natural resources, turn its energies to manufacturing? It was "comparatively advantageous" to sell its raw materials and buy the consumer goods it needed from the developed nations.

It was within this complex tapestry of a mutually beneficial, interdependent free world economy that U.S. policymakers considered their postwar economic aims toward Latin America. That region had not been devastated by war, and therefore did not need to be "reconstructed." And unlike the underdeveloped areas of Asia and Africa, many of which had been in the grip of colonialism for years, Latin America had a long history of close economic contacts with the United States. This did not mean, however, that Latin America was ignored by U.S. officials. Untouched by the direct ravages of World War II, that region had nevertheless felt its economic repercussions and dislocations; these would need to be addressed if it were to be profitably and efficiently meshed with the free world economy.

"The significant economic aspects of the present situation all reflect the degree of economic interdependence between the United States and Latin America. The United States looks to Latin America for the production of certain strategic materials essential to defense mobilization. The Latin

Americans look to the United States as the principal market for their production . . . and as the source of industrial production on which they depend for the maintenance of their economies."[22] Such was the conclusion reached in a briefing book prepared for President Truman in 1951. It reflected the view of most U.S. policymakers that the U.S. economic relationship with Latin America was an extraordinary example of interdependence.

During the postwar years, Latin America was seen as a vital component of the interdependent world economic system. The reestablishment of European trade with that region was deemed essential to the recovery of U.S. allies. More important were the area's links with the United States. As a 1949 State Department report noted, "we need a market for our exports—Latin America offers untold possibilities." Citing the importance of Latin America as a source of raw materials, the memo concluded that, "We need markets and more markets and Europe does not offer sufficient prospect in the near future. We should not neglect our own part of the world which offers almost unlimited possibilities of development."[23]

These possibilities soon became reality. In 1950 the United States imported nearly $2.9 billion worth of products from Latin America (35 percent of total U.S. imports that year). At the same time, the United States was sending $2.7 billion worth of exports to Latin America (50 percent of the area's total imports). That latter figure compared very favorably with U.S. exports to Western Europe in 1950, which amounted to only $200 million more. Latin America was also serving as a magnet for U.S. private investments. By 1950, the United States had invested nearly $6 billion in the region, as compared with only $4.6 billion invested outside of the Western Hemisphere (excluding Canada).[24]

The composition of U.S.–Latin American trade was also well within the parameters of the ideal interdependent relationship between an industrialized and underdeveloped area. Of U.S. exports to Latin America, machinery and vehicles amounted to $1.1 billion. Latin America absorbed 44 percent of U.S. automobile and 30 percent of all machinery exports. It also imported 40 percent of U.S. textile exports ($209 million), 38 percent of chemical exports ($224 million), and 40 percent of iron and steel advanced manufactures ($345 million). Such products made up 75 percent of U.S. exports to Latin America.[25]

On the other side of the coin, raw materials and agricultural products made up the lion's share of Latin American exports to the United States. Coffee was the main item, accounting for $778 million of Latin American exports. Sugar, petroleum, copper, lead, cocoa beans, bananas, and tin accounted for a good deal of the rest. While sugar, coffee, and bananas were big moneymakers (and, as one State Department report noted, "any disruption in the import" of such products "would have extremely serious consequences throughout the United States"), the primary U.S. interest lay in the vital and strategic raw materials Latin America could provide. The following resources (with percentage provided by Latin America in parentheses) give an idea as to the importance of imports from that region: vanadium (100 percent), castor oil and quartz crystals (95 percent), crude petroleum and fuel oil, cordage sisal, vegetable tannin materials (80 percent); antimony, cadmium, and copper (60 percent); beryl, bismuth, and lead (50 percent), "and a significant part of our imports of chromite, manila fibers, fluorspar, manganese, tin, wool, and zinc." Mexico provided 34 percent of graphite imports; Brazil, 68 percent of menthol imports; and Colombia, 73 percent of imports of ipecac.[26]

While Latin America as a whole conducted 44 percent of its international trade with the United States, Central America was even more closely bound to its northern neighbor. Each of the five Central American nations sent from half to over 70 percent of their exports to the United States; the same figures held true for their imports. And, despite the popular view which saw these nations as "banana republics," they also were the producers of a number of more strategic materials. Guatemala, for example, produced 20 percent of U.S. imports of cinchona (a source of quinine) and, along with Costa Rica and Panama, was responsible for 15 percent of the free world's abaca production. A 1952 study by the Technical Cooperation Administration (TCA) pointed out the great potential for increased raw material production in Central America. Already, the area was producing limited amounts of antimony, chromite, copper, lead, mica, rubber, sisal, and zinc.[27]

In this case, at least, numbers did not seem to lie. The economic interdependence between the United States and Latin America was a reality. As a National Security Council (NSC) memorandum stated in 1954, "The *mutual advantage* is inherent in this situation since not only do the Latin Americans have something clearly to gain from us but we have, as well, something clearly to gain from them." What the Latin Americans would get from the United States would be "hope for the future well-being of the Latins," which would be accomplished by the United States, "taking its men, money and materials into Latin American countries where they can be put to work in a mutually advantageous partnership with the Latin

Americans." Perhaps the "good neighbors" were becoming the "good partners."[28]

Hopes for "future well-being" would have seemed particularly applicable to the nations of Central America. According to economic data compiled by the United States, that region was pathetically poor and underdeveloped. A 1944 economic comparison with the other nations of Latin America demonstrated that, with the exception of Costa Rica, the countries of Central America ranked below average in nearly every area of measurement. Perhaps more revealing was a study prepared in 1952, comparing Central America to other less developed regions. All five nations (except Costa Rica) were just above the average for per capita income. All were below the average of percent of males in non-agricultural work. And, excepting Honduras, all had a higher birth rate (which, when combined with their substantially lower death rate, indicated future problems with population size). This study also compared Central American data with that from "more developed regions." Per capita income for the more developed areas was $690; for Central America (Costa Rica included), the average was $94. In every other field— consumption of non-human energy, percent of males in non-agricultural work, infant mortality, life expectancy, crop yields, calories per person per day, persons per physician, illiteracy, and number of teachers— Central America lagged far behind.[29] If interdependence could work economic miracles, here was an area waiting for them.

A World Shrinking in Time and Space

> Today, in a world shrinking in time and space, our experience in three foreign wars in less than half a century and the persistent threat of Communist power in many parts of the earth demonstrate the need for collective action with nations which share our aspirations for world peace. It is to meet this need that our collective security programs have been designed. In building strength an association of those who believe in collective action is of first importance. The United States—with only 6 percent of the world's population—needs the aid of other countries just as they need our assistance.[30]

Though written in 1957, this statement from a report of the President's Citizen Advisers on the Mutual Security Program (the Fairless Committee) aptly sums up the view of U.S. policymakers concerning the need for collective defense arrangements following World War II. In its imagery it echoed those same policymakers' views on economic interdependence. Indeed, as we shall see, economic and military interdependence often overlapped.

Having worldwide economic interests and links after World War II meant that the United States also had to adopt a worldwide defense network to defend those interests. A PPS report of 1949 stated what seemed to be obvious to many policymakers: "U.S. security and welfare are closely bound up with the peace and security of the world community. Aggression, anywhere, may jeopardize the security of the U.S."[31] Such thinking underlay the U.S. support and/or membership in the numerous regional defense organizations which sprang up after the war. As U.S. officials in the NSC realized, however, the glue that would hold these defense lines together would be assistance from the United States: "[I]f they [other "free nations"] are to develop stronger military capabilities it is essential that their own efforts be effectively coordinated and be supplemented by assistance in the form of military supplies, equipment and technical advice from the United States."[32]

Arguing that "free peoples of the world look to us for support in maintaining their freedom," Harry S. Truman initiated the first large-scale U.S. military assistance in 1947, sending aid to Greece and Turkey. With the passage of the Mutual Defense Assistance Act of 1949, such aid was also extended to the members of NATO, Iran, Philippines, Korea, and China. It was the Mutual Security Act (MSA) of 1951, however, that "authorized more appropriations and considerably extended the scope of military aid to nearly all countries."[33]

While the Mutual Security Program (MSP) established by that far-reaching act was also designed to provide a small amount of economic and technical aid to U.S. allies, the main thrust of the program was in the area of military assistance. In arguing the necessity of this assistance, MSP officials stressed the "mutual security" nature of the program: "It is important to bear in mind that this program is a program for mutual security. Our contributions to other countries have as their purpose to enable those other countries to do those parts of the total security task which we could not do alone in any case." U.S. contributions would allow its allies to raise and supply sufficient forces; make more efficient use of their productive facilities; help its allies rebuild their economies; and would raise the morale of its allies by developing "a sense of common interest in mutual security."[34] In addition, U.S. military assistance would "support their political and military orientation toward the United States, augment our own military potential by improvement of our armaments industries, and through progress in standardization of equipment and training increase the effectiveness of military collaboration between the United States and its allies in the event of war."[35]

The development of a "common interest" or correct "orientation" toward the problems of worldwide security was obviously a primary goal of the MSP; in the "smaller" world they faced, U.S. policymakers could have sought no less.   Disturbances to the carefully balanced interdependent system desired by U.S. policymakers would have to be met by military force: "Strength begets strength," an MSP report concluded, "and accomplishment now will strengthen the conviction of free peoples that they can build within their great community the power to repel present threats and to work effectively toward the fulfillment of their basic aspirations."[36]

One particular area that U.S. officials saw a need for strength was in Latin America.   While MSP assistance to Latin America amounted to only $44 million in 1954 (about 1 percent of total MSP expenditures), this is somewhat misleading.[37]   U.S. policymakers were quite concerned with the military situation in Latin America and foresaw the region as playing an important role in mutual defense.[38]   Considering the vital economic relationship that their nation had with the area, this is hardly surprising.

A 1952 State Department report stated that, "Latin America as part of the hemisphere belongs to the inner citadel of United States—and there, one might say without distortion—of free world strength."   The security of the Panama Canal and the protection of raw material outlets and communication lines in the region were priorities.   U.S. military men also noted the significance of Latin America to their nation's defense plans. The "maintenance of the territorial integrity and sovereignty or political independence of other American states, and regional collaboration to maintain international peace and security in the Western Hemisphere" were the basic goals of their postwar plans.   To achieve them, "liaison with and development and training of the armed forces of the American nations" would be necessary.[39]

That final point was not in question.   The Latin America armed forces were judged to be below standard in nearly every area.   In terms of their value to the defense of the hemisphere in case of a direct attack, a 1952 CIA report concluded that "the Latin Americans would never expect to meet attack by a first-class military power without direct US air and naval support." A State Department analysis was even more pessimistic. Their armies were "small and ill-trained. . .their equipment is obsolete." Only Brazil, Chile, Argentina, and Mexico had forces that could adequately defend their national soil. Outside of their borders, they would be "less effective. . .and almost completely ineffective overseas." Argentina, Brazil, and Chile were the only nations that had sufficient naval strength; the first two, of all Latin American countries, had air power of "even minor value for collective defense." As with the armies, "[o]bsolete equipment, poor training, and low technical standards" hampered the effectiveness of the air forces.[40]

Despite these dismal evaluations, U.S. officials did see roles for the Latin American militaries. As explained in a 1950 NSC report, these included "maintaining security within its own territory, including prevention of revolutionary disturbances, prevention of clandestine enemy operations, defense against isolated attacks or raids, protection of the sources and installations of strategic materials, and local security of bases and military facilities."[41]

The benefits of such arrangements to the United States were obvious. First, they would free U.S. troops for more important military duties. During World War II, the United States was forced to station over 100,000 troops in that region. Second, more responsible and efficient Latin American armed forces could see to it that the export of vital materials from their countries was insured. This was critical since, as the NSC concluded, "During 1948–1949 the Latin American nations demonstrated, in Colombia and in Bolivia, their inability to maintain internal order. Were the Bolivian uprisings repeated in time of emergency, the consequent interruption of tin production could result in grave consequences to the United States." Finally, given U.S. perceptions that the armed forces in Latin America "either completely control the government, as in Venezuela and Peru, or at the very least, influence government policy," it made good sense to curry favor with those forces. If the United States did not, it would "not get from them the measure of cooperation we need."[42]

As with the economic relationship between the United States and Latin America, however, interdependent mutual security relations between the two would mean benefits going both ways. As Under Secretary of State Dean Acheson noted in 1947, military assistance to Latin America would obviously help the security needs of the United States. On the other hand, a strong inter-American defense system would "preserve in this

Hemisphere the possibility of the development of democratic institutions and individual freedoms."[43] Milton Eisenhower, after his 1953 visit to Latin America at the behest of his brother, was even more sure of the two-way benefits: "Military relations between the United States and the other American Republics are closely related to economic interdependence. . . .There is. . .a mutuality of interests: with the United States standing guard against potential aggressors, Latin American freedom and independence can be maintained only if the United States continues strong."[44] And Adolph Berle, former U.S. ambassador to Brazil, aired the idea that military assistance to Latin America "might be combined [with] useful economic and ideological operations." A U.S.-trained engineer corps could "build roads as well as fortifications [and] actually turn back to their countries a dividend of economic progress." The United States could also try to see to it that education and technical training were part of the assistance offered Latin American military men. This would be "one way of enlarging the base of education" needed in the region. "Latin American armies (like it or not) do get down to grass-roots; they are, in fact, one of the few avenues by which American influence can reach grass-roots."[45]

The nations of Central America were not overlooked in U.S. military planning. In fact, they seemed to be ideal recipients of military assistance. Their strategic, economic, and political importance, while not as great as that of a Brazil or Mexico, of course, was significant nonetheless. The armed forces of the region were seen as particularly inept and desperately in need of U.S. help. And, finally, military aid to these nations was seen as providing mutual benefits—another link in the chain of interdependence. Strategically, their "proximity to the United States and the Panama Canal, to the routes between them, and to the sea and air routes between the United States and South America" made them key links in any interhemispheric defense plans. Politically, those nations (along with the Caribbean republics) were of "considerable importance to the United States in promoting the concept of hemisphere solidarity and in furthering its policies in the United Nations."[46] Central America also had important economic links with the United States.

Thus, the need for adequate military strength in the region was considered vital by U.S. policymakers, especially since existing forces in Central America were disappointing, to say the least. A Department of Defense estimate concluded that Costa Rica was simply "not in a position to mobilize for a large scale war"; El Salvador's army was basically an "internal security force"; Honduras had some soldiers being trained by a U.S. Army mission, but all other forces were "inferior and unsatisfactory"; and Nicaragua's military was fairly well armed, but training was uniformly poor. Only Guatemala, which had two regiments being trained by a U.S. Army mission, showed signs that it was "steadily improving." As a State Department report concluded, "The armed forces of the Caribbean republics [which included Central America] exist primarily for the maintenance of internal security. . . . In the event of war, the republics could make no contribution to hemisphere defense of more than local significance." However, with the "provision of US assistance, most of the Caribbean republics will probably maintain small units equipped and trained for modern combat and available to assist in an integrated defense of the Caribbean area."[47]

Beyond the military and economic benefits garnered by the United States, military assistance could also have a political impact. Since the "dominant socio-political element [in the Caribbean republics] is the landed gentry in combination with the military," it obviously behooved the United States to gain the support of such elements. And perhaps, as Acheson, Milton Eisenhower, and Berle had suggested, U.S. aid would have a beneficial effect on the Central American political process, since one of the sectors leading the demand for political and social change in that region was composed of "junior army officers."[48] The needs of one would once again serve the needs of the other. The chaotic militaries of Central America would be given training and arms, leading to a new sense of professionalism and responsibility on their part. And the United States would have five more partners in its interdependent security system.

A Better World

> We know that people are very much alike in their basic aspirations wherever they may be or whatever language they may speak. Our goal is self-development, not imperialism. Our goal is peace, not war. Our goal, not only for ourselves but for all peoples, is a better world—materially, morally and spiritually.[49]

Such was the vision of Assistant Secretary of State Edward Miller in a 1951 speech before a meeting of Latin American foreign ministers. It dealt with his belief that most of the world's population found common cause with those ideals—democracy, freedom, and justice—best expressed by the U.S. system of government. As an NSC report observed, the mass appeal of those ideals was behind the worldwide aggressiveness of the Soviet Union: "The Soviet slave state recognizes the contagious nature of the idea of freedom and is determined implacably to eliminate its challenge." The clash between the Soviet state (and its agents throughout the world), desirous of imposing its own system, and the democratic aspirations of the peoples of the free world would undoubtedly cause problems that the United States would have to face up to: "In a shrinking world, which now faces the threat of atomic warfare, the absence of order among nations is becoming less and less tolerable. This fact imposes on us, in our own interest, the responsibility of seeking to build a world society based on the principle of consent and to bring about order and justice by means consistent with the principles of freedom and democracy."[50] Once again, in the smaller—"shrinking"—postwar world, U.S. policymakers saw a commonality of interest among the nations of the free world.

As the comments by Miller and the NSC make clear, U.S. officials believed that the ideals of the United States were those sought after by most of the world's population. The United States, with the most powerful economy and the most satisfied citizenry, had clearly demonstrated the superiority of a system based on such ideals. Their acceptance on a worldwide basis would provide the foundation for peace, prosperity, and meaningful coexistence for all nations. Standing in the way of this, however, was an awesome challenge—the "Soviet slave state." It was not enough, therefore, for the people of the world to aspire to the ideals of the United States. They had to be made aware of the immense challenge those ideals faced and, shoulder to shoulder with the United States, stand strong against the communist threat.

There was little doubt among U.S. policymakers that in the Latin American region as a whole, identification with the democratic ideals of their own nation was strong. As a State Department dramatically noted, the Latin Americans "regard themselves as part of a New World that has a mission to realize the ideals of national independence, human freedom, and equality among men and nations."[51]

According to U.S. officials, such similarities were deeply rooted in the histories of the two regions. Numerous studies during the post–World War II period commented on the shared experiences of the United States and Latin America. "[D]iscovery, colonization, independence, and the establishment of republics based upon the concept of democracy" were essential parts of the "political evolution" of both regions. Other reports pointed to the "possession of common revolutionary ideals," the "common European origins," the fact that both were "born out of a successful revolutionary struggle against imperialistic foreign domination," and that both were part of the "historic concept of a 'New World' dedicated to liberty and the rights of man."[52]

Shared allegiance to that "historic concept" did not mean, however, that the United States and the republics of Latin America were on a par insofar as their development of democratic institutions was concerned. One State Department report characterized "political progress" in Latin America as "slow," concluding that only Uruguay could be said to have "a tradition of democratic stability." A 1952 State Department paper summed up the views of most U.S. officials when it argued that "the independence which most of the countries of Latin America gained during the 19th century did not bring with it the same type of political, social or economic revolution which was the consequence (or the concomitant) of the independence which the United States had earlier achieved from England."[53]

Such reports also made clear that in the same way that the shared historical experiences of the two regions helped explain their similarities, their histories also explained their differences. While the United States and Latin America could trace their beginnings to "European origins," they had inherited very different societies from their specific "Mother Countries." As one report noted, "Spain and Portugal, from which the Latin American countries . . . derived their independence, had themselves never undergone the type of revolution which had occurred in England." The impact on their Latin American colonies had been that the "political, social and economic patterns in Latin America remained largely frozen in the same status in which they had developed in Spain and Portugal during medieval times."[54] While Latin Americans yearned for democracy, therefore, their national institutions—leftovers from years of backward Spanish and Portuguese rule—had not been willing or able to translate those desires into reality.

Another problem in terms of drawing Latin Americans more closely into the fold of the democratic nations making up the Free World was their apparent lack of interest in meeting the communist threat. As explained in a briefing book prepared for President Truman in 1951, since the Latin American nations were not "world powers," it was "difficult for them to feel an immediate menace to themselves in developments that take place in parts of the world from which they are geographically remote."

The Latin Americans tended to "regard themselves as spectators at a battle-of-the-giants." Nevertheless, the threat was present, and "political aggression" (rather than a "military attack") from communism menaced Latin America. As a result of its weaker political institutions, "communist political attempts from within would be more likely to succeed in Latin America than in the United States."[55]

For the United States, therefore, the political problem in Latin America was two-fold. First, it must encourage the development of democratic institutions. "We should use our influence," declared one State Department study, "to promote an orderly evolution towards democracy throughout the hemisphere—to promote general acceptance (*and the practice*) of approximately the same political, economic and social principles to which we adhere."[56] Second, the Latin Americans would have to be convinced of the necessity of standing up to the communist challenge. In practice, U.S. officials believed that the achievement of the first goal would go far in securing the second. U.S. support of groups working toward greater political freedom in Latin America would "further the natural development of democracy in Latin American countries, will increase the wellbeing of their populations, and will help to create an environment conducive to the establishment and maintenance of governments friendly to this country."[57] This all reflected the widely held view that the peoples of the world, given the fruits of democracy, would be staunch defenders of that ideal.

The encouragement of pro-democratic/anti-communist ideals in Latin America would have substantial benefits for the United States. As U.S. officials saw it, Latin American support of the "New World" ideals of freedom, justice, and democracy lent additional weight to U.S. efforts to expand those ideals worldwide. As a study by the Randall Commission put it, "The attitude towards the U.S. of the 20 countries in this area can significantly influence for good or bad the attitude of other countries toward the leadership of the U.S. in the free world." The State Department, in a 1952 report, claimed that Latin America's "support has great moral importance for us and for the cause of democracy in general." It concluded, "By the same token, political chaos and the continuance of misery and ignorance in Latin America are not only a threat to our material interests, but a poor advertisement for the political and economic principles we profess."[58]

In addition, Latin American support for those principles had more direct international implications in terms of their participation in the UN. A

number of State Department reports addressèd this issue. One noted that
the nations of Latin America almost always voted with the U.S. This was
important, since in many crucial votes "the transfer of a handful of votes
would have reversed the outcome." Another noted that the Latin Ameri-
càn votes (making up one-third of the total votes) had "greatly contributed
to the effective functioning of the world organization in resisting the
imperialism of the Soviet bloc. It has also been of inestimable value in
giving our policies the moral authority that comes with the voluntary
support of the great majority of those nations."[59]

The reciprocal benefits to Latin America were obvious, and U.S. officials did not spend much time reflecting on this question. Democracy was
obviously preferable to the stagnant political systems existing in most
Latin American nations. The necessity of battling against the encroach-
ment of communism was similarly plain to see: "it involves everything
they stand for and, ultimately, their survival as free nations," as one
report put it.[60] Political interdependence would bring benefits to both
Latin America and the United States: a vibrant democracy that would
bring development and freedom to the former; important allies in the
battle against communism for the latter.

The five republics of Central America (with one notable exception)
seemed to embody the two goals of political interdependence: support for
U.S. ideals of democracy and opposition to communism. A 1952 State
Department study claimed that relations between the United States and
Costa Rica, El Salvador, Honduras, and Nicaragua were "excellent" and
"friendly." The people of Costa Rica were specifically singled out as
prizing "personal liberty and are highly democratic." The latter three
nations were all supportive of U.S. policies and were sensitive to the issue
of communism. Only Guatemala, which had a government suspected of
being too soft on communism, seemed a possible trouble spot.[61] Another
report from that same year, surveying Communist Party strength in Latin
America, pointed out that the party was illegal in all five Central
American republics. The party's membership was "negligible" in
Honduras, numbered approximately 500 in Nicaragua, El Salvador, and
Guatemala, and only 1,000 in Costa Rica. (These were some of the
lowest figures in all of Latin America; Ecuador, for example, was
estimated to have 3,000 Communist Party members.)[62]

A closer look, however, revealed many of the same problems noted
elsewhere in Latin America. Support for U.S. ideals did not necessarily
translate into their practice in Central America. A State Department study

prepared just after World War II clearly illustrated this problem. In dividing the nations of Latin America into the categories of countries with "good," "uncertain," and "bad" stability, only Costa Rica fit into the first group. In the "uncertain" category were placed the nations of Guatemala, Honduras, and Nicaragua. El Salvador, the only nation in the last, and worst, category, was viewed as a nation on the edge of revolution. An NIE prepared nearly ten years later indicated that the situation had not improved. The Central American nations suffered from "political immaturity" and "rule by military 'strong men' has been normal." Revolution was the generally accepted method of transferring political power.[63]

Nor could U.S. policymakers be complacent about communism in Central America. Despite the pronounced anti-communism of most of the governments in that region, a report prepared by the Division of Research for American Republics in January 1955 indicated that communist agents were assiduously at work. In Guatemala, despite the overthrow of the presidency of Jacobo Arbenz (suspected to be pro-communist in its leanings by U.S. officials) in June of 1954, "a revival of operations on a clandestine basis is taking place." In El Salvador, Costa Rica, and Honduras, the communists had, to various degrees, infiltrated the labor movements. Only in Nicaragua, under Somoza's strict rule, were the activities of communists "negligible."[64]

The status of political interdependence between the United States and Latin America was, therefore, a mixed bag after World War II. The consensus among U.S. officials was that certainly Latin Americans supported the democratic ideal. This was shown in their friendliness for the United States and their support in the UN. Unfortunately, the political situation in Latin America did not always reflect those yearnings for democracy. The history that had given them many of the same ideals as their contemporaries in the United States had also saddled them with impediments to the achievement of true democracy. The Latin Americans also seemed to lack the necessary interest in fighting the communist menace. These same problems were highlighted in Central America. There, despite outward support of U.S. ideals and intense anti-communism, most of its nations were mired in dictatorship, with communism a small, but ominous threat.

Despite these problems, the United States hoped to make the best of the situation it faced. By working with the forces of freedom in Latin America, the United States would help bring about the democratic institutions desired by the people of that region. In so doing, it would also be helping to build a bulwark against the inroads of communism. The United States would acquire real allies, who shared in the "New World" mission. These allies would offer evidence to other nations of the validity of U.S. ideals, and would be twenty more votes in the UN the United States could count on. The Latin Americans would gain the types of government they desired and would be more willing and able to face up to the Soviet threat. For U.S. policymakers, it would be the "better world" that everyone wanted.

They were sweeping ideals, enunciated in often dramatic statements. A world economy bound together in mutual profit and service; a mutual security system based on each nation contributing to the protection and safety of all others; and a shared vision concerning the political ideals of freedom, justice, and democracy (and shared visions, as well, concerning the threat posed by communism). They are so sweeping, so dramatic, in fact, that they are often dismissed as merely the woolly-minded musings of naive idealists; the cynical and misleading remarks of devious *realpolitik* ideologues; or the off-the-cuff "sound bites" of probably well-meaning, but uncommitted, politicians. Some no doubt were, for there were among U.S. officials and policymakers a generous supply of idealists, cynics, and politicians. To dismiss out of hand such statements, however, would be a grievous mistake, for this would overlook what becomes obvious after the reading and re-reading of the words of U.S. officials during the decade after World War II. That is, that most of those officials sincerely believed that economic, military, and political interdependence were worthy goals, capable of being achieved.

They did not believe this out of sheer humanitarianism or fuzzy idealism (although these played a role). Certainly they believed that capitalism, mutual security, and democracy, operating on a worldwide scale, was all to the good. They believed that their operation would bring prosperity, safety, and freedom to peoples everywhere, just as they had to the American people. On the other hand, they were just as aware of the very real benefits to be gained by their own nation. They were not ashamed to admit as much; after all, interdependence was a two-way street not only of responsibility, but of reward. Economic interdependence would aid in the postwar reconversion of the U.S. economy. Mutual security would help the United States in assuring stability among its allies and protection from war. The building of prodemocratic and anticommunist governments would provide reliable allies, sharing its ideals (and fears).

Latin America presented U.S. policymakers with both the realities and possibilities of interdependence. In some ways after World War II, that interdependence was already in place. The long history of the two regions had prepared the ground. The economic links between the two were substantial and growing. Latin America seemed the perfect match for the resource– and consumer–hungry industrial base of the United States. In the field of mutual security, sheer proximity seemed to make for natural allies to protect the hemisphere. The United States would provide the weaponry and training; the Latin Americans could be forged into a first line of defense in the Western Hemisphere. In terms of political ideals, the Latin Americans shared the belief in democracy and freedom. Not always able to translate those beliefs into action, however, they would be aided by the United States in both striving for democracy and in standing strong against communism.

Central America seemed to provide a particularly fertile soil for the growth of interdependence. Its five republics were already engaged in heavy economic activity with the United States, trading their raw materials for U.S. consumer goods. Yet, interdependence had not brought much development to the desperately poor Central Americans. Their geographic location made military cooperation a necessity, but their pathetic armed forces did not indicate that such cooperation would be worthwhile. The political situation was mixed, with apparent support of democracy and anticommunism transposed over the reality of unstable and repressive governments and small, but potentially threatening, communist groups. The promises of interdependence—prosperity, security, and democracy— seemed far from being achieved in this corner of the world.

The job facing U.S. policymakers was to see that the benefits of interdependence found their way to Central America. From an idealistic point of view, it was desirable; from a pragmatic outlook, it seemed absolutely necessary. In the "smaller" and "shrinking" world they lived in, the problems of one area could very easily become the problems of another. Even on the face of things, the chore was daunting. As they attempted to remedy the deficiencies, they found that increasing the interdependence between the United States and Central America often led to ends that contradicted the very aims it set out to achieve. The "chain of interdependence," which was to bind the two regions together in prosperity, security, and democracy, ended up binding the United States to policies that aided in even more poverty, repression, and dictatorship in Central America.

Notes

1.   For Europe, see Michael Hogan, *The Marshall Plan: America, Britain, and the Reconstruction of Europe, 1947–1952* (New York, 1987). For Japan, see Michael Schaller, *The American Occupation of Japan* (New York, 1985).

2.   U.S. policy towards Asia following the war is covered in Robert M. Blum, *Drawing the Line: The Origin of the American Containment Policy in East Asia* (New York, 1982); Andrew Rotter, *The Path to Vietnam: Origins of the American Commitment to Southeast Asia* (Ithaca, NY, 1987); and Gary Hess, *The U.S. Emergence as a Southeast Asian Power, 1940–1950* (New York, 1986). For the Middle East, see William Roger Louis, *The British Empire in the Middle East, 1945–1951* (New York, 1984); and David S. Painter, *Oil and the American Century: The Political Economy of U.S. Foreign Oil Policy, 1941–1954* (Baltimore, 1986). U.S. relations with Africa are covered in Peter Duignan and L. H. Gann, *The United States and Africa: A History* (New York, 1984), a survey that has a good section on the postwar period, and Thomas Noer, *Cold War and Black Liberation: The United States and White Rule in Africa, 1948–1968* (Columbia, MO, 1985).

3.   Some of the books that make this point are LaFeber, *Inevitable Revolutions*, 85; Samuel L. Baily, *The United States and the Development of South America, 1945–1975* (New York, 1976), 54; Immerman, *CIA in Guatemala*, 8–9; Burton I. Kaufman, *Trade and Aid: Eisenhower's Foreign Economic Policy, 1953–1961* (Baltimore, 1982), 6; Rabe, *Eisenhower and Latin America*, 12; and Leonard, *United States and Central America*, 10. Two important articles also note that the developing Cold War significantly influenced U.S. policy towards Latin America: Louis A. Pérez, Jr., "International Dimensions of Inter-American Relations, 1944–1960," *Inter-American Economic Affairs* 27:1 (1973):47–68; and Roger Trask, "The Impact of the Cold War on United States–Latin American Relations, 1945–1949," *Diplomatic History* 1:3 (1977):271–84.

4.   LaFeber, *Inevitable Revolutions*, Ch. II passim. "Maintaining the System" is the title and theme of the chapter.

5.   A good discussion of these changes can be found in Stephen J. Randall, *Co-lombia and the United States: Hegemony and Interdependence* (Athens, GA, 1992), Chs. 5 and 6.

6.   PPS Report No. 63, 23 Nov. 1949, General Records of the Department of State, Record Group 59, Records of the Policy Planning Staff, 1947–1953, National Archives, Washington, DC (hereafter RG 59, Records of PPS, NA).

7.   U.S. Department of Commerce, *Thirty-Fourth Annual Report of the Secretary of Commerce* (Washington 1946), v–vi (hereafter cited as CD, *Thirty-Fourth Report of Secretary*).

8.   Lincoln Gordon, Oral History, 17 July 1975, p. 5, Harry S. Truman Library, Independence, MO (hereafter HSTL).

9.   Bureau of Foreign and Domestic Commerce to William Clayton, 1 May 1943, Records of the Bureau of Foreign and Domestic Commerce, Record Group 151, File 620 (hereafter cited as RG 151, with file number), NA.

10.   CD, *Thirty-Fourth Report of Secretary*, vii–viii, 123.

11.   Rotter, *Path to Vietnam*, 49–50.

12.   "Summary of the Remarks of Assistant Secretary of Commerce Thomas C. Blaisdell, Jr. at the Meeting of the Business Advisory Council, Hot Springs, Virginia, May 6, 1950," Papers of Thomas C. Blaisdell, Jr., Box 7, HSTL.

13.   Rotter, *Path to Vietnam*, is rich in information dealing with U.S. postwar economic planning. Also to be consulted is Thomas McCormick, *America's Half-Century: United States Foreign Policy in the Cold War* (Baltimore, 1989).

14.   Louis H. Bean to Stanley Andrews, 14 June 1950, Papers of Stanley Andrews, Box 3, Government Service File, 1942–1953; Foreign Trade, Declining Importance of Europe, HSTL.

15.   CD, *Thirty-Sixth Report of Secretary, 1948* (Washington, 1948), 171; *Thirty-Fourth Report of Secretary, 1946*, 131.

16.   For a discussion of U.S. foreign economic policy during and after World War I, see Michael L. Krenn, *U.S. Policy Toward Economic Nationalism in Latin America, 1917–1929* (Wilmington, DE, 1990), Ch. One.

17.   "Partners in Progress: A Report to the President by the International Development Advisory Board, March 1951 (Summary)," Papers of Harry S. Truman, Official File (OF) 20–U, Box 20, Folder 2 (hereafter Truman Papers, file, box, and folder number); "President's Materials Policy Commission, 1st Draft," 4 Sept. 1951, Records of the President's Materials Policy Commission, Box 14, First Draft–Foreign Resources Chapter I (hereafter Records of PMPC, box number, file name), HSTL.

18.   "The United States and the Economic Progress of Underdeveloped Countries," 15 Nov. 1953, Records of the President's Commission on Foreign Economic Policy (Randall Commission), Box 56, Studies–Economic Development file (hereafter Records of Randall Commission, box number, file name), DDEL.

19.   Truman to Nelson Rockefeller, 9 Mar. 1951, Truman Papers, OF 20–U, Box 20, Folder 1, HSTL; "Preliminary Department of Defense Views on the Randall Commission Report," 1954, Dwight D. Eisenhower, Records as President, White House Central Files, Box 588, Official File (hereafter OF) 116–M 1954 (1) (hereafter WHCF, box number, file designation), DDEL.

20.   "Final Declaration of the Thirty-Eighth National Foreign Trade Convention, New York, N.Y., October 29, 30 and 31, 1951," enclosed in Walter White to Members of Committee on Latin America, 23 Nov. 1951, RG 59, Office Files of the Assistant Secretary of State for Inter-American Affairs (Edward G. Miller), 1949–1953, Box 3 (hereafter cited as Miller Files with box number), NA.

21.   John Stambaugh, Oral History, 20 July 1976, p. 51, DDEL.

22.   "Meeting of Foreign Ministers of American Republics, 1950 and 1951, Briefing Book, The President," Truman Papers, President's Secretary's File (hereafter PSF), Subject File (hereafter SF), Box 177, Foreign Ministers of American Republics—Meetings folder, HSTL.

23.   Guy W. Ray to Willard Barber and Edward Miller, 30 Sept. 1949, RG 59, Decimal File 710.11/9–3049 (hereafter RG 59, with file number), NA.

24.   "United States Relations with Latin America," 1952, RG 59, Miller Files, Box 3, NA.

25.   Ibid.; "Latin America," March 1951, Truman Papers, Confidential File (hereafter CF), State Department Correspondence, Box 39, 1952 file, folder 30A, HSTL.

26.   Ibid.; "Strategic and Critical Materials of Which Latin America is a Major Supplier," 1951, RG 59, Records of the Office of Regional American Affairs, Bureau of Inter-American Affairs (Mutual Security Program Budget Files), 1951–1955, Box 1, 1951 (hereafter RG 59, MSP Files with box number), NA.

27.   "Latin America," March 1951, Truman Papers, CF, SD Corres., Box 39, 1952 file, folder 30A, HSTL; "Strategic and Critical Materials. . . ," 1951, RG 59, MSP Files, Box 1; "The Economic Importance of the Resources of Selected Areas to the US and Other Free World Countries," 30 Sept. 1953, Records of the U.S. Council on Foreign Economic Policy, Office of the Chairman, Intelligence Reports Series, Box 1, Economic Importance of the Resources of Selected Areas (EIC), DDEL; "Report on the Possibilities of Expanding Production of Strategic Materials in Latin America by Improving Power and Transportation Facilities," 2 Jan. 1952, Truman Papers, CF, SD Corres., Box 38, 1951–1952, loose brown folder, HSTL.

28.   Charles R. Norberg to Col. Byron K. Enyart, 14 Sept. 1954 [emphasis in original], White House Office, Papers of the National Security Council Staff, 1948–1961, OCB Central Files, Box 72, OCB 091.4 LA (File #2) (6) (hereafter cited as WHO, Papers of NSC, OCB CF, box number, and file designation), DDEL.

29.   Coordinator of Inter-American Affairs, Research Division, "Basic Economic Data Concerning the Other American Republics," Oct. 1944, Records of the Department of State: Interdepartmental and Intradepartmental Committees, Record Group 353 (RG 353), Inter-American Economic Affairs Committee, 1945–1950, Box 76, Committee on Inter-American Postwar Economic Policies file (hereafter Records of IAEAC, box number, and file designation); Ernest Siracusa to Gordon Reid, et al., 19 May 1952, RG 59, 813.00/5–1952, NA.

30.   "Report to the President by the President's Citizen Advisers on the Mutual Security Program," 1 March 1957, Dwight D. Eisenhower, Papers as President of the United States, 1953–1961 (Ann Whitman File), Box 26, Mutual Aid–1957 (1) file (hereafter Whitman File, box number, file designation), DDEL.

31.   PPS Report No. 50, 22 Mar. 1949, RG 59, Records of PPS, NA.

32. NSC Report 14/1, 1 July 1948, Truman Papers, PSF, Intelligence File (hereafter IF), Box 204, NSC Meetings 14–27: Meeting No. 14 file, HSTL.

33. A good discussion of early U.S. military aid programs is found in Harold A. Hovey, *United States Military Assistance: A Study of Policies and Practices* (New York, 1966), 3–16. Information about the MSA is found in Robert M. Macy to W. F. Finan, 30 Dec. 1954, Records of CFEP, Chairman, Dodge Series, Subject Subseries, Box 2, Foreign Aid–Factual Data from Bureau of Budget file, DDEL.

34. A breakdown of MSP expenditures for 1954 is found in a series of graphs and charts enclosed in William M. Rand to Dwight D. Eisenhower, 11 May 1953, Whitman File, Box 34, Stassen, Harold, 1952–53 (2) file, DDEL; "The Mutual Security Program for Fiscal Year 1952," Committee Print, 82d Cong., 1st sess. (Washington, 1951), in RG 353, Records of Interdepartmental and Intra-Departmental Committees, 1943–1951, Box 82, 5.32 MSP, 1951: c. MSP Committee Prints, Annexes, President's Message file (hereafter Records of ID/ID Committees, box number, and file designation), NA.

35. NSC Report 14/1, 1 July 1948, Truman Papers, PSF, IF, Box 204, NSC Meetings 14 –27: Meeting No. 14 file, HSTL.

36. "The Mutual Security Program for Fiscal Year 1952," Committee Print, 82d Cong., 1st Sess., RG 353, Records of ID/ID Committees, Box 82, 5.32 MSP, 1951: c. MSP Committee Prints. . . file, NA.

37. Refer to material in Rand to Eisenhower, 11 May 1953, Whitman File, Box 34, Stassen, Harold, 1952–53 (2) file, DDEL.

38. A good introduction is John Child, *Unequal Alliance: The Inter-American Military System, 1938–1978* (Boulder, CO, 1980), especially Ch. 4. For a closer look at that relationship up to the passage of the 1951 Mutual Security Act, see Stephen G. Rabe, "Inter-American Military Cooperation, 1944–1951," *World Affairs* 137 (Fall 1974):132–149.

39. "United States Relations with Latin America," 1952, RG 59, Miller Files, Box 3, NA; James F. Schnabel, *The History of the Joint Chiefs of Staff: The Joint Chiefs of Staff and National Policy, Volume I, 1945–1947* (Washington, 1979).

40. CIA, "Conditions and Trends in Latin America Affecting US Security," 12 Dec. 1952, Truman Papers, PSF, IF, Box 254, Central Intelligence Reports, NIE 67–75; "Latin America," Mar. 1951, Truman Papers, CF, SD Corres., Box 39, 1952 File, Folder 30A, HSTL.

41. NSC Report 56/1, 27 Apr. 1950, Truman Papers, PSF, IF, Box 208, NSC Meetings 56–64, Meeting no. 57 file, HSTL.

42. "Statement in Support of the Mutual Security Program for FY 1954 (Latin America)," 23 Apr. 1953, RG 59, MSP Files, Box 1, 1953, NA; NSC Report 56, 31 Aug. 1949, Truman Papers, PSF, IF, Box 208, NSC Meetings, 56–64: Meeting No. 57 file, HSTL; "United States Relations with Latin America," 1952, RG 59, Miller Files, Box 3, NA.

43. Acheson to Carleton Savage, 8 Apr. 1947, RG 59, 710.11/4–847, NA.

44. "A Summary of Dr. Milton Eisenhower's Report to the President: United States–Latin American Relations," 1953, WHCF, Box 25, Confidential File (hereafter CF), Subject Series, Eisenhower, Milton, Trip to South America (3) folder, DDEL.

45. Berle, "For the Discussion Group on Political Unrest in Latin America, Council on Foreign Relations, May 15, 1953," 12 May 1953, RG 59, 720.00/5–1253, NA.

46. NIE, "The Caribbean Republics," 24 Aug. 1954, *Foreign Relations of the United States, 1952–1954* (Washington, 1983):4:382 (hereafter *FRUS*, with date).

47. "Data on the Armed Forces of Latin America," c. 1952, Records of the Office of the Secretary of Defense, Record Group 330, Assistant Secretary of Defense (International Security Affairs), Office of Military Aid Programs, Operations Division. Control Branch, Subject File, 1950–1953, Background Info Title IV file (hereafter RG 330, Office of MAP, Subject File, 1950–1953, with file designation), NA; *FRUS, 1952–54*, 4:382, 390.

48. *FRUS, 1952–1954*, 4:382–83.

49. Miller, "Address to Meeting of Ministers of Foreign Affairs of American Republics," 1951, RG 59, Miller Files, Box 4, NA.

50. NSC, "Draft: A Report to the President," 29 Mar. 1950, Truman Papers, National Security Council Files, Box 19 (hereafter cited as NSC Files, with box number), HSTL.

51. "Briefing Book. . . ," 1951, Truman Papers, PSF, SF, box 177, Foreign Ministers of American Republics–Meetings file, HSTL.

52. "Latin America and U.S. Policy," 1952, RG 59, 720.00/12–452; Untitled problem paper, 5 July 1949, RG 59, Miller Files, Box 10, NA; "Statement in Support of the Mutual Security Program for FY 1954 (Latin America)," 23 April 1953, RG 59, MSP Files, Box 1, NA; "Briefing Book. . . ," 1951, Truman Papers, PSF, SF, Box 177, Foreign Ministers of American Republics–Meetings file, HSTL; "United States Relations with Latin America," 1952, RG 59, Miller Files, Box 3, NA.

53. "United States Relations with Latin America," 1952, RG 59, Miller Files, Box 3; "Latin America and U.S. Policy," 1952, RG 59, 720.00/12–452, NA.

54. "United States Relations with Latin America," 1952, RG 59, Miller Files, Box 3, NA.

55. "Briefing Book," 1951, Truman Papers, PSF, SF, Box 177, Foreign Ministers of American Republics–Meetings file, HSTL.

56. "Latin America and U.S. Policy," 1952, RG 59, 720.00/12–452 (author's emphasis).

57. Untitled problem paper, 5 July 1949, RG 59, Miller Files, Box 10, NA.

58. "LA Study, Section Six: Conclusions and Recommendations," 13 Oct. 1953, Records of Randall Commission, Box 59, Studies–Study of U.S. Problems

and Policy Toward Latin America file, DDEL; "United States Relations with Latin America," 1952, RG 59, Miller Files, Box 3, NA.

59.   "Latin America," Mar. 1951, Truman Papers, CF, SD Corres., Box 39, 1952 file, folder 30A, HSTL; "United States Relations with Latin America," 1952, RG 59, Miller Files, Box 3, NA.

60.   "Briefing Book," 1951, Truman Papers, PSF, SF, Box 177, Foreign Ministers of American Republics–Meetings file, HSTL.

61.   Untitled report, 3 Oct. 1952, RG 59, 720.5 MSP/10–352, NA.

62.   "Communism in Latin America," RG 59, Miller Files, Box 3, NA.

63.   "Statement for Joint Intelligence Staff on the Political Situation in the Other American Republics as it May Affect American Plans for Military Commitments," 28 Sept. 1945, RG 59, Records of the Office of American Republic Affairs, 1918–1947, Box 16 (hereafter Records of OARA with box number), NA; "The Caribbean Republics," 24 Aug. 1954, *FRUS, 1952–1954*, IV:380.

64.   Division of Research for American Republics (hereafter DRAR), "Communism in Middle America," 14 Jan. 1955, RG 59, Records of the Office of Middle American Affairs, 1951–1956: Miscellaneous Records, Box 1 (hereafter Records of OMAA, Misc. Records, with box number), NA.

2

A Definite Ferment

Democracy or totalitarianism; free markets or statism; "the free world" or communism. Such were the choices provided by U.S. theories of interdependency. There seemed to be little room for compromise. A state could not be *somewhat* totalitarian; support a "halfway" free market; or be just a little bit communistic. In an ideal world, there was little doubt among U.S. policymakers what choices states and peoples would make. In the postwar decade, however, the situation was far from ideal, and those policymakers were well aware of the problems they faced.

It is somewhat surprising, considering events elsewhere in the world, that U.S. policymakers gave a good deal of thought to Central America. While no immediate emergencies were present in the region, Washington was alive to the proposition that such a state of affairs was not necessarily permanent and that there existed serious impediments to its policies of interdependence. The three most threatening problems, as seen by U.S. officials, were general instability, economic nationalism, and communism. And the more that they considered those problems, the more U.S. policymakers began to back away from the "either/or" choices posed by interdependence.

A Definite Ferment

"No region in the western hemisphere has been more subject to political unrest than has the Caribbean area [including Central America]. Nor has any region been more subject to dictatorial rule and generally undemocratic practices."[1] That 1952 assessment by historian Charles C. Cumberland was widely shared by U.S. policymakers. While there were some encouraging signs concerning Central American political development during the postwar years, in general the region was regarded as almost inherently unstable, where democracy—if it existed at all—was of only recent advent.

For Washington, political stability in postwar Latin America as a whole was suspect. A 1945 State Department study claimed that only seven Latin American republics could be rated as having "good political stability." Eight others were in the "uncertain" category, while the remaining five were stamped as "bad." Seven years later, the department's evaluation was perhaps even gloomier, concluding that only Uruguay had "a tradition of democratic stability."[2]

The CIA also cast a pessimistic eye toward political developments in Latin America. The year 1948, so the agency claimed, saw the region "approaching a political and institutional crises [sic] which may seriously affect its ability to afford valuable cooperation to the United States," and concluded that Latin American requests for U.S. aid provided "evidence that Latin American leaders cannot find within themselves or their countries the means to restore stability and achieve real authority for their governments."[3]

As Cumberland's remarks made clear, however, Central America was viewed as particularly unstable. Writing in 1945, William Cochran, chief of the State Department's Division of Caribbean and Central American Affairs, warned that, "I think there is a definite ferment working in all of Central America and foresee a general period of unrest and disturbance."[4]

Not much had changed by 1954. An NIE of that year was positively dismal in its evaluation. "The generally prevailing characteristics of the Caribbean republics," it began, "are social immobility, economic underdevelopment, and political immaturity." Revolution seemed to be the preferred method of political change. Strong men, military despots, dictators, and other unpleasant characters formed the backbone of political leadership. "In any case," the estimate shrugged, "no substantial improvement in basic conditions is likely to occur for many years." The situation in Guatemala was uncertain, following the revolution led by Colonel Carlos Castillo Armas. The government of Costa Rica, under the "erratic" leadership of José Figueres, was involved in an internal struggle with conservative opposition. Honduras, facing an election for president, was full of "mounting tensions" and a "possibility of civil war." Only

Nicaragua, under its dictator Anastasio Somoza, and El Salvador, led by another, seemingly more progressive military figure—Oscar Osorio—were quiet.[5]

As the CIA's 1948 report made clear, the basic problem for U.S. policymakers caused by the unstable situation in the Latin America area was that it might "seriously affect its ability to afford valuable cooperation to the United States."[6] Only stable allies could provide the United States with secure sources of essential resources and communications and transportation lines. Indeed, internal stability was the primary contribution the Latin Americans could make to hemispheric security. Instability, especially in the event of conflict, meant the diversion of U.S. manpower and resources to police the region; at the least, it meant unnecessary anxiety and uncertainty.

It was imperative, then, for U.S. officials to understand the forces behind instability in Latin America (particularly Central America). Only then might they come to some useful conclusions concerning how to combat it. In their search for understanding, they looked to the history of the region, analyzed the various political players and forces at work, examined economic weaknesses, debated the impact of cultural and racial factors on internal stability, and finally took note of the recent rise to prominence of new (and demanding) sectors in Latin America.

The colonial heritage of Latin America was often cited as a factor in the history of instability in the region. A 1949 State Department paper claimed that, "Democratic self-government" had been "alien" to Spain and Portugal, and "incipient tendencies toward it in the colonies were deliberately suppressed." "Ecclesiastical control, oppressive economic measures and political vassalage" were ingrained in the Latin American colonies. The church, armed forces, and land-owning oligarchies held on to power after independence, and had "continued to exert a restraining influence upon the process of democraticization." In sum, "Freedom without a prior apprenticeship in self-government forced the new Latin American states to assume a 'developed stage without first having had the preliminaries.'"[7]

Adolph Berle and John Cabot echoed those sentiments. Berle, in a paper prepared for a Council on Foreign Relations (CFR) discussion group, commented that the majority of Latin American nations were still controlled by oligarchies, and bemoaned the "limited heritage of popular education." Speaking in 1953, Assistant Secretary of State Cabot noted the "grievous handicaps" Latin America had to cope with upon its independence: lack of education and widespread illiteracy; a society nearly "feudal" in composition; a reigning oligarchy of large landowners, with "practically no middle class"; and a huge mass of "ignorant mestizos or Indians." The result had been extremely unstable dictatorships. The Latin Americans "yearned for democracy," but "were accustomed to authoritarian rule. . .and that is what they got often as not from their native governments."[8]

A 1952 State Department paper laid out the problems in no uncertain terms. Latin America suffered from a "great lack of a trained group of public servants capable of efficiently administering affairs of state." Corruption among government officials was the norm. Another report two years later lamented that in the region "politics have revolved around persons rather than public issues, the continued or shifting favor of the army has been the decisive political factor, and rule by military 'strong men' has been normal." "Intrigue and conspiracy" were the inevitable results of "such political immaturity."[9]

Such a state of affairs had persisted due to the inability of the Latin American masses to bring about change. As a CIA report put it, independence had found the wealthy oligarchs and military ruling over masses who were "dependent, inarticulate, and politically impotent." The passing of over one hundred years had done little to alleviate the situation, as noted in an NIE in 1954: "The vast majority of their [the Caribbean republics] heterogeneous population is illiterate, poverty-stricken, and socially and politically inert." The depressing conclusion of a 1951 State Department report was that the people of Latin America were so poor and badly educated that "they cannot be regarded as reliable adherents to the cause of democracy."[10]

Such was the hard historical soil in which U.S. officials saw themselves toiling in their efforts to sow stability and bring about an interdependent relationship. In addition, many of those policymakers were also plagued with doubts about the human crop they wished to reap—the Latin Americans themselves. Throughout the postwar decade, the racial make-up of Latin America was of great interest (and concern) to Washington. A 1949 study detailing the differences between the United States and Latin America listed as one of the eight criteria "% white population." Argentina scored highest (97 percent), while Honduras was at the bottom with 2 percent. A later report focusing on the Caribbean and Central American region noted that the 21,000,000 people living there were "of diverse racial stocks and admixtures." The specific nations ran the gamut from "preponderantly white" (Costa Rica), to "negro" (Haiti), to "Indian" (Guatemala), with the remaining countries being populated by *mestizo* (mixed Indian and white)."[11]

The problems with the racial mixture of Latin America were numerous. Economic and political development had been hampered "by the efforts to assimilate millions of Indians who are heirs of a different type of civilization." It also caused problems in the implementing of U.S. policies, since it faced a "great variety of breeds of people reacting in their own way to our public and diplomatic behavior (origins, including European, and African, Moorish and indigenous, and complex crisscrossing)." Derogatory comments about the Latin American "breeds" were commonplace among U.S. officials. Costa Ricans were "not a logical people and have short memories." Guatemalan statesmen were noted for their "mental deviousness and difficulty of thinking in a straight line." One report concluded that to approach the Latin Americans on the subject of discontinuing showy U.S. special missions to presidential inaugurations would be "rather like consulting with babies as to whether or not we should take candy away from them."[12]

Despite the pessimism inherent in these evaluations, there was one de-velopment that was cause for hope. The old order in Latin America was being challenged by newly emergent forces. In Central America particularly, the rise of these groups—the middle class, labor, and (to a lesser extent) intellectuals—might mean the end of oligarghic rule, economic backwardness, and social stagnation, and the beginning of democratic stability.

> [D]uring the last twenty years there has been increasing public awareness of political issues in Latin America; increasing sensitivity of governments to public opinion; decreasing dictatorships of the Leguía type in Peru; and fewer revolutions of simply the "outs" versus the "ins". . . .Latin America is passing through a period of inevitable and very far-reaching adjustment as between classes.[13]

That assessment by the State Department in 1946 was evidence of a strongly held belief in Washington: Latin America was going through a social and political revolution. The spearheads of this attack were the middle class, labor, and intellectuals.[14] As a 1952 report concluded, their demands had resulted in the rise to power of figures such as "Cardenas in Mexico, Arevalo in Guatemala, Figueres in Costa Rica. . .Peron in

Argentina. . .and Vargas in Brazil," all of whom promised the "masses a greater voice in government and a greater degree of social justice."[15]

This was true even in the less-developed nations of the Caribbean and Central America. The "traditional ruling elements" were confronted with "increasing demands for social, economic, and political change." As elsewhere in Latin America, "These demands come, not from the peasant masses, but from urban elements: students and intellectuals, business and professional men, labor leaders, and junior army officers." The pressures brought to bear by these groups had had uneven results in Central America. They were enough to "shatter the traditional order" in Guatemala in 1944, but had been "less spectacularly effective" in nations such as Costa Rica. In El Salvador and Honduras, they were "only beginning to be felt," and were "effectively contained" in Nicaragua. Nevertheless, such "pressure for change will continue to grow."[16]

The meaning for the United States seemed patently clear to members of the Randall Commission in 1953:

> We will do better to recognize the Latin Americans' right to manage their own affairs, as well as the inevitability and indeed the desirability of many of the political, economic, and social changes for which they strive. We should seek in this way to identify ourselves with emerging rather than decaying forces on the Latin American scene.

The U.S. role would have only a "second effect" on the "outcome of Latin America's current revolutionary trend." Yet, in cases of "evenly balanced power. . .even a second effect may be of considerable significance. Certainly, the stakes are too high to countenance a failure on our part to maximize, and to direct to constructive purposes, such potential influence as we have." In somewhat plainer language, a 1952 State Department report stated that, "We should use our influence to promote an orderly evolution towards democracy throughout the hemisphere—to promote general acceptance (and the practice) of approximately the same political, economic and social principles to which we adhere."[17] John Cabot agreed, explaining that, "We do not wish to interfere with constructive social ferment and nationalism; on the contrary, we should like to see our sister republics develop into progressive self–reliant democracies."[18]

The strong emphasis on "*orderly* evolution" and "*constructive* social ferment" belied some nagging reservations about the situation in Latin

America. Certainly, it was gratifying to see the people of that region breaking down the traditional barriers to democracy and justice. As officials such as Cabot liked to note, the United States could take a bit of the credit for those developments, having "thrust such ideas as free compulsory education, equality before the law, a relatively classless society, a fabulous standard of living for the masses" into Latin American society.[19] Nevertheless, the very fact that in terms of their political outlook the Latin Americans were coming more to a U.S. point of view concerned U.S. policymakers. The "all-prevading (sic) drive for social justice imposes upon governments an intense preoccupation with domestic problems." Such Latin American "preoccupation" often meant calling into question the prevailing economic relationship with the United States through policies more statist than the latter found comforting. In addition, "people, in and out of government, are simply not in a mood to fight against a supposedly revolutionary movement such as Communism when they consider themselves part of a revolutionary movement of their own."[20] In other words, democracy and social justice were all to the good—as long as they did no damage to the economic networks and anticommunist bulwarks the United States was trying to build in Latin America. All too often, however, U.S. policymakers found that two forces—nationalism and communism—were causing a bit too much ferment.

The Bug of Virulent Nationalism

> Life among the Latinos is much as you left it some years ago. We worry about Bolivian tin, Chilean copper, bananas in Guatemala and coffee from Brazil. Fortunately for the time being, we do not worry too much about sugar which is being sold at a good healthy price with the result that the current dicho in Cuba is that the only difference between a rich man and a poor man in Habana is that the poor man has to wash his own Cadillac.[21]

These off-the-record comments by Assistant Secretary of State Edward Miller to Philip Bonsal reveal an appalling misunderstanding of conditions in Cuba. More important, his "worries" over Latin American natural resources underline a general uneasiness in Washington concerning the U.S.-Latin American economic relationship following the war. Those concerns focused on the spread of economic nationalism in Latin America.

Economic nationalism, in its most general terms, "sought national economic growth through freeing the domestic economy from the constraints imposed on it by uncontrolled foreign ownership of land and resources and the dictates of what was perceived as an unfair world trade system."[22] Its development in Latin America was not a new phenomenon, having begun during the late nineteenth and early twentieth centuries, and maturing during and after World War I.[23] It reflected both economic concerns (dissatisfaction with an unstable world market, generally depressed prices for natural resources, and fears of "economic imperialism" through foreign investment) and political (the demands for a better standard of living from the masses and workers and for a bigger slice of national power from the middle class). It sometimes meant the expropriation of foreign-owned properties (oil in Mexico, oil and tin in Bolivia, for instance), calls for national industry (substitution of domestically produced goods for expensive imports), and "economic independence." U.S. policymakers had not cared for it after World War I;[24] by the time World War II was over, it raised a distinct challenge to the ideals of interdependence.

Even before the end of the war, U.S. officials sensed a "rise of strong nationalistic sentiments" in Latin America. The fact that the United States had insisted on inserting a call for a "policy of international collaboration to eliminate the excesses which may result from economic nationalism" into the "Economic Charter of the Americas" (which had been approved at the Inter-American Conference on Problems of War and Peace in March 1945) signaled its concern.[25] After the war, U.S. officials were emphatic in their statements that economic nationalism had taken hold in Latin America. A 1948 paper on Latin America's actions at a recent UN economic conference stated that, "Extravagant claims of economic nationalism have been made. . . .the obsession regarding economic nationalism is generally a fundamental conviction." George Messersmith, who had served as U.S. ambassador to Cuba, Mexico, and Argentina, cited the "*extreme* nationalism" brewing in "practically every country of Latin America" in 1952; Milton Eisenhower's report to his brother in 1953 noted the "rising tide of nationalism" in most of the region; and notes prepared for Under Secretary of State Walter Bedell Smith for use in briefing some members of Congress pointed to the fact that, "Nearly all of them [Latin American nations] are just emerging from their rigid colonial economies and have also been bitten with the bug of virulent nationalism."[26]

That "bug," it was apparent, was also infesting the Caribbean and Central American region. A 1954 NIE stated that, "Throughout the area, agitation against the traditional order of society has had strong nationalistic overtones. Frequently this nationalistic sentiment has been directed against the special privileges granted in former times to foreign economic enterprises." Economic nationalism had taken hold most definitely in Guatemala after the 1944 revolt. A 1951 report from the American embassy in that nation laid out the problem. The government of President Jacobo Arbenz "aspires toward extensive industrialization." Economic nationalism was "an apt phrase for describing the economic orientation of the regime."[27]

Yet Guatemala was not the only scene of potential troubles. In Costa Rica, the rise to power of José Figueres was met with considerable anxiety in Washington. A State Department intelligence report alerted the reader to the new president's "proclivity toward statism." "Figueres," it concluded, "appeals to nationalists by promising a broader program of economic development and firmer control over foreign investment —primarily US—in Costa Rica."[28]

El Salvador, too, proved troubling to U.S. policymakers. A 1948 coup in that nation had brought to power a military junta, called the Council of Revolutionary Government. While a 1949 State Department assessment claimed that the coup had done little to change the relationship between the United States and El Salvador, there was "one troubling element." That came in the form of a draft of a new constitution which, as characterized by U.S. Ambassador George Shaw, was "based upon a concept of excessive nationalism and would undoubtedly promote anti-foreign sentiment." In the ambassador's opinion, attempts at new U.S. investment "would not receive a warm welcome," and investments already made "would be endangered by a basic national charter such as envisaged."[29]

Even Honduras was not immune. After the long rule of General Tiburcio Carías Andino had ended in 1949, U.S. officials noted some distinct changes taking place. A 1953 report on conditions in that nation revealed that "economic nationalism has grown in Honduras during the last four years," and that "Honduras cannot be said to be a safe place for American investment except under the strictest terms and under-standing."[30] Only Somoza's Nicaragua stayed free from such pestilence.

The spread of economic nationalism throughout Latin America meant problems both immediate and long-term in nature. The most pressing problem it caused was the fear it put into U.S. investors and businessmen. Where economic nationalism flourished, U.S. capitalists were not likely to be found in great abundance. Such were the conclusions of a study published by the Department of Commerce in 1953. Nationalizations in Latin America had been "a major factor in the reduction of much of the earlier foreign investment (mainly European) in Latin America." The "threat of expropriation or nationalization. . .remains an obstacle to investment in Latin America."[31] That there were plenty of U.S. concerns that might be under the gun was pointed out in a 1952 State Department paper. These included copper and nitrate in Chile, tin in Bolivia, "mining interests" in Peru and Mexico, United Fruit in the Caribbean and Central America, sugar in Cuba and the Dominican Republic, and petroleum in Venezuela, Colombia, and Peru.[32] With so much at stake, it was little wonder that the PMPC in 1951 noted "widespread hesitancy in making or increasing private investments" on the part of U.S. businesses.[33]

The ultimate outcome, U.S. officials feared, would be a serious break in the interdependent economic (and political) relationship with Latin America. Another PMPC report laid out the parameters of the problem:

> Price controls, credit controls, exchange controls, import quotas, investment limitations, etc. . . .represent rigidities that interfere with ready adjustments to changing materials requirements. This is particularly true of underdeveloped areas at the very time that the United States and other industrialized countries of the Free World have come to rely more and more and more on such areas to meet basic materials needs. . . .Entrepreneurs may be as venturesome today as ever, but there is a lot more to discourage investment abroad in 1951 than there was a quarter century ago.[34]

The report cut to the crux of the problem. Economic nationalism was not simply a case of bad business sense. In its more "extreme" forms, it struck at the very basis of the economic interdependence between the United States and Latin America. That basis rested on the exchange of the latter's raw materials for the former's consumer products. The United States needed those natural resources for its booming factories and its growing arsenal. Latin America needed capital to develop. A logical system, or so thought U.S. policymakers. The Latin Americans' fascination with economic nationalism, therefore, was completely illogical.

Yet, U.S. fears of economic nationalism in Latin America went beyond the purely economic sphere. Thomas Mann of the State Department clearly stated his belief that "the principal threat to Latin American support of our political, economic and military policies is an excessive nationalism. . . . This is not just a problem of protecting American interests; it affects and conditions the whole range of our relations." Reports from both the State Department and the CIA in 1952 seconded Mann's fears. "Excessive" nationalism would be a "serious deterrent to hemisphere solidarity and to our efforts to obtain Latin American support for our foreign policy objectives"; "extreme" nationalism would "make it difficult for Latin American governments to render on all occasions the degree of diplomatic, military, or economic support desired by the United States." In sum, concluded George Messersmith, U.S. relations with Latin America "have been becoming more and more a one-way street."[35] Such a situation was hardly acceptable for the United States, intent as it was on constructing two-way highways.

The situation was deemed even more unacceptable when U.S. officials pondered the relationship between Latin American nationalism and communism. Communists were much like leeches, attaching themselves to nationalism, sucking it dry in pursuit of their own revolutionary goals, and then, once in power, discarding the empty carcass to fulfill their Marxist ideology. As one State Department report explained, the mixture of unstable governments, dissatisfied masses, and nationalistic appeals was "tailor-made for exploitation by the Communists who, constituting a relatively small part of the total population, exert an influence out of all proportion to their number. In doing this they make full use of the dogma and slogans of the extreme nationalists and try to associate themselves in the popular mind with these nationalists."[36]

This troublesome situation was in evidence in Central America, where communists had gained some influence due to "the skill with which they have identified themselves with progressive and nationalistic movements." Guatemala served as a symbol of what might happen if the communists were successful, as explained in a 1953 report: "In Guatemala, commun-ism has had its greatest success in Latin America. While Guatemalan hostility toward and mistrust of United States interests derives largely from intense nationalism, this feeling has been deepened and aggravated by the communists."[37]

While many U.S. officials were sure of the distinct links between "extreme nationalism" and communism in Latin America, others were not so certain. Those uncertainties were reflected in a fascinating discussion during a 1952 CFR meeting, attended by a number of former State Department members and businessmen.[38] Old State Department hand Dana Munro, then at Princeton University, opened the meeting by enumerating the challenges to U.S. policy in Latin America: "anti-American scoundrels, i.e., communists, Peronistas, nationalists, etc." Was it possible, he wondered, to take them all on at the same time? "Must we," he asked the group, "put up with nationalism, for example, while we are combating communism? In other words, exactly what are we fighting?" Spruille Braden, another department veteran, quickly responded that the problem in Guatemala was communism, and John McClintock from the United Fruit Company generally agreed. He believed that communists were taking advantage of nationalism in Latin America, but felt that the United States, being a bit nationalistic itself, should show more understanding. The job for the United States was to "winnow the wheat from the chaff, and devote most of our energies to combating communism, while channeling nationalism into constructive paths." Perhaps, Munro suggested, the two forces could be played off against one another.

That suggestion returned the debate to Munro's original query concerning exactly what the United States was facing. Langbourne Williams, Jr., of the Freeport Sulphur Company, believed that the problems plaguing U.S. interests in Latin America would be there with or without communism. Another businessman, H.W. Balgooyen of American and Foreign Power Company, Inc., agreed, pointing to Argentina "where nationalism is the problem instead of communism." Indeed, nationalism was "harder to combat than communism itself." Douglas Allen, of the Otis Astoria Corporation, argued that the "problem is not nationalism *per se*, but the use of nationalism by communism. . . .nationalism itself is a fundamentally different thing and is dangerous only in conjunction with communism." Balgooyen was not convinced, noting that it was "hard to draw the line" in many instances. Given the inconclusive nature of that exchange, Rutgers scholar Charles Cumberland reiterated Munro's question once again: was it "nationalistic or communistic propaganda that is making the situation difficult?" McClintock could only restate his earlier position, concluding that "the problem would not be the same if communism were not a factor."

The CFR debate raised a number of questions concerning the link between nationalism and communism in Latin America. Like the chicken and the egg, which came first? Was nationalism alone a force to fear, or might it be turned to "constructive paths?" Was it, like some inert element, a threat only when it combined with a more dangerous compound—communism? Or was it "harder to combat than communism itself?" Even Milton Eisenhower, after his 1953 trip, seemed to hedge a bit in tackling those questions, arguing that nationalism had two faces. "Nationalism as such contains praiseworthy elements of pride in achievement and desire for improved living standards. But ultra-nationalism, with its blindness of long-term interests, is today a definitely retrogressive influence, fostered by communist agitators."[39] It was, perhaps, better than no answer at all and, in a somewhat murky fashion, summed up two of the more consistent views held by U.S. officials. First, that nationalism in Latin America (aside from a rather nebulous "praiseworthy" sort emanating from "pride in achievement") was a potentially dangerous thing. And second, that the "virulent bug of nationalism," when combined with the plague of communism, was judged by one and all to create a far deadlier and more dangerous strain.

In searching for answers to the problem, U.S. officials began by trying to locate its causes. Some looked to the history of Latin America to discern the origins of such an ideology. A Department of Commerce publication noted that, "Partly as the result of historical evolution and partly owing to the characteristics of segments of the population. . . , Latin America has been accustomed to a larger measure of governmental intervention in political, social. . . , and economic affairs than in the United States."[40] Such an evaluation was entirely consistent with other comments on the deleterious effects of Spanish and Portuguese rule; just as the colonial rule of those nations had slowed the later development of democratic governments, so too had it affected the future economic development of the region.

Contemporary factors, however, were deemed to be much more important in fomenting anti-U.S. economic nationalism in Latin America. One centered around what a 1952 State Department report called the "jealousy and feelings of inferiority common to the weak and poor with regard to the rich and powerful." It was not unnatural, other reports noted, that Latin America would view the United States with "jealousy" or "envy." The disparity in "economic, political, and military power is fantastically great." Such disparity "naturally creates envy of the United States on the part of Latin Americans and also leads them to excuse their nonperformance of international obligations by pointing to tremendously superior United States power."[41] While somewhat understandable, such policies were nevertheless unacceptable, since they sought to punish the United States for something it had little control over (its own obvious superiority) and/or excuse the Latin Americans from doing something more constructive concerning their own dismal situation.

Latin American jealousy, it was thought, was compounded by a resentment springing from the belief that the United States had abandoned the region after World War II. Milton Eisenhower's 1953 report cited the fact that some in Latin America "mistakenly believe that the United States turns its attention to the other American Republics only in time of crisis," and "hold a persistent feeling that the United States could, if it wished, have made substantial sums for development available to them when it was providing billions for the rest of the world." They felt "disappointment" over the failure of the United States to "establish the equivalent of the Marshall Plan" in their region, and were "deeply disturbed by the preference which they feel the United States is showing for Europe." Somewhat less charitably, a U.S. delegate to a UN conference complained about the "Latin American self-pity arising from, if not always an honest, at least a strong, feeling that American dollars should be going to Latin America instead of to Europe."[42]

Jealousy and resentment may have gone far in explaining some of the anti-U.S. sentiment emanating from Latin America; but why did that resentment find expression in policies of economic nationalism? The analysis of U.S. officials revealed a fairly simple equation. The United States, being the dominant power in the hemisphere, was naturally thought by the Latin Americans to be "responsible for everything." "Everything" included the fact that "90 percent of the wealth [in the hemisphere] is produced by one of the American republics—the United States—leaving 10 percent for division among the remaining 20 American states with a total population greater than ours."[43] Increasingly, the thought was gaining credence in Latin America that such a state of affairs was not simply a product of natural market forces, but a result of U.S. "imperialism" or "colonialism."[44] Moreover, Latin Americans believed that they were "prevented by the more highly indus-trialized countries from diversifying their economies. United States and other foreign companies doing business in Latin America are considered to be major perpatrators [sic] of this exploitation and therefore fair prey for expropriation."[45]

Some U.S. reports dismissed these ideas as wrong-headed, characterizing them as "psychological" or "emotional rationalizations of their own political, economic, and social failures."[46]   Many others, however, recognized that there were concrete reasons for the growth of economic nationalism in Latin America. Both the Great Depression and World War II had "left a profound impress." During the depression, prices for the primary exports of Latin America fell disastrously. During the war, the region had experienced a shortage of consumer goods. These developments underscored a growing belief that an economy dependent on the export of natural resources and the import of needed consumer products "becomes subject to wide and violent fluctuations whenever importing countries experience the cyclical swings that seem endemic to a condition of industrialization." The result was a "greater emphasis on diversification and self-containment and reduced concern with international trade and investment."[47]

Politically, economic nationalism provided either a solution or a scapegoat for various sectors in Latin America. According to a 1952 State Department report, there existed in Latin America "a popular demand for better living and health standards, that is to say, for diversification of their economies . . . , for industrialization. . . , for increased productivity. . . and for solution of the perennial problem of dollar shortages." Those "demands" emanated from some of the same sectors cited by U.S. officials when discerning the source of the new instability in Latin America. A new middle class, full of nascent entrepreneurs, had arisen. While "once comparatively indifferent to technology and trade," they were now "business- and machine-minded." It had gotten to the point that "production managers now receive some of the prestige formerly reserved for poets or politicians." Many of them had "vigorous appetites [sic] for industrial conquest, and hence are at times inclined to favor limitations on, or discrimination against, outside financial control."[48]

As a 1953 State Department paper revealed, however, economic nationalism also provided a handy scapegoat for some groups in Latin America. It was a "useful screen" for indigenous businessmen "who rely upon limited volume and high unit profit and who wish to avoid competition." It also was a "tempting refuge for the wealthy, since it diverts attention from age-old abuses in the Latin American social and economic structure." Even the governments themselves used economic nationalism to their own ends, explaining their failures to produce better standards of living by blaming the United States.[49]

Central America, with its undeniable poverty, economic backwardness, and dependence on primary product export/consumer product import economies, was a fertile region for the growth of economic nationalism. According to a 1954 report, the nations of the area were dissatisfied with "a 'colonial' economic status," and this feeling found "expression in antagonism toward the large US corporations operating" there. Communists were ready to "exploit this dissatisfaction for their own purposes, but the sentiment is real and general." Especially was this true among the rising economic groups, the middle class and labor.[50]

In addition to jealousy, resentment, disappointment, and other more concrete reasons for the development of economic nationalism in Latin America, U.S. policymakers also considered the peoples of that region as a factor. By and large, those officials believed the Latin Americans to be quite ignorant concerning economics; such views were often tainted with a dash of racism, in which the Latinos were depicted as children trying to play with toys that were much too complicated. One of the most damning portrayals of this kind was made by J. Robert Schaetzel, who served as the technical secretary for the U.S. delegation to the 1947–48 UN Conference on Trade and Employment.[51] The Latin Americans were so "fixated" on industrialization that "practicality, soundness, and even likelihood of success are ignored." Their proposals were "preposterous," formed in an "atmosphere of unreality." Their conference delegates showed "a lamentable tendency on the part of many to talk in direct ratio to their ignorance." Arguments used by them were "emotional," with "only rare instances of good preparation and tight reasoning." In particular, "The influence of the Central Americans was negligible."

While Schaetzel was particularly harsh in his indictment of the Latin Americans, other officials seemed to share his general viewpoint. Former ambassador Spruille Braden, responding to a letter from Assistant Secretary Miller, commented that, "Not infrequently, I have had a feeling that some of our Latino friends were playing at economics, just as a child will pretend in his games to be something he isn't and has no immediate possibility of becoming." U.S. Ambassador to Costa Rica Nathaniel Davis bemoaned the fact that in Central America it seemed impossible to "get it through their heads that without genuine (and demonstrated) adherence to the Pan American system they may not find it easy to attract American capital or get international bank loans." He wondered whether there was "some way to get the Pan American family to admonish its naughty members." A Department of Commerce report tried to alleviate the fears of readers concerning statist economics in Latin America: "Experience and responsibility frequently have a sobering effect."[52]

The inherent dangers of economic nationalism in Latin America were of such pressing concern, however, that the United States could not wait for the Latin Americans to "sober up." Irregardless of whether they had some grounds for complaint, economic nationalism was obviously not the proper response. Yet, the fact that their complaints were based on some concrete factors meant that the United States must propose some alternate road to economic development.

There was widespread support for the "economic development" of Latin America among U.S. policymakers. The necessity for it seemed apparent. The "continued cooperation" of Latin America in the political and economic plans of the United States and the Free World made it essential that the United States "demonstrate that we are interested in helping to raise the status of the masses in Latin America," argued a 1953 State Department report. A preliminary report by the Randall Commission in 1953 pointed out that U.S. aid to Latin America would, "by contributing to genuine economic advance, increase the likelihood that moderate factions will gain and maintain ascendancy in the political movements responding to demands for social change." Thus, an added bonus would be political stability—killing two birds with one stone.[53]

Still, what did all of this really mean? A 1954 report dealing with the MSP in Latin America outlined some of the means and goals. The United States had to "develop a clearer understanding" of the "constructive role which foreign private capital can and does play" among the people of Latin America. It also needed to "encourage" the Latin Americans to set up a "favorable environment for such investment." It all sounded very "constructive" and "favorable" and "encouraging," but to what end? The ultimate goal was to "encourage the continued production in Latin America of commodities on which our consumers, industries and defense effort depend. We also wish to develop and expand the market for exports in Latin America."[54]

The "commodities" to which the report referred were, of course, the raw materials needed by the United States for its industrial and defense plants. All in all, it seemed to call not for radical change, but simply a continuation of the present situation, albeit on a more "constructive" footing. Perhaps, as alluded to in a 1951 State Department document, that was the only possible answer, since the whole question of economic cooperation raised the "matter of continuance of economic development in Latin America while we are expanding our plant facilities in the United States."[55] In plain terms, how could the United States promise the kinds of "economic development" apparently desired by the Latin Americans, if by so doing it cut into the needs of its own industries and defense interests? Didn't the existing interdependence depend on the continual exchange of goods—Latin American raw materials for U.S. consumer goods? Were development and interdependence compatible? Obviously, this issue was not quite as simple as it seemed.

To Reach the Minds and Hearts of Our Fellow Americans

A lot of people assume that Latin America is in the bag. Perhaps this is true from the military point of view, but in terms of ideology Latin America is by no means a sure thing. Throughout the Hemisphere we are presented with very serious problems in our efforts to extend the American ideology—to reach the minds and hearts of our fellow Americans, so as to solidify them against our common enemy.[56]

Aside from the hauntingly familiar phrasing employed, those words from Assistant Secretary Miller summed up the view of many U.S. policymakers concerning the threat of communism in Latin America. The region apparently shared with the United States a general adherence to the ideas of democracy, freedom, and justice. Nevertheless, the fact that the governments and peoples of Latin America seemed to take a rather lackadaisical approach to the Cold War bothered officials in Washington. This, combined with the belief that certain groups in Latin America were extraordinarily susceptible to the sirens' song of communism, was enough to raise distinct questions as to just how "safe" Latin America was. Reports of the spread of communism in the region, particularly Central America, indicated that Latin America was "by no means a sure thing." Somehow or another, the United States would have to "solidify" the peoples of that region.

Apathy on the part of Latin Americans toward the problem of international communism often infuriated U.S. officials. A number of reports noted that while Latin American governments were more than willing to give lip service to the cause, positive action was rarely forthcoming. One report cited the "dismal performance" of the Latin Americans in sending troops to Korea as part of the UN force. Another echoed that sentiment, with the stinging comment that Latin American "restraint" in the battle against communism was "felt especially at the point at which Latin American support for the cause of the free world threatens to entail sacrifices for the general public." Communist propaganda, to the effect that the United States was "bleeding them [Latin Americans] for its own exclusive interests," was part of the problem, appealing as it did to "the millions of Latin Americans who live in the direst poverty, feel they have little to lose, and are therefore disposed to listen favorably to its promises." Another factor was the "latent rather than. . .immediate menace" of communism in Latin America; the people of that region simply did not feel any urgency about the situation.[57]

Inaction in the free world–communist world struggle was barely tolerable. When it became obvious that communism was making inroads into Latin America, the situation took on more ominous overtones for U.S. policymakers. As a State Department report from the early 1950s declared, "At present Communists are disturbingly able to use the growing aspirations of Latin American peoples for higher levels of living, their disappointed hopes, and a considerable pessimism about the future." More important, perhaps, was that, "Key Latin American sectors—labor, students, nationalists—have been surprisingly vulnerable to Communist propaganda."[58] We have previously noted U.S. views of the role communism played in the nationalist movements in Latin America. Yet, the apparently favorable responses of "labor" and "students" (and intellectuals as a whole) to communist dogma were also commented on with some concern. U.S. interest was at least partially motivated by the fact that the working class and intelligentsia were considered to be leading forces in the widespread attacks on the old regimes in Latin America and as such would probably be playing larger roles in the future of that region.

One of the "success stories" for communism in Latin America, at least according to U.S. officials, was the "capture of Latin American intellectuals who turned away from capitalism to socialism during the great depression when so many of our own intellectuals passed through a time of confusion as to the ability of capitalism to deal with the economic problems confronting the world." While this was but a handful of individuals, "These fuzzy-minded intellectuals have not only obtained control of many schools and universities where they have influenced youth, but they have supplied the imagination needed to adapt the dogma of socialism and communism so as to reconcile them with nationalistic prejudices."[59]

The impact of communism on the nascent labor movements in Latin America seemed even more concrete. As a 1946 State Department research paper bluntly stated, "The most important single ideological force in Latin American labor today is Communism." One of the most important aspects of communism's role in Latin American labor was the "intense nationalistic and anti-imperialistic character" it imparted to the movement. An earlier report had cited the "Marxian ideology of class warfare" gaining influence in the labor movements in Latin America. Many workers, it claimed, went beyond mere "affiliation" with communism and belonged to the Communist Party.[60]

The situation in Central America and the Caribbean was much the same. The lack of urgency in confronting the issue of communism was demonstrated in the region's response to the Caracas Conference and the overthrow of the government of Guatemala in 1954. "From their point of view, a question of US intervention in the internal affairs of a Caribbean republic is a matter of far more urgent importance than that of an indirect and long-term Communist threat." Here, too, communists were seen to "exert an influence far out of proportion to their limited numerical strength." This was done through linking up with "progressive and nationalistic movements" and by exploiting the "susceptibility of the intelligentsia to Marxist cliches." Labor also played an important role, since "Caribbean Communist international contacts are maintained through the Communist-controlled Latin American Confederation of Labor."[61]

According to U.S. officials, the fact that the Latin Americans were not inclined to keep up their guards against the communist menace, combined with the fact that communism was making rapid inroads into some increasingly important groups in that region, was inexorably leading to the growth of communist power in many of its nations. To be sure, that growth had not been even or consistent. Beginning with a peak party membership of 330,000 in the immediate postwar years, by the early 1950s, the Communist Party could count only 200,000 members in Latin America (and most of those were located in Brazil, Chile, or Cuba).[62] Nevertheless, as a report by the Operations Coordinating Board (OCB) stated, "Latin American Communists continue to pour their energies into Moscow-directed activities and to proclaim their loyalty to the USSR." Communists had "managed to attract an increasing number of sympathizers and to build numerous front organizations." Aid from "international Communism" was another indicator of their continued presence in Latin America. In 1953, the report claimed, "approximately 1,000 Latin Americans traveled to the Soviet orbit under Communist auspices"— ten times the number of 1950. Increasing numbers of Latin Americans were attending "non-hemisphere Communist front conferences." All of this, combined with "intensified Communist propaganda" and numerous Radio Moscow stories concerning the region, "indicate the Kremlin's interest in its collaborators in the area." This revealed, as a CIA study concluded, that "Latin America will continue to be a fertile ground for demagogues of the ultra-nationalist as well as the Communist type."[63]

In many ways, U.S. policymakers saw Central America as a microcosm of the "communist problem" in Latin America. In strictly numerical terms, the Communist Party was indeed weak in the area. Officially illegal and with 1,000 or less party members in each of the five nations, communism seemed to pose, on paper at least, little threat.[64] However, none of the Central American nations—save Nicaragua—seemed entirely secure from communist machinations.

In Costa Rica, the problem manifested itself in three main areas. The first was the Popular Vanguard Party (PVP), described as a "Communist-line party" in a 1947 State Department report. The report went on to note with some dismay that "there are probably more key members of the international Communist organization in Costa Rica, proportionately, than in almost any other American republic." And while, by 1955, the PVP had been declared illegal and its membership had fallen to somewhere between 1,500 and 3,000 (from 20,000 in 1947), the party's "old-line leadership has remained intact."[65]

The second problem was José Figueres, who, after leading a succesful 1948 revolt, was elected president of Costa Rica in 1953. While not viewed as a communist, Figueres, according to Washington, was about as close as one could come without crossing the line. A 1953 intelligence report portrayed the Costa Rican leader as "demagogic," "socialistic," "volatile," "opportunitistic," and as a "strong nationalist [who] advocates statism and. . .is inclined toward dictatorial methods." None of this made Figueres a communist, but it did mean that his stances on several issues were "likely to increase Communist capabilities in Costa Rica."[66]

The final ingredient of danger in Costa Rica was the increased presence of communists in the labor groups of that nation. It was among "certain element of organized labor" that Costa Rican communists found "their chief support." The nation's labor movements were linked to the Con-federation of Latin American Workers and the World Federation of Trade Unions, "both of which are communist-dominated." Inside Costa Rica, the communists centered their strength in the General Confederation of Costa Rican Workers, which operated throughout the nation and "claimed a membership of about 6000, about 4000 of whom were in agricultural unions, including the banana workers."[67]

The situation in El Salvador was somewhat more comforting, but still contained overtones of concern. Here again, the problem was not the number of communists (it was estimated in 1955 that there were probably no more than 300 party members, and 500 "sympathizers"), but their success in penetrating the labor movement. Ambassador Shaw, in 1949 and 1950, commented with some anxiety on the communist efforts in this regard. Although there was but a "small group of active communists," it obviously intended to "continue its efforts to stir up trouble in the form of strikes and similar measures." While they had not met with much success, "more problems of like nature may be expected to arise from time to time in the relatively near future." A few months later, in February 1950, Shaw wrote of the "public agitation" in the country, claiming that there "seems to be a strong Communist imprint." A State Department report five years later, however, pointed to 1950 as a turning point, with the rise of Oscar Osorio to the presidency. By "making sweeping arrests and exiling various leaders," he had made a successful counterattack against communist infiltration. Problems remained, however. Communist efforts in the labor movement, while conducted among a "small and somewhat nebulous segment of workers, is nevertheless significant." The tone of the report was guarded optimism.[68]

Communism in Honduras, as befit the general U.S. view that there was very little indigenous to that nation save poverty and backwardness, was seen as a stepchild of stronger movements in El Salvador and Guatemala. The Honduran Communist Party had few members, but had "gained a strong foothold in the labor element and, to a lesser extent, in intellectual circles." The party itself was illegal, but still operated through a "front"—the Honduran Democratic Revolutionary Party. Communists were active in the unions, among students and in the schools, and even had a "feminine auxiliary." The situation had deteriorated since 1948, when the election of Juan Manuel Gálvez Durón produced a "free atmosphere" in Honduras, which meant that "communist leaders have had a more favorable climate in which to operate." The climax of their efforts had been a May 1954 strike among nearly 22,000 Honduran agricultural workers. As the U.S. embassy reported, "This must be considered as a very strong Communist offensive in Honduras." The peaceful solution to the strike, combined with a new Honduran government that demonstrated a "more enlightened policy toward labor" and aided the "anti- communists in their organizational efforts" seemed to have stemmed the tide for the time being. Nevertheless, even before the overthrow of the suspected communist government in Guatemala in June 1954, Honduras was the only Central American nation listed in the "First Priority" group of Latin American nations in an NSC directive calling for intelligence on communist activities in Latin America.[69]

Guatemala, of course, was cited as the most significant example of communist infiltration in Central America. Using their time-honored tactic of boring from within, Guatemalan communists had ridden the wave of the 1944 revolution in that nation, making use of "visionary intellectuals and opportunists," as well as labor, to push for their own purposes. By identifying themselves with nationalism, they were able to insert themselves into positions of power in the new government. The real base of their power, however, was the General Confederation of Guatemalan Labor, which "combined into a single organization under communist domination the principal unions of the country." From there, the communists had moved into "influential youth, women's and mass organizations" of the nation, including student and intellectual groups. The communists had performed their work so well, in fact, that a 1952 State Department report lamented, "So intimate is the relationship between communists and certain non-communist elements in Guatemala that it is difficult to distinguish between them." The U.S.-supported overthrow of Guatemalan president Jacobo Arbenz in 1954 had "removed the most immediate and dangerous threat to stability and order in the region, but, in Guatemala and throughout the Caribbean, the Communists will continue to make the most of plentiful opportunities for agitation."[70]

Nicaragua, according to a 1955 State Department report, was the least hospitable nation in Central America for communists. Their party—the Socialist Party—had "lost their dominant position in the General Confederation of Labor" and had its "key leaders in exile." President Somoza had outlawed the party, and it had since survived as "a tolerated nuisance." Membership in the underground party was probably less than 500, and since neither major party in Nicaragua had "any sympathy" for the communists, their "activities were negligible."[71]

The threat to U.S. interests in Latin America was obvious to officials in Washington. Specifically, the ability of communism to secure a toehold in Latin America would damage U.S. credibility, pose a threat—in the form of sabotage and terrorism—to U.S. business and strategic interests, undoubtedly spread to other areas, and, most important, lead to the inability or unwillingness of Latin American nations to participate in the interdependent economic, political, and military arrangements so important to the United States.

The issue of credibility was raised in a letter from Assistant Secretary of State Henry Holland to Secretary Dulles in May of 1954. He began by noting that the communists often engaged in "frontal tests of strength" around the globe, and cited the cases of Korea and Indochina to make his point. Now, he claimed, another threat was to be found in Guatemala. What was being tested was the will and trustworthiness of the United States: "the test is whether the world Communist organization has the strength to establish a satellite nation in this hemisphere and, conversely, whether the free nations have the power to resist that attempt." Just a few weeks later (after the overthrow of the government of Guatemala), Secretary Dulles, in an address to the nation, put the issue in a somewhat simplistic manner by claiming that, "This intrusion of Soviet despotism was, of course, a direct challenge to our Monroe Doctrine—the first and most fundamental of our foreign policies."[72] Such challenges could hardly be allowed to pass without response.

The more direct threat posed by communism to U.S. interests in Latin America was also a cause of concern. A 1947 CIA report on "Soviet Objectives in Latin America" painted a distressing picture of what might happen in case of a world emergency—a time when the United States would depend on stability and the smooth flow of necessary raw materials from Latin America. "Soviet activity in the area has recently shifted to measures that can be counted on to prevent, reduce, or place in doubt US access to the area's strategic materials or military support." It summed up the bleak situation by arguing that

> Communist nonpolitical organization in Latin America has already proceeded so far and so effectively that in the event of war with the US, the USSR can, by merely giving the necessary orders, paralyze the economies of Chile and Cuba and thus deny to the US, at least temporarily, the copper and sugar that they would otherwise contribute to the US war effort.

Perhaps the CIA was a bit too heavy-handed in its portrayal of the communist danger; attached reports from the Department of State and Office of Naval Intelligence dissented (although the latter agreed that the Soviets would emphasize "sabotage in the form of strikes, etc.").[73]

Despite such skepticism, however, the fear of communist sabotage and disruption was constantly expressed in following years. An example of what might possibly occur was cited by Assistant Secretary Miller in 1951. Already in Guatemala, "American business interests. . .are being persecuted and hard-pressed by extremist labor demands which are motivated and sparked by Communist leaders." And if that was what U.S. interests were facing in a time of peace, what would happen during a national emergency? A note from the JCS in 1952 provided the answer, pointing to the "indigenous Communist movements and. . .the probability of extensive operations by small numbers of Communist agents" as the "chief covert threats to the strategic areas of Latin America" in time of war. A CIA assessment from that same year also noted the danger, claiming that the communists, "Through their influence in labor, . . .have a capability for interrupting the operations of strategically important industries by means of strikes and sabotage." It concluded that, "The greatest danger from Communists in Latin America in time of global war would be that of sabotage in strategic industries."[74]

Quite naturally, considering the belief in the expansionist nature of the Soviet state held by many U.S. policymakers, one of the biggest fears concerning a communist foothold in the Western Hemisphere was that it would quickly infiltrate elsewhere. The focus of U.S. attention during the early 1950s was on the communist "beachhead" in Guatemala. Few officials believed that the communists would be content to merely maintain their hold on that nation. As early as 1951, Assistant Secretary Miller complained about the "alarming amount of subversive travel into Honduras and El Salvador" from neighboring Guatemala. An NIE study of 1954 cited a specific case where Guatemala, acting as a "base for international conspiratorial action," had been the source of "subversive activity. . .in the strike of Honduran plantation workers. That technique was capable of further extension." And the official history of the JCS conveyed the fear that once having secured their hold on Guatemala, the communists "might seek to expand, particularly at the expense of their less populous neighbors to the south—El Salvador, Honduras, and Nicaragua."[75] Obviously, Southeast Asia did not have a monopoly on dominoes.

Finally, as a CIA paper reported, the most obvious, and potentially most harmful, aspect of communist penetration in Latin America would be the demise of intrahemispheric cooperation—the breakdown of U.S.-Latin American interdependence. The communists were actively pursuing policies designed "to curtail Latin American cooperation with the United States. The social, economic, and political conditions which have been described will afford them opportunities for anti-US agitation." For now, they aimed at giving "such direction to nationalism as will most effectively hinder Latin American cooperation with the United States."[76] Little needed to be said about how much "cooperation" would be "hindered" if communists actually secured control of a nation or nations in the region.

With those ominous concerns in the backs of their minds, U.S. officials sought solutions to the communist menace in Latin America. For Thomas Mann, the solution was to be found not in what the United States could do, but in what it could convince the Latin Americans to do. "Freedom," he stated, "is something that each people and each nation must themselves achieve and defend. If we can get our friends to thinking along these lines instead of standing by with crossed arms waiting for the United States Marines or the United States Treasury to pull their chestnuts out of the fire we will soon have the Communist problem under control in this hemisphere." That same conclusion was reached in a State Department study a year earlier. "We must make the case for cooperation so strong that it will override. . .the case for neutrality and opportunism. We must make active adherence to free world policy the fashionable thing in Latin America by persuading those groups whose good will is decisive that it is a) the virtuous thing, b) the smart thing, and c) the inevitable thing."[77] And exactly who were "those groups"? According to a CIA analysis, "The best immediate prospects for a check upon the extremist forces of social and economic change are to be found in countries. . .where moderate urban groups have been established as a political factor."[78]

The CIA's solution meant courting the emerging middle class in Latin America. As a State Department study claimed, that class "has as a whole been the proponent of Western concepts of political and economic democracy." Even here, however, there was danger. The middle class was often "torn" between the traditional conservative forces and left-leaning extremists. In some cases, where "trade unionism and Communism are regarded as the most menacing," the middle class tended to align with the old conservatives. In other cases, though, it had "aligned itself with labor, and in some instances, as in Chile and Cuba, for example, even with the Communists."[79] The middle class, then, could not be entirely trusted. And what of those Latin American nations, such as in Central America, where the middle class was so small as to be nearly negligible?

The answer, provided in another State Department report, was to look elsewhere: "Among the effective forces to combat communism, although they do not necessarily promote representative democratic government, are the church, the armed forces, and certain student groups and non-communist labor elements." Certainly, most of those "forces" did not sound like protectors of "representative democratic government"; indeed, they sounded like the old, traditional, oligarchic forces that were being rooted out by the new "forces" in Latin America. As the wording of the report demonstrates, U.S. aid or encouragement of such sectors would have to be done with two or more fingers clamped tightly to the nose. Nevertheless, as a memorandum from Assistant Secretary Miller in 1951 suggested, in combating a menace like communism, stringent measures were often called for. The removal of "agents from positions of influence in their governments"; the separation of "such agents from control and direction of organized labor"; the adoption of "measures to prevent sabotage by such agents"; the imposition of "effective restrictions to prevent travel by such agents from one state to another"; and requiring "the registration of such agents so that they can be readily identified" were some of his ideas on battling the "agents of Russian imperialism."[80]

The problems confronted by U.S. policymakers intent on constructing a web of interdependent economic, political, and military relations with Latin America, and specifically Central America, were immense. Like the system they were trying to build, the problems themselves seemed interdependent. Instability was caused by the rise of various new forces against the traditional ruling classes; that instability often took as its rallying cry economic nationalism; communist agents, waiting in the shadows, took advantage of the instability and extreme nationalism to make a push for their own goals. So closely related were these factors that more than one U.S. official wondered whether the United States was facing three problems or one. In the overall scheme of things, of course, it did not matter. Instability hurt opportunities not only for the development of stable democratic governments but for U.S. investors, who rarely put money into the middle of a revolution. Economic nationalism, with its decidedly anti-U.S. overtones, also marked a stumbling block. Nations determined to pursue their own courses did not seem to have the right spirit of cooperation. And communism, the least of all but perhaps the worst of all problems, always stood at the ready, fanning the flames of anti-U.S. sentiment, contributing wherever it could to instability, and waiting for its opportunity to grab the reins of power.

At first glance, the solutions seemed perfectly obvious. To bring about stability, the United States must encourage those new forces that appeared to be the best chance for the development of democracy in Latin America. To defuse the arguments of economic nationalism, the United States had to demonstrate the miraculous powers of private enterprise and promote "economic development" in the region. The battle against communism must be carried on by finding appropriate anticommunist forces in Latin America and supporting them.

That was the first glance; anyone looking deeper was confronted by some troubling questions. How was the United States to encourage democracy in a region that historically, culturally, institutionally, economically, and even racially seemed uniquely unfit for its growth? And what was one to make of those "new forces"? The intellectuals and middle and working classes were seen as both possible harbingers of a new democratic era in the region and as unreliable forces that might easily get carried away. The very democracy they strove for, in fact, could be unsettling, involving as it often did violent strains of economic nationalism and an attitude toward the communist threat that U.S. officials regarded as reckless. Where was the basis for political interdependence?

Even more confounding was the Latin American infatuation with economic nationalism. It was one thing for the Latin Americans to be jealous of U.S. power and wealth. And one could understand Latin American claims that they were being ignored after World War II, while Europe and Japan were showered with U.S. gifts. Their attachment to economic nationalism as a solution to their economic woes, however, was nearly inexplicable. Yes, they had a valid argument about the prices they were paid for their natural resources and the much higher prices they paid for imported goods. And, yes, their demands for economic diversification sounded fairly reasonable. But relying on the statist notions of economic nationalism was a case of sadly misguided naivete. Here, racism entered the picture, as U.S. officials pondered the notion that the Latin Americans were simply incapable of understanding the higher economic laws they were calling into question. The problem, of course, was what to do about it. "Economic development" was a phrase that could mean a great deal. To Latin Americans, it meant breaking their import-export dependency and diversifying their economies. For U.S. policymakers, however, that raised the troubling question of how to "develop" Latin America without breaking down the fundamental mechanism of its interdependence with the United States—the exchange of its raw materials for U.S. consumer goods.

And finally, there was the problem of communism. The Latin Americans, according to Washington, did not have the proper appreciation of the threat it posed, and therefore seemed reluctant to take the steps necessary to eradicate it from the hemisphere. This was all the more troubling since communism seemed to be making important inroads into new and influential groups in Latin America. Entirely oblivious to the problem, however, Latin America seemed to view the struggle against communism as basically a United States–Soviet Union battle. Meanwhile, the communists—exploiting both the instability and economic nationalism in the region—moved to co-opt the "fuzzy-headed" intellectuals and nationalistic workers to serve their own ends. Again, what was the United States to do? Having apparently given up the "big stick," it would have to rely on groups within Latin America to rouse themselves to stem the communist tide. But what groups were to be roused? The middle class seemed a likely candidate, but its connection to economic nationalism and its unreliability made it suspect. Might the United States be better off by supporting some groups—not particularly democratic-minded, unfortunately—that were proven communist fighters? Yet, where might a policy of this sort lead—to repression, police-state tactics, the thwarting of the nascent democratic movements in the region?

Democracy, economic nationalism, dictatorship, anticommunism, development, instability, communism, repression, freedom. Suddenly, they no longer seemed like black and white choices. In terms of the U.S.-Latin American relationship, they seemed to flow one into the other, resulting in a dull gray. The promise of interdependence seemed to be slipping away.

Notes

1.   Charles Cumberland, "The Caribbean Area," Working Paper No. 2, 11 Nov. 1952, for CFR Discussion Group on Political Unrest in Latin America, Council on Foreign Relations, Records of Groups, Vol. XLV, Archives of the Council on Foreign Relations, New York, NY.

2.   "Statement for the Joint Intelligence Staff. . . ," 28 Sept. 1945, RG 59, Records of OARA, Box 16; "United States Relations with Latin America," 1952, RG 59, Miller Files, Box 3, NA.

3.   CIA, "Review of the World Situation. . . ," 14 July 1948, p. 9, Documents of the National Security Council, 3rd Supplement (Microfilm) (Bethesda, MD), Reel 1 (hereafter NSC Documents, 3rd Supplement, and reel number).

4.   Cochran to Finley, 23 Feb. 1945, RG 59, 817.00/2–645, NA.

5.   "The Caribbean Republics," 24 Aug. 1954, *FRUS, 1952–1954*, 4:379–399.

6.   CIA, "Review of the World Situation. . . ," 14 July 1948, p. 9, NSC Documents, 3rd Supplement, Reel 1.

7.   Problem paper, 29 Aug. 1949, RG 59, Miller Files, Box 10, NA.

8.   Berle, "For the Discussion Group. . . ," 12 May 1953, RG 59, 720.00/5–1253, NA; John Cabot, "Summary of Remarks at Conference on U.S. Foreign Policy, June 4 and 5, 1953," John Foster Dulles Papers, Box 75, Seeley G. Mudd Manuscript Library, Department of Rare Books and Special Collections, Princeton University Libraries, Princeton, New Jersey (hereafter cited as Dulles Papers, box number, Mudd Library).

9.   "United States Relations with Latin America," 1952, RG 59, Miller Files, Box 3, NA; "The Caribbean Republics," 24 Aug. 1954, *FRUS, 1952–1954*, 4:381.

10.   CIA, "Conditions and Trends in Latin America. . . ," 12 Dec. 1952, Truman Papers, PSF, IF, Box 254, Central Intelligence Reports, NIE 67–75 folder, HSTL; "The Caribbean Republics," 24 Aug. 1954, *FRUS, 1952–1954*, 4:380; "Latin America," Mar. 1951, Truman Papers, CF, SD Corres., Box 39, File 1952, Folder 30A, HSTL.

11.   Untitled problem paper, 5 July 1949, RG 59, Miller Files, Box 10, NA; "The Caribbean Republics," 24 Aug. 1954, *FRUS, 1952–1954*, 4:383.

12.   Problem paper, 29 Aug. 1949, RG 59, Miller Files, Box 10; Walter N. Walmsley to Paul Nitze, 9 May 1952, RG 59, Miller Files, Box 10; Hallett Johnson to DS, 15 Oct. 1946, RG 59, FW818.00/10–1546; Rudolf Schoenfeld to Miller, 5 Sept. 1952, RG 59, Miller Files, Box 7; Miller to Paul Daniels, 7 Apr. 1952, RG 59, Miller Files, Box 7, NA.

13.   "United States Relations with Latin America," 19 Nov. 1951, RG 59, Miller Files, Box 10, NA.

14.   Such an analysis is best presented in a report prepared in 1946; see "III. Summary of Issues and Trends in the Other American Republics," RG 59, Records of OARA, Box 16, NA.

15.   "United States Relations with Latin America," 1952, RG 59, Miller Files, Box 3, NA.

16.   "The Caribbean Republics," 24 Aug. 1954, *FRUS, 1952–1954*, 4:380, 383.

17.   "Section Six: Conclusions and Recommendations," 13 Oct. 1953, Records of the Randall Commission, Box 59, Studies–Study of U.S. Problems and Policy Toward Latin America file, DDEL; "U.S. Policy With Respect to Latin America," 1952, RG 59, 720.00/12–452, NA.

18.   John Cabot, "Summary of Remarks. . . ," Dulles Papers, Box 75, Mudd Library.

19.   Ibid.

20.   "United States Relations with Latin America," 1952, RG 59, Miller Files, Box 3, NA.

21.   Miller to Bonsal, 25 Jan. 1952, RG 59, Miller Files, Box 3, NA.

22.   Krenn, *U.S. Policy Toward Economic Nationalism*, 22. For more on economic nationalism and its development in Latin America, see Shoshana Tancer, *Economic Nationalism in Latin America: The Quest for Economic Independence* (New York, 1976).

23.   For the early growth of economic nationalism in Latin America, see Christopher Abel and Colin M. Lewis, eds., *Latin America, Economic Imperial-ism and the State: The Political Economy of the External Connection from Independence to the Present* (London, 1985), particularly Sections III and IV; and Bill Albert, *South America and the First World War: The Impact of the War on Brazil, Argentina, Peru and Chile* (Cambridge, 1988), especially Ch. 7.

24.   See Krenn, *United States Policy Toward Economic Nationalism*.

25.   "Proposed Circular Instruction on the Post-War International Economic Program of the United States, with Particular Reference to the Other American Republics," 10 July 1944, RG 59, Records of the Office of Intelligence Research, Division of Research for the American Republics, Box 9 (hereafter Records of OIR, box number); "Economic Charter of the Americas: Declaration of Princi-ples," RG 353, Records of IAEAC, Box 1, EA Documents, 1/45–10/45 file, NA.

26.   J. Robert Schaetzel, "Analysis of Latin American Proposals, Tactics and Behavior at the United Nations Conference on Trade and Employment," 30 March 1948, RG 353, Records of IAEAC, Box 2; Messersmith to Mann, 17 Dec. 1952, RG 59, Records of Deputy Assistant Secretaries of State for Inter-Amer-ican Affairs, Subject File, 1945–56, Box 4 (hereafter Records of Deputy for I-A Affairs, box number), NA; "Summary of Milton Eisenhower's Report . . . ," 1953, Eisenhower Papers, WHCF, CF, Subject Series, Box 25, Eisenhower, Milton, Trip to South America (3) file, DDEL; "Notes for Use of Under Secretary Smith at White House Briefing for Congressional Leaders," 14 Apr. 1953, RG 59, Records of PPS, Foreign Policy, 1948–1952 file, NA.

27.   "The Caribbean Republics," 24 Aug. 1954, *FRUS, 1952–1954*, 4:384; Douglas K. Ballentine to DS, 21 Mar. 1951, RG 59, 814.00/3–2151, NA. For more on the development of economic nationalism in Guatemala after the 1944 revolt, and the U.S. view of that development, see Immerman, *CIA in Guatemala*, Chs. 3 and 4; Rabe, *Eisenhower and Latin America*, Ch. 3; and Gleijeses, *Shattered Hope*, 85–133.

28.   Intelligence Report, No. 6238, 21 Aug. 1953, RG 59, Records of OIR, NA. For the best treatment of Figueres, see Charles D. Ameringer, *Don Pepe: A Political Biography of José Figueres of Costa Rica* (Albuquerque, 1978).

29.   Shaw to Acheson, 10 Dec. 1949, RG 59, Miller Files, Box 6, NA.

30.   Gordon Reid to Raymond Leddy, et al., 12 June 1953, RG 59, 715.00/6–1253, NA.

31.   CD, *Factors Limiting U.S. Investment Abroad: Part 1—Survey of Factors in Foreign Countries* (Washington, 1953), 3, 5.

32.   "U.S. Policy with Respect to Latin America," 1952, RG 59, 720.00/12–452, NA.

33.   "Obstacles to U.S. Private Investment," 19 July 1951, Records of PMPC, Box 1, General Records A–W: Finance file, HSTL.

34.   Preliminary Draft, "Foreign Resources: Introduction," 13 June 1951, Records of the PMPC, Box 11, Preliminary Draft for Foreign Resources file, HSTL.

35.   Mann to Miller, 9 May 1952, RG 59, Miller Files, Box 10; "United States Relations with Latin America," 1952, RG 59, Miller Files, Box 3, NA; CIA, "Conditions and Trends in Latin America. . . ," 12 Dec. 1952, Truman Papers, PSF, IF, Box 254, Central Intelligence Reports, NIE 67–75 file, HSTL; Messersmith to Mann, 17 Dec. 1952, RG 59, Records of Deputy for I-A Affairs, Box 4, NA.

36.   "Statement in Support of the Mutual Security Program for FY 1954," 23 Apr. 1953, RG 59, MSP Files, Box 1, NA.

37.   "The Caribbean Republics," 24 Aug. 1954, *FRUS, 1952–1954*, 4:388; "Guatemala," 13 Mar. 1953, RG 59, Records of OMAA, Records Relating to El Salvador and Guatemala, 1952–1954, Box 1, Guatemala, 1954:   Briefing Materials file (hereafter cited as Records of OMAA, El Salvador and Guatemala, with box and file designation), NA.

38.   CFR, Discussion Group on Political Unrest in Latin America, 1st Meeting, 15 Oct. 1952, Records of Groups, Vol. XLIII, CFR Archives.

39.   "Summary of Milton Eisenhower's Report. . . ," 1953, Eisenhower Papers, WHCF, CF, Subject Series, Box 25, Eisenhower, Milton, Trip to South America (3) file, DDEL.

40.   CD, *Factors Limiting U.S. Investment Abroad*, 1:5.

41.   "U.S. Policy With Respect to Latin America," 1952, RG 59, 720.00/12–452; "Anti–United States Sentiment in the Other American Republics," 3 July 1944, RG 59, Records of OARA, Box 16; "United States Relations with Latin America," 1952, RG 59, Miller Files, Box 3, NA.

42.   "Summary of Milton Eisenhower's Report. . . ," 1953, Eisenhower Papers, WHCF, CF, Subject Series, Box 25, Eisenhower, Milton, Trip to South America (3) file, DDEL; DuWayne G. Clark to Woodward and Daniels, 1 Feb. 1949, RG 59, 710.11/2–149; "Suggested Plan for Economic Aid to Latin America," 22 Jan. 1948, RG 353, Records of ID/ID Committees, Box 78, Finance: Inter-American Bank Proposal file; Schaetzel, "Analysis of Latin American Proposals. . . ," 30 Mar. 1948, RG 353, Records of IAEAC, Box 2, NA.

43.   "United States Relations with Latin America," 1952, RG 59, Miller Files, Box 3; "U.S. Policy With Respect to Latin America," 1952, RG 59, 720.00/12–452, NA.

44.   "United States Relations with Latin America," 1952, RG 59, Miller Files, Box 3, NA.

45.   "State in Support of the Mutual Security Program for FY 1954 (Latin America)," 23 Apr. 1953, RG 59, MSP Files, Box 1, NA.

46.   "Foreign Resources: I. Introduction," 13 June 1951, Records of the PMPC, Box 11, Preliminary Draft for Foreign Resources file, HSTL; "U.S. Policy With Respect to Latin America," 1952, RG 59, 720.00/12–452, NA.

47.   CD, *Factors Limiting U.S. Investment Abroad,* 1:5; "Foreign Resources: I. Introduction," 13 June 1951, Records of the PMPC, Box 11, Preliminary Draft for Foreign Resources file, HSTL.

48.   "U.S. Policy With Respect to Latin America," 1952, RG 59, 720.00/12–452; CD, *Factors Limiting U.S. Investment Abroad,* 1:5.

49.   "Statement in Support of the Mutual Security Program for FY 1954 (Latin America)," 23 Apr. 1953, RG 59, MSP Files, Box 1, NA.

50.   "The Caribbean Republics," 24 Aug. 1954, *FRUS, 1952–1954,* 4:391–93.

51.   Schaetzel, "Analysis of Latin American Proposals. . . ," 30 Mar. 1948, RG 353, Records of IAEAC, Box 2, NA.

52.   Braden to Miller, 6 June 1950, Papers of Edward G. Miller, Box 1, Correspondence File, 1949–52, B (Folder 2) (hereafter Miller Papers, box and file designation), HSTL; Nathaniel Davis to Paul Daniels, 5 Nov. 1948, RG 59, 813.00/11–548, NA; CD, *Factors Limiting U.S. Investment Abroad,* 1:5.

53.   "Significance and Status of United States Economic Relations with Latin America," 22 June 1953, RG 59, Records of Deputy for I-A Affairs, Box 3, NA; "Section Six: Conclusions and Recommendations," 13 Oct. 1953, Records of Randall Commission, Box 59, Studies–Study of U.S. Problems and Policy Toward Latin America file, DDEL.

54.   "Regional Narrative Justification of Mutual Security Program for Latin America for FY 1955," 8 Mar. 1954, RG 59, MSP Files, Box 1, NA.

55.   "Briefing Book," 1951, Truman Papers, PSF, SF, Box 177, Foreign Ministers of American Republics–Meetings file, HSTL.

56.   Miller to William Benton, 2 May 1950, RG 59, Miller Files, Box 1, NA.

57.   "United States Relations with Latin America," Draft #2, 19 Nov. 1951, RG 59, Miller Files, Box 10, NA; "Briefing Book," 1951, Truman Papers, PSF, SF, Box 177, Foreign Ministers of American Republics–Meetings file, HSTL.

58.   "Information on Mutual Security Program for the Bureau of the Budget," c. 1951, RG 59, MSP Files, Box 1, NA.

59.   "United States Relations With Latin America," 1952, RG 59, Miller Files, Box 3, NA.

60.   Policy Report, enclosed in Hussey to Butler, 23 Aug. 1946; Statement for Joint Intelligence Staff, 1 Oct. 1945, RG 59, Records of OARA, Box 16, NA.

61.   "The Caribbean Republics," 24 Aug. 1954, *FRUS, 1952–1954,* 4:388, 390, 398.

62.   "Information on Mutual Security Program for the Bureau of the Budget," c. 1951, RG 59, MSP Files, Box 1; "Communism in Latin America," 1952, RG 59,

Miller Files, Box 3; Policy Statement, enclosed in Hussey to Butler, 23 Aug. 1946, RG 59, Records of OARA, Box 16, NA; CIA, "Conditions and Trends in Latin America. . . ," 12 Dec. 1952, Truman Papers, PSF, IF, Box 254, Central Intelligence Reports, NIE 67–75, HSTL; "Communism in Latin America," OCB, 8 Dec. 1954, WHO, Papers of NSC, OCB CF, Box 72, OCB 091.4 LA (File #2) (9), DDEL.

63. "Communism in Latin America," OCB, 8 Dec. 1954, WHO, Papers of NSC, OCB CF, Box 72, OCB 091.4 LA (File #2) (9), DDEL; CIA, "Conditions and Trends in Latin America. . . ," 12 Dec. 1952, Truman Papers, PSF, IF, Box 254, Central Intelligence Reports, NIE 67–75, HSTL.

64. "Communism in Latin America," 1952, RG 59, Miller Files, Box 3, NA.

65. W. Bennett to Robert Newbegin, et al., "Communist Strength in Costa Rica," 10 Nov. 1947, RG 59, FW 818.00B/10–3047; DRAR, "Communism in Middle America," 14 Jan. 1955, RG 59, Records of OMAA, Misc. Records, Box 1, NA.

66. Office of Intelligence Research, "The Probable Position of Jose Figueres with Respect to Costa Rica's Domestic and Foreign Policies," 21 Aug. 1953, RG 59, Records of OIR, Box 3, No. 6238, NA. For a very interesting look at U.S. relations with Figueres after 1953, see Kyle Longley, "Resistance and Accommodation: The United States and the Nationalism of José Figueres, 1953–1957," *Diplomatic History* 18, No. 1 (Winter 1994):1–28.

67. DRAR, "Communism in Middle America," 14 Jan. 1955, RG 59, Records of OMAA, Misc. Records, Box 1, NA.

68. Shaw to Acheson, 10 Dec. 1949, RG 59, Miller Files, Box 6; Shaw to DS, 12 Feb. 1950, Record Group 84, Records of the Foreign Service Posts of the Department of State, El Salvador, San Salvador Embassy, Classified General Records, 1950–1952, File 350, NA.

69. DRAR, "Communism in Middle America," 14 Jan. 1955, RG 59, Records of OMAA, Misc. Records, Box 1; DRAR, "Communist Penetration of Honduras from Guatemala," 31 Mar. 1950, in Lester to Clark, 5 Apr. 1950, RG 59, 715.001/ 4–550; Wymberley DeR. Coerr to DS, 12 May 1954, RG 59, 815.062/5–1254, NA; Horace S. Craig to Robert Amory, 9 June 1954, WHO, Papers of NSC, OCB CF, Box 72, OCB 091.4 Latin America (File #1) (7), DDEL.

70. DRAR, "Communism in Middle America," 14 Jan. 1955, RG 59, Records of OMAA, Misc. Records, Box 1; "United States Relations with Latin America," 1952, RG 59, Miller Files, Box 3, NA; "The Caribbean Republics," 24 Aug. 1954, *FRUS, 1952–1954*, 4:399.

71. DRAR, "Communism in Middle America," 14 Jan. 1955, RG 59, Records of OMAA, Misc. Records, Box 1, NA.

72. Holland to Dulles, 14 May 1954, RG 59, 714.00/5–1454, NA; "International Communism in Guatemala," Text of Radio and Television Address by John Foster Dulles, 30 June 1954, Dulles Papers, Box 81, Mudd Library.

73.   CIA, "Soviet Objectives in Latin America," 1 Nov. 1947, Truman Papers, PSF, IF, Box 254, CIA, ORE 1947, No. 15–39 file, HSTL.

74.   Miller to Barrett, 16 Aug. 1951, RG 59, Miller Files, Box 7; "Note by the Secretaries to the Joint Intelligence Committee on *Estimate of Soviet Capabilities in the Latin American Area in a War Commencing 1 July 1952*," n.d., Records of the Joint Chiefs of Staff, Record Group 218, Geographic File, 1951–1953, CCS 381 Western Hemisphere (3–22–48), Sec. 10 (hereafter GF, 1951–1953, with file name), NA; CIA, "Conditions and Trends in Latin America. . . ," 12 Dec. 1952, Truman Papers, PSF, IF, Box 254, Central Intelligence Re-ports, NIE 67–75, HSTL.

75.   Miller to Barrett, 16 Aug. 1951, RG 59, Miller Files, Box 7, NA; "The Caribbean Republics," 24 Aug. 1954, *FRUS, 1952–1954*, 4:388–389; Robert J. Watson, *The History of the Joint Chiefs of Staff: The Joint Chiefs of Staff and National Policy, Vol. IV, 1953–1954* (Washington, 1986), 353.

76.   CIA, "Conditions and Trends in Latin America. . . ," 12 Dec. 1952, Truman Papers, PSF, IF, Box 254, Central Intelligence Reports, NIE 67–75, HSTL.

77.   Mann to Whelan, 22 Oct. 1952, RG 59, Records of OMAA, Records Relating to Costa Rica and Nicaragua, Box 1, Nicaragua 1952, Communism file (hereafter Records of OMAA, Costa Rica and Nicaragua, box number, and file designation); "United States Relations with Latin America," 19 Nov. 1951, RG 59, Miller Files, Box 10, NA.

78.   CIA, "Conditions and Trends in Latin America. . . ," 12 Dec. 1952, Truman Papers, PSF, IF, Box 254, Central Intelligence Reports, NIE 67–75, HSTL.

79.   Policy Statement, enclosed in Hussey to Butler, 23 Aug. 1946, RG 59, Records of OARA, Box 16, NA.

80.   Problem Paper, 5 July 1949, RG 59, Miller Files, Box 10; Miller memorandum enclosed in Mann to Elsey, 9 Jan. 1951, RG 59, Records of Deputy for I-A Affairs, Box 2, NA.

3

The Scope of Normal Political Change

The U.S. military assistance programs begun after World War II seem to be relatively easy to understand in terms of the interdependent world they were established to support. The United States, fearing for the safety of the Free World, set out to supply and train the armed forces of its allies. The United States would have competent allies in the Cold War; those allies would find safety from both external invasion and internal instability and, thus, protection from communist expansionism. As is so often the case with postwar U.S. policies, however, a closer look at those programs reveals that they were designed to bring about more than simply military interdependence and, therefore, to cope with more than just the threat of communism. Focusing on the specific example of the 1954 bilateral military assistance agreement between the United States and Honduras, this chapter will demonstrate that the U.S. pursuit of military interdependence through such means raised troubling contradictions that U.S. policymakers were unable or unwilling to resolve.

Links in the Chain

The challenges to an interdependent world in Latin America forced U.S. officials to consider methods by which they could simultaneously construct the framework of interdependence and contain the forces working against it. Military assistance was one answer they came up with. To place U.S. military assistance to Latin America in its proper perspective, it will be useful to provide a brief analysis of the program's development.[1]

In principle, U.S. defense goals in Latin America were behind efforts to extend military assistance to that region. In the Cold War mindset of U.S. policymakers, the establishment of some sort of mutual defense system with Latin America was seen, as John Child has put it, "as merely another link in the chain of anti-communist containment alliances."[2] To that end, the Truman administration sought Congressional approval of a program of military aid to Latin America, but to no avail. One factor working against the passage of any such legislation was the opposition of State Department members such as Spruille Braden, who resented the interference of the military in U.S. diplomacy with Latin America and believed that any military aid to most nations of that region would reinforce dictatorial regimes.[3]

There matters stood until the passage of the MSA in 1951 which allowed the United States to negotiate bilateral agreements for the provision of grant military aid with the nations of Latin America.[4] The primary factors behind this sudden change of heart were the outbreak of the Korean War in 1950 and the persistent arguments by the Department of Defense that Latin America be included in the nation's mutual defense program.[5]

Secretary of Defense George C. Marshall made the strategic goals plain in January 1951. Foremost was the need to "establish an Inter-American defense structure which associates the military and strategic resources of the other American Republics with those of the United States." The economic implications of that association were made clear as Marshall pointed out the need for "an increased production and delivery of essential strategic materials." The secretary also noted the "strategic interests" that the United States had in the region and the "undesirability of diverting United States forces to this area in time of emergency." Therefore, the JCS supported military aid for Latin American nations.[6]

Political goals also played a role. As a 1952 Office of American Republic Affairs (ARA) paper noted, the sale of arms to Latin America "has political implications as well, since the Latin American military establishments either completely control the government. . .or at the very least, influence government policy." Therefore, "if we do not give adequate attention to the military in those countries, we do not get from them the measure of cooperation we need." John Cabot told an audience at a 1953 Conference on U.S. Foreign Policy that "in practically all of the American republics the loyalty of the armed forces rather than the amount of arms they have is the determining factor in the stability of the government." "In practice," he concluded, "it is better therefore to cooperate with the armed forces of our sister republics and to seek a greater identity of ideals than it is gratuitously to offend them by refusing them arms."[7]

It was clear that in order for Latin America to effectively participate in any hemispheric defense proposals, the United States would have to provide the training and materials. With those necessities in mind, a presidential finding was proposed by President Truman late in 1951 which stated that under the auspices of the MSA, twenty nations of Latin America (all of the nations of Central and South America, as well as Cuba, Haiti, and the Dominican Republic) were deemed to be eligible for economic, technical, *and* military assistance.[8]

Allowing Scope for Normal Political Change

In nearly every government paper and study produced during the postwar period dealing with the question of military assistance to Latin America, the issue of how that aid would impact on the governments and societies of that region was raised. Again and again, it was reiterated that the United States would do all in its power to see that the assistance was not turned to anti-democratic uses by the armed forces. A State Department report from mid-1949 laid out the basic ground rules for U.S. military aid: it "should not strengthen military dictatorships at the expense of progress toward representative civilian government; and should most carefully guard against the military strengthening of any Latin American country in which there is risk of the establishment of a police state system." NSC Report 56/1, produced in April 1950, clearly stated that, "In accordance with the democratic principles that the United States represents and upholds throughout the world. . .every effort should be made to assure that U.S. training and equipment not be used to deprive the peoples of the American republics of their democratic rights and liberties."[9] After all, weren't those the very values that the interdependent military defensive system would protect?

But just as U.S. policymakers had tempered their evaluations of democratic progress in Latin America with numerous reservations, so too did they begin to inch away from analyses that suggested a quid pro quo between U.S. military assistance and the growth of democracy in Latin America. Even in NSC 56/1, one noted some caveats. One of the primary purposes of U.S. military assistance was "the maintenance within each nation of political stability and of internal security," although "allowing scope for normal political change."[10]   Seemingly a simple enough directive, such a passage was nevertheless filled with potential points of friction or confusion.   United States officials were aware of the tremendous changes taking place in Latin America which promised to move that region toward a more democratic ideal.   Supportive of the general goal, those same officials were also wary of the disruption such changes would involve.   If the aim of U.S. military aid was to "maintain political stability," would this perforce mean a stifling of the forces working toward a more democratic form of rule in Latin America?   The way out of this seeming contradiction, as proposed by NSC 56/1, was that "normal political change" would be allowed.   It was not much of a solution, for what was "normal political change" in Latin America?   If normal were defined in historical terms, then there would be almost no change at all.   If it were to be defined by using the United States as a standard of measurement, then one had to consider the serious questions raised by U.S. officials as to the applicability of their nation's democratic experience to the backward institutions and peoples of Latin America.

A year later, the State Department was still looking for an answer.   In July 1951, the department formulated a paper for use in a "'rehearsal'" of Assistant Secretary of State Edward Miller and General Charles L. Bolté (Chairman of the Inter-American Defense Board), in preparation for their appearance before Congress dealing with U.S. military assistance to Latin America.   It began with some general observations about the goals of that assistance, and admitted that the "risk that this grant aid will contribute to strengthening dictatorial or other anti-democratic elements in some countries must be recognized in answering questions that may be asked."   As with NSC 56/1, it concluded that "the problem of overriding importance is to secure effective military cooperation from countries capable and willing to cooperate, and that the political risks must be taken."   Later in the paper, the rehearsing went so far as to propose possible questions and suggest possible answers.   One of the most troubling questions, apparently, would be, "Will this grant aid help dictator governments perpetuate themselves in power?"   The answer: "Our estimate is that these American Republics which we feel can handle defense tasks are all sincerely united in their opposition to Communism and we feel that they are now big enough to keep their hemisphere mission ahead of any local political angles."   That was obviously not very convincing, even to the person writing it, and in the next sentence the author issued a "call upon the Department of State to develop this answer more completely." This was done in a brief supplement. Rehashing the usual arguments that such aid was for mutual defense, and that the United States would take every precaution to see that the aid was not misused, it was finally admitted that

> This can be no absolute assurance, however, that groups with anti-democratic objectives will not be strengthened in some places. Embarking on a program of this kind is and must involve a calculated risk. However, the chance of achieving the main objective of a stronger and more effective system of collective security, in which the other governments will assume greater military responsibilities, is of over-riding importance.[11]

For the time being, then, the question of exactly what benefits "collective security" would bring to Latin America was left hanging. The "risk" that military assistance would be turned to anti-democratic uses would have to be taken.

The Apotheosis of the Negative

In many ways, the discussions by U.S. officials of internal stability, military aid, dictatorships, and the "scope" of "normal political change" in Latin America paralleled their analysis of what was going on in Honduras during roughly that same period. In the postwar years 1945–1954, U.S. officials noted with some alarm the pace and direction of economic and political change in that nation. They also pondered what steps the United States might take to bring those changes more in line with U.S. interests. An examination of the U.S. decision to grant military assistance to Honduras in 1954 provides us with an interesting case study of how the United States came to perceive such aid in terms of its goal of an interdependent military defense system in the Western Hemisphere.

For U.S. officials commenting on Honduras during the immediate post-war years, internal stability was not an issue much in question. A 1946 report from the U.S. chargé in Honduras summed up the situation:

> the place [Honduras] might better be described as the Apotheosis of the Negative: no volcanoes, no earthquakes, no hurricanes, no railroads, no tramways, no labor unions, no strikes, no unemployment, no presidential elections (since 1932), no social security laws, no income

tax, no price controls, no rationing, no Fascists, no Falangists, no Nazis, no Japs, no Communists (known), no central bank, no stock exchange, no millionaires, and no admitted problems of any kind.[12]

The lack of presidential elections was due to General Tiburcio Carías Andino, who had exercised power in Honduras since elected president in 1932. As one of his first acts, he had his term of office extended from four to six years; in 1939, his tenure was extended until 1949.[13] His rule brought a reprieve from the nearly constant revolutions that had plagued Honduras, but at the price of a sometimes harshly repressive regime.[14] And while other Central American dictators such as Martínez in El Salvador and Ubico in Guatemala were gone by 1945, Carías remained solidly in power. As U.S. Ambassador John D. Erwin reported in March 1945, "It appears unlikely that there will be any strikes or other serious difficulties as long as the Carías Government remains in power."[15]

As many U.S. policymakers would do in the years to come, Erwin wrestled with the question of the proper U.S. attitude toward dictators such as Carías. In June 1945, he explained his rationale for his positive view of the strongman's regime. "This Embassy holds no brief for President Tiburcio Carías," he began, pointing out the lack of civil rights in Honduras. Nevertheless, the alternatives were not very attractive, "and it is reasonably certain that life and property would be less safe than under the present regime. . . .The choice is not between Carías and Democracy, but rather between Carías and chaos." The State Department's rather tepid rejoinder to Erwin's logic was that "this GOVT is not in sympathy with the Carías dictatorship."[16]

Even that mild rebuke brought forth an impassioned plea for understanding from U.S. Chargé d'Affaires John B. Faust. The Carías regime was of the "well-known personal type" so common to Latin America. Admittedly, Carías had unconstitutionally lengthened his tenure of office; however, "it seems a bit late to object now." And, yes, the Carías government did repress civil rights. Yet, as Faust claimed in a statement of truly heroic proportions, "Sam Houston, Andrew Jackson, Oliver Cromwell, or Robert Bruce (Great champions of freedom who sometimes found a little dictating necessary after appeals to sweet reason proved fruitless) would have understood and appreciated President Carías very well." History had shown that dictatorships often showed a "gradual softening towards democracy." Given all this, Carías deserved "more sympathy than has been given him up to now."[17]

One factor that was cited as having helped Carías maintain Honduran stability was the military.[18] While pointing out that it was "unlikely that Honduras could furnish an effective combat force" for "hemispheric defense," it was clear that the armed forces had an internal role to play. As the U.S. military attaché to Honduras noted in a 1947 report, Carías had had to fight his way to power, having defeated Liberal opponents in 1932 who sought to block his ascension to the presidency. He wryly noted that "air power" had been vital to Carías's victory. A single plane, piloted by two Americans, had "caused consternation in the ranks of the Liberal troops, thus assuring the victory of the Carías adherents." As he concluded, "it can be said that the Honduran Air Force has been the most important stabilizing factor in Honduras in recent years."[19]

Nor had Carías been hesitant in using the military since his 1932 victory. As Ambassador Erwin reported during early 1945, the Honduran armed forces had repelled an invasion of Honduran exiles coming from Guatemala. The Carías regime claimed complete and absolute victory. While Erwin expressed some doubts concerning the casualty figures, he also pointed out that the man in charge of Carías's forces, General Carlos Sanabria, was "pretty ruthless." His "reputation being what it is no one who knows him doubts that he would have killed all of the rebels if given the opportunity." In any case, the defeat had "thrown a damper over the hopes of the revolutionists which may presage a prolonged period of tranquility."[20]

The United States, in keeping with its philosophy of staying on friendly terms with politically powerful Latin American armed forces, did not ignore Honduras in the postwar years.[21] In May of 1946, the United States agreed to send both army and air force missions to Honduras (these missions, by 1952, consisted of seven personnel each from the Army and Air Force). In 1947, a contract between the U.S. Foreign Liquidation Commission and Honduras called for the sale of up to $450,000 of surplus war supplies.[22]

In 1948, however, the situation in Honduras changed, and this precipitated some uneasiness among U.S. policymakers. The year before, Carías had announced that elections would be held in October 1948 and that he would not seek another term as president.[23] Carías's reasoning for these moves is unclear; perhaps after witnessing the downfall of other Central American dictators such as Martínez and Ubico he had decided to not overstay his welcome. Whatever the reasons, he made it apparent that he would not be completely out of the picture. His chosen successor was his minister of war, Juan Manuel Gálvez Durón. In February 1948, the National Party duly nominated Gálvez as its candidate.[24] The election itself went off in October 1948, with the National ticket winning by a large margin.

While the new U.S. ambassador, Harold Bursley, commented that the election was a "pathetic travesty," he was nevertheless optimistic. Despite its failings, the election had been "a significant step forward to an eventual day which may bring truly democratic life for this struggling country." A few months later, he happily reported that the new Gálvez government seemed interested in extending the life of the U.S. military missions.[25] Perhaps the ideal was coming to pass: from the Carías dictatorship—and the stability it had provided—Honduras was now slowly passing into the first stages of democracy.

The election of Gálvez was at once the catalyst and symbol of significant changes taking place in Honduras. In contrast to Carías, the new president attempted to open the stifling Honduran political system by calling upon political exiles to return, freeing political prisoners, relaxing contraints on the nation's nascent labor movement, and allowing freedom of the press. He also sought to modernize the nation's backward economy.[26] These actions, however, did not so much *bring* change to Honduras as *allow* the forces of change in that nation, surfacing since the war, to reach fruition. As James Morris notes, "The overlay of political peace was peeled away after World War II."[27]

With the passage of the Carías era, new social and economic groups began to make an impression on Honduran politics and society. The freer political and economic atmosphere, together with improved communication and transportation, brought forth new and relatively unified labor and peasant organizations, as well as social and professional groupings among the emerging middle class.[28] Unfortu nately, despite the trappings of democracy and development employed by Gálvez, the ruling National Party, composed largely of old and powerful elite groups, was unwilling or unable to integrate these new forces into the government. The Liberal Party, weak and disorganized after years of exile of its leaders, could not absorb these new forces either.[29] Morris explains the consequences:

> A political vacuum was formed between the faltering grasp on power by old elites and the untested political viability of urban middle-class and popular-sector groups. The dispersal of power among declining political institutions, emergent sociopolitical groups, and the potential

military governors made the Honduran political system vulnerable to domestic unrest and external influences.[30]

It was not long before reports about these disturbing developments began to emanate from the U.S. embassay in Honduras. Bursley was the first to raise the alarm, commenting in August 1949 that tensions were developing in the new Honduran government between the new Gálvez people and the leftovers from the Carías regime. The entire situation was "complicated at the present time by increasing nationalism. . .and feeling of independence and self-confidence." A few weeks later, he was even more anxious, claiming that the situation was deteriorating while the Gálvez administration seemed unduly slow in organizing and pressing reforms. The result was "a tendency recently towards agitation against the Government" with students "spearheading" this.[31]

A more ominous problem seemed to be the presence of communist elements in Honduras, and during the early 1950s this issue came to be of more interest and concern to U.S. policymakers. Of particular interest were the activities of the Partido Democratico Revolucionario Hondureño (PDRH). As discussed by Chargé Harold Montamat in March 1950, the ideology of the PDRH was fuzzy—a bit taken from Mexican leftists, together with some "diluted" ideas from communism. Whatever it was, he did not seem much impressed. The PDRH had probably less than 20 members, did not appear "directly violently hostile" to U.S. interests, and had little impact although it might find some response among the Honduran employees of the United Fruit Company. American Vice Consul John Morrison agreed and disagreed with Montamat's assessment. The PDRH was certainly small, but its ideology appeared to be "definitely Communistic." John Erwin, back for his second tour of duty as U.S. ambassador to Honduras, added fuel to the fire by reporting that "outside sources" were stirring up the political waters in Honduras, especially among labor circles.[32]

Gordon Reid, in charge of Central American and Panama affairs in the State Department, in 1953 offered a more thoughtful appraisal of events transpiring in Honduras.[33] According to Reid, the changes taking place in Honduras appeared threatening only because U.S. diplomats and businessmen in that country had "lulled themselves into a belief that Honduras would never change." Change had come, however. A more democratic climate was present in the country. The "paradise" that Erwin had described during the mid-1940s had "disappeared." Economic nationalism had sprung up in Honduras, but that was not surprising considering the dictatorial rule Carías had exerted for sixteen years. U.S. companies had not been much deprived, although he cautioned that "Honduras cannot be said to be a safe place for American investment except under the strictest terms and understandings." He also noted the fine work Gálvez had done in the economic development of Honduras and in streamlining the military. He ended on a cautionary note:

> If one believes that a "paradise" is not possible in Honduras at the present time it is necessary to think ahead to what may be forthcoming in that country. In my mind, Honduras is awakening from a long sleep and is beginning to understand that it has potentialities not yet exploited. I am fearful of the weaknesses of its Foreign Minister and its general tendencies to believe that one can live with communism on an equal basis. Therefore, I come to the conclusion that the job ahead for the United States is to protect our citizens from economic nationalism, communist infiltration in the form of men and ideas and, lastly, to preach the importance of emphasizing that Honduras is part of an area of major interest to the United States where communism must be faced and defeated.

The battle against the forces of nationalism and communism, for which the United States was already preparing by early 1953, would be met sooner than Reid had perhaps imagined.

Edward Miller showed remarkable prescience in a January 1952 letter to Philip Bonsal. While he noted that less than one hour of his time in ARA had been spent on Honduras during his two and a half years as assistant secretary, he concluded that, "The very fact that I have recorded this will probably cause the roof to fall in on the United Fruit Company down there or some other disaster to happen in the near future."[34] In late April and early May 1954, a strike began among United Fruit Company workers, which eventually spread to thousands of other laborers in the employ of Standard Fruit and other companies.[35]

Secretary of State Dulles was unnerved enough about this development to write a memorandum to President Eisenhower. The strike itself was bad enough. Furthermore, "there have been reports of suspicious movements and planes and men from Guatemala." Obviously, Dulles saw a relationship between the two events. He informed Eisenhower that "negotiations between the United States and Honduras for a grant-aid bilateral military assistance agreement are scheduled to begin on May 17."[36]

Two days later, Dulles called his brother Allen (who was serving as director of the CIA) to ask whether he would be giving a briefing on Guatemala and Honduras. Allen Dulles replied that he would be giving one on Honduras and further noted that things in Honduras seemed to be "quieting down, and mentioned getting arms down and also a military mission," although he did not know the details concerning negotiations. Just two minutes later, the secretary was on the phone to Henry Holland, assistant secretary of state for inter-American affairs, inquiring about those negotiations between the United States and Honduras. Dulles mentioned that Allen "thought this would help." Holland noncommittally replied that "it would help some." On May 20, 1954, the bilateral military agreement was signed with Honduras.[37]

The preceding sequence of events might lead one to believe that the decision to pursue a military aid agreement with Honduras was spur of the moment. This was not the case, however, as the United States had initiated the effort over a year before the May 1954 crisis. On 9 April 1953, Secretary of State Dulles wrote to Secretary of Defense Charles E. Wilson asking that the latter's department "determine the specific hemisphere defense missions which each of these countries [Honduras, Nicaragua, and El Salvador] could effectively perform with limited United States grant assistance" (a necessary step for the granting of such aid). The JCS responded that the desired defense missions "would be of almost insignificant military value."   In conclusion, the JCS could not "conscientiously recommend at this time either diverting funds from existing Title IV programs or requesting additional funds for even minor roles in hemisphere defense for El Salvador, Honduras and Nicaragua."[38]

Less than two weeks later, however, the JCS reevaluated its recommendations and agreed that Nicaragua should be eligible to receive grant military assistance. By October 1953, the JCS had completely reversed itself and now found El Salvador and Honduras also eligible for such aid.[39] This radical change in outlook was due to heavy pressure from the State Department which argued that despite the negligible military value of the aid, U.S. interests in the region would be well served by its immediate provision.

Dulles laid out the main arguments in his April letter to Wilson. He noted that his department was "making every practicable effort at the diplomatic level to diminish the strength of communist elements in Central America, particularly in Guatemala."   Military aid to Nicaragua, Honduras, and El Salvador would convince them of the U.S. commitment to help them fight communist advances. Furthermore, Guatemala's absence from the list might "help establish a political climate in Guatemala of benefit to anti-communist Guatemalan elements, including elements in the Guatemalan armed forces." To obtain these "political and psychological objectives," Dulles issued a plea that the Department of Defense develop "hemispheric defense missions," even if these were "only relatively minor roles."[40] When Defense made its decision to approve grant military assistance only to Nicaragua, Deputy Under Secretary of State H. Freeman Matthews argued, in a letter to Secretary Wilson, that U.S. objectives in Central America could "have the greatest opportunity of attainment" if the aid were "extended to other Central American Governments which express a desire for such aid, and which are not under the influence of Communism." He hoped that such aid to El Salvador and Honduras would be reconsidered.[41]

Obviously, U.S. officials believed that grant military aid to Honduras would have a beneficial effect vis-à-vis the situation in Guatemala. But the "Guatemalan problem" was not the only factor behind the U.S. desire to negotiate an agreement with Honduras. Instead, events in Honduras itself (notably the strike in May) brought the military aid pact to fruition. That this was the case is more vividly demonstrated by the fact that even after the overthrow of the Arbenz government in June, U.S. policymakers continued to see military aid to Honduras as a valuable remedy to problems in that nation.

Throughout the summer of 1954 the strikes in Honduras began slowly to come to an end. In June, a U.S. official on the scene reported that United Fruit was optimistic. Gálvez had set up an arbitration committee and had also cracked down on the supposed communists in the labor unions, arresting four. Another report in July stated that strike activity in general was subsiding, with Standard Fruit already having reached an agreement with its workers. The Honduran government had reacted cautiously on the whole, but had at one point seized control of a railroad line and issued a statement linking "international communism" to the strikes. Finally, in September, the main strike against the United Fruit Company's railroad line was settled, with the workers gaining a raise in their minimum daily pay from $1.64 to $2.04. "Honduran labor," the report concluded, "could no longer be taken for granted and was now a force to be reckoned with."[42]

What impact the announcement of the Honduran-U.S. military aid a-greement had on the strike settlements cannot be empirically demonstrated. It may be argued that such a show of support by the United States during the period of greatest strike activity must have strengthened the resolve of the Honduran government in dealing with the strikers. The importance of the episode lies more in the U.S. perception of the events in Honduras. The strike, obviously, was seen as a threat to U.S. interests, and was further viewed as evidence of communist infiltration into the ranks of Honduran labor. U.S. military assistance to Honduras, which up to that time had been discussed primarily in terms of its impact on the situation in Guatemala, was now seen as having value in terms of what it might do in helping salvage the situation in Honduras.

With labor problems subsiding, a more complex situation arose in Honduras, one that alarmed U.S. observers just as much and one in which military aid would again play a part. As noted, 1954 was a presidential election year in Honduras. The new U.S. ambassador to Honduras, Whiting Willauer, explained to the State Department in early June that he expected trouble and argued for quickening the pace of U.S. assistance to the Honduran military. His logic was that with rapid aid, the Honduran armed forces might be ready by the 10 October election date "when there is every expectation of internal disorder." That fear was based on "the new situation created by present Communist infiltration of the Honduran labor movement." A "strategic reserve" might be needed to "handle riots or attempts to overthrow the Government." Willauer specifically requested that the Honduran military be furnished with four C-47 transports.[43] In a personal letter to Julian Harrington, U.S. consul general in Hong Kong, Willauer laid out the political problems in simple terms. Three parties would be vying for the presidency in October; none were expected to receive a majority of the votes. Some sort of coalition would undoubtedly be necessary, but he was not optimistic about its coming together. The result would be that "the Commies again have a beautiful choice of targets." By this, he meant that the communists could either "foment a revolution" or "deliver the labor vote" to one or another of the candidates. In any event, the communists would come out of the resulting mess with more power.[44]

The initial response from the State Department to Willauer's request for increased and speedy aid to Honduras was not promising. Assistant Secretary Holland, while expressing appreciation of the ambassador's argument that with such aid "we might come very close to assuring ourselves that subversion, wherever it might appear, in Honduras, would be repressed effectively with armed force," was skeptical about gaining support from the Department of Defense. The primary problem would be in convincing Defense that there was a real *military* need in Honduras for the additional aid. He doubted that a very strong argument could be made on that level. And even on the political level, what with the fall of the Arbenz government in Guatemala, the old argument about containing communist aggression lacked its original impact. Nevertheless, he promised to forward Willauer's request to Defense.[45]

Despite his skepticism about securing Defense's approval, Holland pressed forward with Willauer's request. In early August, following a visit from the ambassador, he wrote to Deputy Under Secretary of State Robert Murphy concerning the preparation of "an effective infantry battalion which could be used to the advantage of our interests, in the event of an emergency" in Honduras. He reported that Willauer had met with Major General George C. Stewart, director of the Office of Military Assistance in the Department of Defense, and had revised his request—two C-47s would be adequate. Such a request, in Holland's opinion, was "a modest one, considering the interests we have at stake in the area," and recommended that it be formally made to Defense. Four days later, Murphy sent the request to Assistant Secretary of Defense for International Security H. Struve Hensel, with the following explanation:

> The Department of State is of the opinion that communist activity within Honduras, which has recently been manifested in labor strikes and riots, and that other types of communist activity in the Central American area, pose a threat to the stability of the present Honduran Government. It is of overriding political importance to the interest of the United States that such disturbances be prevented at this time.

With such considerations in mind ("which are in part political"), Murphy asked Defense to approve the delivery of the C-47s, even if this required "small adjustments in other Latin American country programs."[46]

Hensel's reply arrived back at the State Department two months later, and it completely justified Holland's earlier pessimism. He reported that the JCS had met and decided that the C-47s could not be spared. Furthermore, it was concerned that extra aid for Honduras would set a bad precedent, in which other Latin American nations, such as Nicaragua, would also request additional support. It reiterated once again its belief that Honduras's military value was "negligible."[47] Perhaps another factor in the JCS decision, which Hensel did not mention, was its feeling that having once been pushed by State into approving military aid for such "negligible" nations as Honduras and El Salvador, it was willing to compromise no more.

Despite the fact that additional military aid was not forthcoming, Willauer was to discover that while he had been accurate in predicting an electoral stalemate in the presidential election, the scenario turned out fairly well. In a February 1955 letter to a personal friend, Willauer explained that none of the three candidates had received a majority of the votes nor were they willing to make compromises. Instead of a communist revolt, however, the country found itself ruled by Gálvez's outgoing vice president, Julio Lozano Díaz, who was "forced to take over as a caretaker" until the mess could be worked out. While the new government was "a dictatorship by consent of a very benevolent type," Willauer was optimistic. The elections had gone quietly; new labor and social legislation was being drawn up; and, with the elimination of the Guatemalan problem, "it is just possible that such a new era is just ahead of us."[48] In that new era, the U.S.-supplied and -trained Honduran military would play an increasingly important role.

Lozano attempted to solidify his position with fraudulent elections in 1956.[49] While his party swept the vote, he was unsuccessful in continuing his rule, when two weeks after the election a military junta seized power. The junta promised elections as soon as the situation stabilized. These took place in September 1957, with regular military units overseeing the voting, and resulted in the election of the Liberal candidate, Ramón Villeda Morales. Villeda served until 1963, when he was also ousted by a military coup.[50]

The seizure of power in 1956 by a military junta marked, as James Morris has noted, "the entry of a refurbished, professionalized military into Honduran politics." The military had developed an "institutional identity," and no longer saw itself as a force splintered by regional or personalist dissension. The passage of a new Honduran constitution in 1957 gave the military "substantial autonomy vis á vis civilian authority." The Honduran armed forces had "come of age." Morris credits much of that coming of age to the U.S. support after World War II. The arms and training provided by the United States "inspired the organization of a professional armed force in Honduras." Alison Acker more emphatically states that, "The army did not in fact acquire any sense of professionalism until 1950, and then it was the United States that provided it. The Honduran military learned quickly and was soon able to parlay its new sense of authority and discipline into political control." The military's impact on the politics of Honduras would be felt to the present day. As Acker notes, "From 1954 until 1981, no chief of the Honduran armed forces retired without having first served as president of Honduras."[51]

The United States was generally pleased with what had transpired. A copy of a statement Ambassador Willauer used in a speech to President Villeda in December 1957 is worth quoting at length:

> It is with satisfaction that the Government of the United States has noted the part played by the Armed Forces which in cooperation with the people of Honduras returned the Government to constitutional order through processes of democracy. My Government has also followed the development of the new role of the Armed Forces with much interest. . . . Cooperation with the Government of Honduras in realizing this unique and new role of the Armed Forces is an aim of the United States to the end that Honduras will begin a sound development.[52]

United States "cooperation" was heavy indeed. Between 1950 and 1968, it sent $6.4 million in military assistance to Honduras. From 1980 through 1987, it sent over $391 million more. Before being closed down in 1986, nearly three thousand Honduran officers received training at the School of the Americas in the Panama Canal Zone.[53]

As the record makes clear, U.S. military assistance to Honduras during the mid-1950s was not simply a spur-of-the-moment decision, made in the heat of the Guatemalan crisis. It meshed nicely with general U.S. perceptions of the need for strong militaries in the region, necessary to counter instability and chaos. Honduras seemed to fit into that general framework: it was an underdeveloped nation, ruled for years by a "benevolent" dictator, but by the late 1940s and early 1950s, open to new and dangerous incursions of nationalistic and communistic ideas. Given such views by U.S. policymakers, it was not surprising that their nation pursued a military assistance pact with Honduras or that officials such as Ambassador Willauer were content with the "new role" of the Honduran military that transpired after such assistance was given. In evaluating the overall necessity for the military assistance program in Latin America during the 1950s, John C. Dreier, the U.S. Permanent Representative to the OAS, commented in 1958 that "the military in the Latin countries has participated to a larger degree in politics than in most countries and, in so doing, has helped in many cases to preserve a form of government. If the military did not intervene. . .there would at times be greater chaos." In 1959, Brigadier General James W. Coutts wrote to William Draper, head of the U.S. President's Committee to Study the U.S. Military Assistance Program, outlining the many benefits the United States had received in Latin America. Internal stability had been increased; officers trained by the U.S. military were "completely oriented toward the United States"; and economic and military advantages had been accrued.[54]

It would be wrong to conclude, of course, that events in Guatemala had no impact on the signing of the military assistance agreement with Honduras in 1954. It would be equally erroneous, however, to assume that the agreement was simply a knee-jerk reaction to the "Guatemalan problem." Military assistance to Honduras during the 1950s fit the general pattern of U.S. policy toward Latin America. It is also clear that events in Honduras pressed State Department officials to quickly seal the deal and, as the situation seemed to deteriorate, to push Defense to provide even more aid. The pace and direction of political change in Honduras frightened U.S. officials and seemed to threaten that nation's stability—and stability was a prerequisite for the interdependent military arrangement the United States was seeking. The "political risk" of military assistance, therefore, was not a risk at all, as U.S. policymakers came more and more to accept the idea that such aid could protect U.S. interests just as well by containing democracy (at least in its "chaotic" form in Central America) as by protecting it.

The issue of U.S. military assistance to Latin America had always been a touchy one. On the surface, such aid was seen as simply a necessary component of military interdependence. That interdependence would bring benefits to both the United States and the nations of Latin America: extra security and a dependable supply of vital raw materials for the former; the preservation of the "possibility of the development of democratic institutions and individual freedoms" (as Dean Acheson had put it in 1947) for the latter.

The doubts concerning U.S. military assistance were centered on the second half of that equation. Had not the armed forces of Latin America been cited by U.S. policymakers, not only as "stabilizing" influences in the region, but also—historically speaking—as impediments to the growth of democratic institutions and ideas? Would U.S. military aid enable those forces to be even more of an impediment? If so, problems would certainly arise in the interdependent relationship U.S. officials were intent on constructing. Some of those problems were more pragmatic: Would non-democratic Latin American states become inherently more unstable (as the conservative militaries tried to stem the tide of change that even U.S. policymakers knew was coming), and therefore less reliable allies? Other problems dealt more with idealism: If the Latin American nations did become less democratic due to the influence of the new and improved armed forces, what, exactly, was the United States, in association with those forces, trying to defend?

Central America was a prime example of the dilemma posed by U.S. military assistance. To be sure, its militaries, to fulfill their defensive functions, would need U.S. help. The nations of the region were wracked with instability; some force would have to stand against "extreme nationalism," apparently endless political instability, and, to a lesser degree, the intrusion of communist ideology. Again, the military—a traditional force of stability—filled the bill. Yet, as U.S. policymakers were well aware, the Central American armed forces were not known as positive forces for democratic change. What price would the U.S.-desired stability and protection of its interests in the region incur?

Eventually, it was decided that military aid served the "national interest" and should be pursued. The instigation of this assistance was not brought on solely by fears of communist expansion and Cold War strategy (although such considerations were always present). It evolved, instead, as U.S. policymakers began to come to grips with the almost inevitable consequences of their views on military interdependence (which, as we have seen, overlapped with those on political and economic interdependence). The protection of U.S. interests depended on a stable, pro-U.S. Latin America, and one of the best ways to secure those goals seemed to be through assistance of the Latin American armed forces. Hence, the first and, for U.S. officials, most important element of the interdependent relationship would be fulfilled. Having made this judgement, those officials were willing to hedge a little on the other element—the "opportunity for democracy" that would result in Latin America. After all, what real opportunities would be impeded by military assistance? The area was viewed by Washington as a not very promising place for the growth of democratic institutions. Certainly its history was not very encouraging. And, yes, changes were being called for. But the very groups calling for those changes were suspect. Labor and intellectuals were infiltrated by communists; the middle class, in many instances, was far too nationalistic. The Latin American people (themselves racially suspect) did not seem to understand or be prepared for democracy, and therefore provided tempting targets for nationalistic demagogues and communist rabble-rousers. Their officials, corrupt and lazy, seemed far too complacent about the communist threat.

By the mid- to late-1950s, remaining U.S. doubts about military assistance had apparently been put to rest. It was the "lesser of two evils"; it recognized the more pressing need of survival and protection of U.S. interests—ideals would have to wait. Any thought that such aid would actually help promote democracy dissipated. Military interdependence had acquired a new, and harder-edged, definition. The United States still needed the Latin American armed forces to promote stability in their nations. The Latin Americans still needed stability—and that is what they got. Stability did not necessarily mean democracy, of course, but it was, after all, "better than the alternative" (chaotic instability, fed on by radicals of all shades, inevitably resulting in anarchy or extremism). Such an interpretation relied on the assumption that only two alternatives existed: pro-U.S. stability (even if it had to be enforced by antidemocratic forces) or instability that threatened the entire fabric of U.S.-Latin American relations. To consider a possible third alternative—the slow, perhaps halting, perhaps not-quite-to-their-liking development of democracy in Latin America—strained their understanding of interdependence to the breaking point.

Notes

1. For military assistance in the postwar years and its applications in Latin America, see Chester J. Pach, Jr., *Arming the Free World: The Origins of the United States Military Assistance Program, 1945–1950* (Chapel Hill, 1991), especially Ch. 2; Child, *Unequal Alliance,* Ch. 4; Hovey, *United States Military Assistance,* particularly Ch. 4; Edwin Lieuwen, *Arms and Politics in Latin America* (New York, NY, 1961), Part Two; and two articles by Stephen Rabe: "Inter-American Military Cooperation," 132–49, and "Eisenhower and Latin America: Arms and Dictators," *Peace and Change* 11 (Spring 1985):49–61. Two other books, which focus on the period of 1960 and beyond, also contain some good background material: Don L. Etchison, *The United States and Militarism in Central America* (New York, 1975), and Willard Barber and C. Neale Ronning, *International Security and Military Power: Counterinsurgency and Civic Action in Latin America* (Athens, OH, 1966).

2. Child, *Unequal Alliance,* 71.

3. Ibid., 90–95; Hovey, *United States Military Assistance,* 49–50; Lieuwen, *Arms and Politics,* 196–197; Rabe, "Inter-American Military Cooperation,"

132–142; and Chester J. Pach, Jr., "The Containment of U.S. Military Aid to Latin America, 1944–49," *Diplomatic History* 6 (1982):225–43.

4.   There were many other programs designed to supply and train Latin American armed forces. An excellent summary of these programs, as of 1952, can be found in Cale to Czayo and Mann, "Military Assistance Provided Latin American Countries," 23 Sept. 1952, RG 59, 720.56/9–2352, NA.

5.   Child, *Unequal Alliance*, 119–122; Hovey, *United States Military Assistance*, 50; Lieuwen, *Arms and Politics*, 198–200.

6.   Marshall to Acheson, 10 Jan. 1951, RG 59, 720.5 MAP/1–1051, NA.

7.   "United States Relations with Latin America," RG 59, Miller Files, Box 3, NA; "Summary of Remarks at Conference on U.S. Foreign Policy, June 4 and 5, 1953," pp. 61–62, Dulles Papers, Box 75, Mudd Library.

8.   Hoover to Cardozo, 29 Dec. 1951, RG 59, MSP Files, Box 1, NA.

9.   SD, Draft Report, 29 Aug. 1949, RG 59, Miller Files, Box 10, NA; NSC 56/1, 27 Apr. 1950, Truman Papers, PSF, IF, Box 208, NSC Meetings 56–64: Meeting No. 57 file, HSTL.

10.   NSC 56/1, 27 Apr. 1950, PSF, IF, Box 208, File: NSC Meetings 56–64: Meeting no. 57, HSTL.

11.   "General Points of Background in Questioning on Latin American Military Aspects of MSP," 1951, RG 59, 720.5–MAP/7–1751, NA.

12.   Faust to DS, 29 Mar. 1946, RG 59, 815.001 CA, T/3–2946.

13.   Using dubious legal means to overcome constitutional limits on the tenure of office (which came to be known as *continuismo* in Latin America) was not unique to Carías. Somoza in Nicaragua, Martínez in El Salvador, and Ubico in Guatemala all resorted to political subterfuge to remain in office past their legal limits. For an analysis of *continuismo*, see Russell H. Fitzgibbon, "'Con- tinuismo' in Central America," *The Inter-American Quarterly* 2 (July 1940): 56–74.

14.   James A. Morris, *Honduras: Caudillo Politics and Military Rulers* (Boulder, CO, 1984), 8–9; Steve Lewontin, "'A Blessed Peace': Honduras Under Carías," in *Honduras: Portrait of a Captive Nation*, Nancy Peckenham and Annie Street, eds. (New York, 1985), 85–88; Robert MacCameron, *Bananas, Labor, and Politics in Honduras: 1954–1963* (Syracuse, NY, 1983), 17; James A. Morris and Steve C. Ropp, "Corporatism and Dependent Development: A Honduran Case Study," *Latin American Research Review* 12, no. 2 (Summer 1977), 31–42; Alison Acker, *Honduras: The Making of a Banana Republic* (Boston, 1988), 73–75.

15.   Erwin to DS, 21 Mar. 1945, RG 59, 815.00/3–2145.

16.   Erwin to DS, 28 June 1945, RG 59, 815.00/6–2845; Byrnes to Erwin, 9 Mar. 1946, RG 59, 815.001 Carías Andino, Tiburcio/3–946. This was a far cry from the original draft of the message to Erwin which read, "this GOVT strongly disapproves of the Carías dictatorship."

17. Faust to DS, 3 Apr. 1946, RG 59, 815.001 Carías Andino, Tiburcio/ 4–346, NA.

18. For more on the military's role in the Carías regime, see Acker, *Banana Republic*, 74; Lewontin, "'Blessed Peace,'" 87; MacCameron, *Bananas, Labor, and Politics*, 17; and Steve C. Ropp, "The Honduran Army in the Sociopolitical Evolution of the Honduran State," *The Americas* 30, no. 4 (April 1974):509.

19. Lt. Col. Nathan A. Brown, Jr., "Paper for Military Attaché Conference, Panama, 12 to 18 January 1947," enclosed in Erwin to DS, 15 Jan. 1947, RG 59, 815.00/1–1547, NA.

20. Erwin to DS, 29 Mar., 12, 16, 20, 21 Apr., 7 May 1945, RG 59, 815.00/ 3–2945, /4–1245, /4–1645, /4–2045, /4–2145, /5–745, NA. Sanabria had gained infamy in Honduras long before this episode. Five years earlier, he had gone about "wiping out entire villages" in his efforts to put down protest against the Carías government. For Carías, Sanabria was the living embodiment of his political philosophy: "Round them up, throw them out, and bury them." See Acker, *Banana Republic*, 74.

21. The United States had not entirely ignored Honduras even before the war. In 1922, U.S. advisors had been on the scene training pilots for the Honduran air force; twenty years later, pilots trained by the United States were flying the 22 planes that comprised that force. See Ropp, "The Honduran Army," 509; MacCameron, *Bananas, Labor, and Politics*, 17.

22. Brown, "Paper for Military Attaché Conference, Panama, 12 to 18 January 1947," RG 59, 815.00/1–1547; Cale to Czayo and Mann, "Military Assistance Provided Latin American Countries," 23 Sept. 1952, RG 59, 720/56/9–2356; Daniels to DS, 2 Sept. 1947, RG 59, 815.00/9–247, NA.

23. For the political manuevering in Honduras at that time, see Daniels to DS, 18 July 1947, RG 59, 815.00/7–1847, NA.

24. Morris, *Honduras*, 9; Montamat to DS, 22 Feb. 1948, RG 59, 815.00/2–2248, NA.

25. Bursley to DS, 11, 15 Oct. 1948; 3 May 1949, RG 59, 815.00/10–1148, /10–1548; 815.20 Missions/5–349, NA.

26. Morris, *Honduras*, 10; Acker, *Banana Republic*, 75; Morris and Ropp, "Corporatism and Dependent Development," 42–43; and MacCameron, *Bananas, Labor, and Politics*, 17–18.

27. Morris, *Honduras*, 123.

28. Ibid., 78–81; Morris and Ropp, "Corporatism and Dependent Development," 42–43.

29. Morris, *Honduras*, 124–126; Ropp, "The Honduran Army," 513–514.

30. Morris, *Honduras*, 125.

31. Bursley to DS, 2, 26 Aug. 1949, RG 59, 815.00/8–249, /8–2649, NA.

32. Montamat to DS, 12 Mar. 1950; Morrison to DS, 19 Mar. 1950; Erwin to DS, 24 July 1951, RG 59, 715.00/3–1250, /3–1950, /5–2252, /7–2451, NA.

33.   Reid to Leddy, et al., 12 June 1953, RG 59, 715.00/6–1253, NA.

34.   Miller to Bonsal, 25 Jan. 1952, RG 59, Miller Files, Box 3, NA.

35.   Morris, *Honduras*, 10–11; LaFeber, *Inevitable Revolutions*, 132–134; Acker, *Banana Republic*, 82–84; Longino Becerra, "The Early History of the Labor Movement," in Peckenham and Street, *Captive Nation*, 98–101; MacCameron, *Bananas, Labor, and Politics*, 21–64.

36.   Dulles, Memorandum for the President, 11 May 1954, RG 59, Records of the Assistant Secretary of State for Inter-American Affairs: Records of Henry F. Holland, RG 59, Box 4 (hereafter Holland Records with box number), NA.

37.   Dulles, phone call to Allen W. Dulles, 13 May 1954; Dulles, phone call to Holland, 13 May 1954, Papers of John Foster Dulles, Telephone Calls Series, Box 2, telephone memos file, May 1, 1954–June 30, 1954 (#3), DDEL (hereafter cited as Dulles Papers, series, box number, and file designation); Wymberley D. Coerr to DS, 2 June 1954, RG 59, 715.5 MSP/6–254, NA.

38.   Copy of Dulles to Wilson letter enclosed in John Cabot to Dulles, 3 April 1953, RG 59, F.W. 716.5 MSP/4–953; Copy of JCS response enclosed in Joint Strategic Plans Committee, 842/102, 8 May 1953, RG 218, Central Decimal File, 1951–1953, 092 (8–22–46), Sec. 90, NA (hereafter cited as RG 218, CDF, and file number).   Funds for the Mutual Security Act of 1951 (under which the military assistance program operated) were divided up along geographic lines: Title I (Europe); Title II (Near East and Africa); Title III (Asia and Pacific); and Title IV (American Republics).

39.   Joint Chiefs of Staff, 2099/289, 19 May 1953, RG 218, CDF, 092 (8–22–46) Sec. 90; Joint Strategic Plans Committee, 842/118, 29 Oct. 1953, RG 218, CDF, 092 (8–22–46), Sec. 98, NA.

40.   Dulles to Wilson, 9 Apr. 1953, enclosed in Cabot to Dulles, 3 Apr. 1953, RG 59, F.W. 716.5 MSP/4–953, NA.

41.   Matthews to Wilson, 23 July 1953, RG 59, 717.5 MSP/7–2353, NA.

42.   Leddy to Holland, 3 June 1954, RG 59, 715.00/6–354; Lindberg to DS, 9 July, 21 Sept. 1954, RG 59, 815.00/7–954, /9–2154, NA.

43.   Willauer to DS, 8, 11 June 1954, RG 59, 715.5–MSP/6–854, /6–1154, NA.

44.   Willauer to Harrington, 15 June 1954, Papers of Whiting Willauer, Box 18, Mudd Library (hereafter cited as Willauer Papers with box number).

45.   Holland to Willauer, 16 July 1954, *FRUS, 1952–1954*, 4:1308–1311.

46.   Holland to Murphy, 6 Aug. 1954; Murphy to Hensel, 10 Aug. 1954, RG 59, 715.5 MSP/8–654, /8–1054, NA.

47.   Hensel to Murphy, 30 Oct. 1954, RG 59, 715.5 MSP/10–3054, NA.

48.   Willauer to Warner, 10 Feb. 1955, Willauer Papers, Box 19, Mudd Library.

49.   Morris, *Honduras*, 10–11.

50.   For Ambassador Willauer's perspective of the events leading up to the junta's seizure of power in 1956, see a paper he prepared in late 1956 or early 1957,

"Political Background of Current Honduran Governmental Structure," Willauer Papers, Box 20, Mudd Library. Morris, *Honduras*, 11–12, 35–39; and Ropp, "The Honduran Army," 514–518, contain brief analyses of the events in Honduras during the years 1956–1963.

51.   Morris, *Honduras*, 35–59, 83–85; Acker, *Banana Republic*, 109; Ropp, "The Honduran Army," 510–518; Morris and Ropp, "Corporatism and Dependent Development," 52.

52.   Statement enclosed in Mr. Taylor to Willauer, 20 Dec. 1957, Willauer Papers, Box 20, Mudd Library.

53.   Philippe C. Schmitter, *Autonomy or Dependence as Regional Integration Outcomes: Central America* (Berkeley, 1972), 29; Acker, *Banana Republic*, 162, 110. One of the best studies of U.S. relations with Honduras after the late 1950s is Donald E. Schulz and Deborah Sundloff Schulz, eds., *The United States, Honduras, and the Crisis in Central America* (Boulder, CO, 1994).

54.   Kenneth Iverson to James Webb, 29 Dec. 1958, Box 22; Brigadier General James Coutts to William Draper, 13 Jan. 1959, Records of the U.S. President's Committee to Study the U.S. Military Assistance Program, Box 9 (hereafter cited as Records of Committee to Study MAP, box number), DDEL.

4

The Path of Progress

In the immediate post-World War II years, the issue of economic interdependence between the United States and Latin America seemed to require little additional debate. The interdependence was, after all, a reality, with the trade between the two reflecting a "logical" exchange: U.S. consumer products for Latin American raw materials. In this exchange, both would receive what they needed: the United States acquiring markets for its production and resources for its factories; Latin America gaining necessary products and capital for its own development.

Despite the apparent logic of this theory, however, U.S. policymakers were aware that serious problems threatened its application. The economic backwardness of most of Latin America, political instability, and the growth of extreme nationalism were all obvious impediments to the development of economic interdependence. One solution was to use economic aid to further the development of Latin America.

Economic aid to Latin America raised a number of questions: how much aid should, or could, be offered; what kind of aid would achieve the desired results; and, finally, what *were* the desired results? The official debates over those questions, and the answers arrived at—focusing on the specific example of the Point Four program and its application in Central America—highlighted the contradictions U.S. policymakers faced as they attempted to make economic interdependence a reality.

As True in China as It Is in Kansas

In the years immediately following World War II the idea of economic aid to underdeveloped foreign nations began to slowly develop. In the beginning, "aid" was talked about primarily in terms of increased private U.S. investment in these regions.[1] The belief in the miraculous results that might be forthcoming from this action was optimistically expressed in a memorandum from the IDAB in 1950: "The cooperative approach to the problem of backward economies has proved very successful in certain areas. Where local capital is scarce, if not absent altogether, the cooperative technique makes it possible to undertake enterprises which could not be ordinarily financed at all. This is just as true in China as it is in Kansas."[2]

What was good enough for China (and, apparently, Kansas) was also good enough for Latin America. This belief was certainly driven home during the 1945 and 1948 inter-American conferences. At the latter meeting, Secretary of State George Marshall informed the audience that "capital required through the years must come from private sources. . . . As the experience of the United States has shown, progress can be achieved best through individual effort and the use of private resources."[3]

Yet, even while the Latin Americans were being told this, debate was already taking place within the Truman administration concerning more direct forms of foreign aid to that region. Those discussions focused on the inescapable facts that tremendous changes were taking place in Latin America, that some of those changes challenged U.S. interests, and that U.S. economic aid would be one way to meet those challenges head-on.

For Latin America, the war had been, as Shoshana Tancer has put it, a "watershed" in the region's "movement toward economic growth and independence." World War II had a tremendous impact on Latin America's trade and investment, with the result being the development of the belief that "each nation would have to protect itself from the vicissitudes of international affairs."[4]

Latin American demands for more diverse, developed, and nationally based economies were not lost on U.S. officials. A 1946 State Department report noted the war had "greatly intensified the long existing efforts of some of the other American republics to broaden the basis of their economies to make them less subject to the fluctuations of world conditions." The changes, and possible dangers, which resulted from such efforts were also recognized in the report. They "necessitated or [have] been the pretext for more government control and government assistance, in the form of tariff protection, restrictions on imports, direct and indirect subsidies, directed investment, and immediate government participation in enterprise."[5]

For U.S. policymakers, the danger was that those kinds of policies tended to take on quite a nationalistic tone, to the point of possibly endangering U.S.-Latin American economic relations. And such nationalism could be subverted by communists. These results, of course, were worst-case scenarios, but as one ARA official put it in 1949 (referring, in this case, specifically to recent occurrences in Brazil), "If the nationalistic ball ever really starts rolling, there may be no limit to its application."[6]

United States officials were cognizant of the fact that what got that "ball" rolling in the first place was the dire economic situation faced by most Latin American nations. One State Department memorandum in 1949 pointed out that "some of the American nations have made little progress either toward better government or prosperity." It went on to cite eleven "small" nations—including all five of the Central American republics—as examples of "lamentably slow" progress. A CIA review from 1948 concluded: "It is becoming increasingly evident that Latin America is approaching a political and institutional crises [sic] which may affect its ability to afford valuable cooperation to the United States."[7]

Faced with such ugly facts and possible consequences, U.S. officials began to come around to the idea that economic aid to Latin America might be in everyone's best interests. As a 1949 State Department memorandum put it, the many problems being faced in Latin America "should lead us to wonder whether there is not something more we could do for our neighbors—not as Santa Claus but in our own interest." President Truman and Under Secretary of State Acheson echoed those sentiments. Truman, in a 1948 speech calling for more U.S. loans to Latin America, claimed that, "The United States has long recognized the importance of economic and political stability in the Western Hemisphere. Such stability rests substantially upon the continuation of a satisfactory rate of economic progress." Acheson, in 1947, also accented the relationship between economic development and the securing of Western Hemisphere allies in the Cold War: "It is plain to us that to achieve the fundamental objective of having willing allies and strong allies, we must pursue the course of aiding all of these countries to increase their productivity, for only on this basis can strength and free institutions develop."[8]

A regional statement of the Bureau of Inter-American Affairs in 1951 succinctly summarized the role U.S. aid could play in the furthering of U.S.-Latin American economic interdependence. "As their friend," the report claimed, "we may reasonably be expected to assure them a fair share of the things they need to maintain their economies to help them achieve their aspirations toward fuller national development. As leader we may be expected to help them increase their productivity and diversify their production, and see that the economic policies we are obliged by the common interest to follow injure their economies as little as possible."[9]

It was, perhaps, the purest expression of the theory of interdependence. The success of one partner equaled the success of the other and, multiplied together, led to even more success for all. Yet U.S. policymakers would find that such an equation worked better in the abstract than it did in practice. Having come to the conclusion that U.S. aid was essential to the workings of economic interdependence, those officials now confronted the stickier questions of what kind of aid would bring the necessary success in Latin America and, more fundamentally, what kind of "success" really served the interests of interdependence? In answering those questions, U.S. officials found that the only things that multiplied were the contradictions.

As True in Central America as It Is in Detroit?

In casting about for ideas as to the kind of economic assistance to offer Latin America, the most obvious basis for comparison was the much-heralded Marshall Plan.[10] As a State Department memorandum of 1949 explained, the Latin Americans were certainly aware of the comparison, and that there had been "much publicized disappointment among the Latinos that we have been unable to establish the equivalent of the Marshall Plan in that area." United States officials emphasized the inability of their nation to provide an equivalent amount of aid, such as when Secretary Marshall announced at the 1948 Bogotá conference that "it is beyond the capacity of the United States Government itself to finance more than a small portion of the vast development needed."[11] More than thinly stretched resources figured into the U.S. refusal to consider a "Latin American Marshall Plan," however. George Elsey, a former special assistant to Truman, stated in a 1969 interview,

> The Marshall Plan was to help a highly industrialized intricate economy get back on its feet. South America did not have a highly industrialized, intricate economy comparable to that of Western Europe. . . .One could no more impose a Marshall plan on Central America than you could pick up Detroit and put it down in the middle of a Brazilian jungle. The basis for it wasn't there.[12]

The question of what kind of aid to Latin America would help cement the interdependent relationship was thus left hanging. If there was to be no "Latin American Marshall Plan," what was to be done for the under-developed nations of that region?

That question, of course, was intimately linked with another: what was the program decided upon supposed to accomplish in terms of development in Latin America? The search for answers led U.S. officials to a wide-ranging debate about how much development could or should be promoted in Latin America. A number of troubling conclusions soon raised serious doubts about whether their pursuit of economic inter-dependence would result in "[e]conomic maturity, equality, and in-dependence" for Latin America.[13]

One conclusion, discussed at length in Chapters One and Two, was that for both economic and military reasons, the United States viewed the continuance, and even expansion, of raw material production in Latin America to be of paramount importance. Economically, the increase of raw material exports from underdeveloped regions such as Latin America was necessary not only for the production but also for the sale of U.S. goods. Without the income derived from the sale of their natural re-sources, how would such countries buy U.S. products? It was obvious that for everyone's benefit, production of those materials must be increased. Their sale would allow those other nations to slake their desire for U.S. goods.

Furthermore, the need for increased raw material production from areas such as Latin America was not limited to the United States; in the interdependent world economic system, other nations—in Western Europe and Japan—also looked to those regions. Militarily, the U.S. needed the strategic materials the underdeveloped nations provided. And strong economies meant strong allies.

Another conclusion seemed to temper the degree to which economic aid could help in the development of U.S.-Latin American ties. By and large, the Latin Americans seemed incapable of understanding complex eco-nomic issues and would, therefore, not likely use the economic assistance they clamored for in an efficient or useful manner. New York lawyer Francis Adams Truslow, writing to Assistant Secretary Miller in 1951, summed up the view of many U.S. observers concerning Latin American plans for economic growth by stating, "Some or all of these ideas are near-sighted or plain cockeyed, but they are widespread and accepted and they underly even the words of ministers who may deny them."[14]

Others specifically addressed Latin American plans and possible uses for U.S. economic aid. J. Robert Schaetzel commented in 1948 that most Latin American proposals for U.S. aid were designed to "permit underdeveloped countries special liberties and/or to demand unequal and more onerous obligations from the industrialized countries"; most of these were "the stuff of fantasy."[15] Two other officials, interviewed years after their service with the U.S. government was over, expressed somewhat harsher views. Dennis FitzGerald, who from 1946 to 1956 was intimately involved with U.S. foreign aid programs, stated when asked what kind of aid underdeveloped regions such as Latin America desired:

> I think frequently they didn't know for sure. And I also presume it's not unfair to say that if they could get a check, that would be very satisfactory to them. What they wanted and what they needed were very frequently entirely different. It used to be said, in exaggeration, that what every under-developed country wanted was a great big steel mill complex and other, great big, physical entities; that somehow or other they thought one just pressed a button and out spewed steel or whatever. Perhaps too frequently we gave them that when we may have known better.[16]

Ellis Briggs, who served as U.S. ambassador to six different nations between 1944 and 1959 (including the Dominican Republic, Uruguay, Peru, and Brazil), expressed a more definitively racist viewpoint when recalling the successes and failures of U.S. aid to underdeveloped nations. The successes occurred in Greece, South Korea, Taiwan, and Israel, "But those four that I have mentioned deal with people who are not disadvantaged [the original word, scratched out during editing, had been "tribal"], just out of the palm trees, and our experience has been that the closer to the palm tree the object of American aid is, the less likely it is to utilize American assistance to his or our advantage."[17]

Despite these view, U.S. officials were also aware that the Latin Americans were demanding *something* in the way of aid, and that they were voicing some serious doubts about the manner in which an interdependent relationship would work. A 1951 State Department analysis of upcoming negotiations between the United States and Latin America delineated the differences in the positions that each side would take. In the case of nearly every U.S. position, the Latin American response would be "agree, *but*. . . ." Some of the basic goals of the United States were to "increase

LA production of strategic materials"; "grant highest priority to requirements defense production"; "secure cooperation on price controls"; and "facilitate requirements of non-defense economic development in so far as possible." The Latin Americans would agree to raise production, "but will raise questions of long term purchase commitments, . . . post-emergency markets"; would "probably agree" to accent defense production, "but may seek qualifications favoring essential civilian needs"; would "support price controls in theory *but* will seek highest prices for LA exports *and* will attempt obtain reaffirmation Chapultepec Res. XV emphasizing price ceiling relation to cost production and 'just relation' between raw materials and manufactured goods"; and would "recognize retarding influence defense requirements on economic development projects *but* strongly desire continuance non-defense economic development and will seek most liberal interpretation of 'in so far as possible.'"[18] In sum, there seemed to be definite differences.

These differences did not seem insurmountable to U.S. officials. The basic problem was to convince the Latin Americans that it was really in their best interests to continue to expand their involvement in the interdependent economic relationship with the United States. Schaetzel, speaking in 1953 at the Conference on U.S. Foreign Policy, summarized the issue:

> Also there has been inadequate new discovery, exploitation and development of raw material resources in the underdeveloped countries. One important reason is that many of the countries having these materials object to the development of them. This resistance stems from a desire, which is psychologically, politically, and economically based, to industrialize. They do not want to be dependent on the exploitation of strategic materials. They want to husband their wealth and keep it in the ground. . . .Here then is a problem of meeting the long-range needs of an expanding world in the face of strong resistance by the host country.[19]

Throughout the period 1945–1954, U.S. policymakers conducted an arduous search for answers to that perplexing problem. One focus of that search was on the role that economic assistance might play in meeting those Latin American "needs" while simultaneously eroding that "resistance."

A Bold New Program: Point Four

Perhaps the best known postwar program of U.S. economic assistance to Latin America was Point Four, called for by President Truman in his 1949 inaugural address, and finally passed by Congress as Title IV of the Foreign Economic Assistance Act of 1950.[20]   That it was a part of Truman's inaugural speech was evidence of the president's fascination with the idea of using his nation's technical expertise to both develop the poorer nations of the world and throw up another rampart against communism. Point Four would be a "bold new program"; it would be a "key to prosperity and peace"; and "in countries where the choice is between communist totalitarianism and the free way of life is in the balance, this program can tip the scales toward the way of freedom."[21]

Not everyone was quite as excited as the president. Stanley Andrews, who later headed the Technical Cooperation Administration (TCA), recalled that when Truman had wanted something in his speech dealing with aid to the "underdeveloped countries," his "speechwriters began to scurry around about what the hell to have." When the speech was made, "the State Department was caught flatfooted. They didn't have the faintest idea in terms of a program or anything else. So the bureaucracy began to debate on what in the hell this all means, and who would run it."[22]

Once recovering its balance, the bureaucracy began to portray Point Four as a program to simultaneously uplift the masses of the under-developed nations and provide a bulwark against communist infiltration into those countries. A memorandum from the Executive Committee on Economic Foreign Policy in March 1949 explained that the goals of Point Four were "broadly economic"; the program would "[seek] the advance-ment of peoples of underdeveloped areas." Nevertheless, there were political concerns that would also be well served by Point Four; namely, that by "building good will" toward the United States, this would "lessen greatly the effectiveness of sabotage and subversion by unfriendly nations and can unify our friends and make them more effective." Assistant Secretary Cabot made the same points in 1953, declaring that, in relation to Latin America, the Point Four program was "Pan Americanism in action. . . . This is a demonstration that we do care for their well-being, that we do value their friendship, that we want them to rise in splendor in the constellation of nations. It shows the ignorant peon that communist propaganda is clap-trap and that democracy is the path of progress."[23]

All of this sounded very fine, and the rhetoric certainly represented the interdependent outlook. Yet, a closer look at the debates that took place from the time of Truman's speech in 1949 until the mid-1950s suggests that the Point Four program was something much more (or, perhaps, less) than simply a hazy, somewhat half-cocked reply to the demands of underdeveloped nations for U.S. economic aid, or, as Thomas Paterson has claimed, "a Cold War program to meet the Communist threat."[24] Those debates revealed the inherent contradictions posed by the U.S. pursuit of economic interdependence between itself and Latin America. Point Four represented a first attempt to reconcile those contradictions.[25]

First and foremost, the Point Four program was designed to increase the production of raw materials in Latin America. This was not a new idea; in 1948 the Department of the Army had argued for "generous financial and technical assistance to our Latin American neighbors in return for their cooperation in making their strategic raw materials available to us." Assistant Secretary Miller stated in 1950 that "his conception" of the program was that the application of U.S. "technical know-how" would "help Latin America increase its productivity and thereby make its positive contribution toward the closing of the dollar gap." That increase, of course, should come in the form of "exportable products." A 1953 FOA report claimed that such assistance was "much broader in scope than materials development alone. Nevertheless," it concluded, "many specific projects and some of the larger projects are directly connected with expansion of materials production." Some of these projects included "geological surveys, aerial photography and mapping. . .research, training and professional advice is given for specific problems encountered in materials recovery."[26]

Expanded production of natural resources from Latin America fit in well with U.S. perceptions of the interdependent world economy. Henry G. Bennett, administrator of the TCA, pointed out in 1951 that technical assistance would result in "improving methods for securing more and higher quality materials from existing sources and interesting private enterprise in promoting the various kinds and stages of development." In his opinion, the "results and benefits to the United States as well as the foreign government are obvious from the point of view of the local economies and international trade." That "point of view" revolved around the idea of "comparative" or "natural" advantages accruing from the production of readily available resources. A 1949 report by the Advisory Committee on Technical Assistance (ACTA) explained this concept more clearly by examining the benefits of the Point Four program. The program would allow "international trade" to expand—both in terms of materials flowing to the United States and consumer products going to the materials-producing countries. "Productivity both at home and abroad can be expected to increase as production is expanded along lines allowing the greatest benefit to be derived from natural advantage." "The objective of the United States in the field of international production and trade," it concluded, "is the achievement of effective international specialization along the lines of so-called comparative advantage."[27]

Effectiveness, therefore, depended on productivity, and Point Four was designed to directly promote accelerated production of raw materials for export in Latin America. The aforementioned surveys, photography, mapping, and research and training were the most obvious methods to achieve that goal, but U.S. policymakers were well aware that that kind of assistance was not enough. Transportation and power were two prerequisites, as were improved health care and food production. A 1951 report by the PMPC was clear on these points:

> Technical assistance which contributes to materials development through improved health, education and living conditions of workers and through the expansion of transportation and power facilities may also be necessary. . . . For example, in Venezuela iron ore development had to be delayed until malaria control measures were taken. In Indonesia, the Standard Vacuum Oil Company was faced with a shortage of skilled labor and had to institute its own educational program to train local labor. In the Belgian Congo the mining program was limited by the low productivity of the native farmers, and the Union Miniere Company had to take measures to increase local food production through increased agricultural efficiency in order to provide food for the miners.[28]

There were also political benefits from an application of the Point Four program to Latin America. An NSC memorandum of 1951 stated that the program was also considered to be a "political and psychological measure," whereby its work at the "'village level'" would "promote political stability and popular morale, create attitudes favorable to the United States and render the people of the underdeveloped countries less susceptible to communist subversion." The contribution that Point Four might make to stability was also highlighted in a 1952 MSP report. "Existing social unrest and political instability," the report noted, "which stem from hunger, poverty, sickness, and ignorance, are being exploited by extreme nationalists, Communists, and other agitators to fan anti–United States sentiment." One goal for technical assistance was to "assist in overcoming those present weaknesses in the Latin-American economic structure which contribute to political and economic instability."[29]

Point Four had obvious attraction as an anti-communist weapon in Latin America, as the NSC memorandum duly noted. Economically and politically, the program could help build pro-U.S. sentiments in the region. President Eisenhower certainly saw the value when, in considering U.S. aid to Latin America as a whole, he opined that "the $130 million [in economic aid] was a good investment in Latin America if we could be sure that by expenditure of this amount we could secure the allegiance of these republics to our camp in the cold war."[30]

Countering nationalism was one way of containing dangerous "anti–United States sentiment." Here again, Point Four had a role to play. A 1949 study by ACTA revealed that some nations' economic policies might show a preference for "regional or national autarchy," or be designed to avoid "a repetition of the wartime situation in which some markets were cut off from traditional sources of supply," or might simply be "in response to local political pressures." Studies for technical assistance to any nation, therefore, must consider whether the "existing policies" in a given nation were "consistent with a pattern of economic development in accord with the general principle of international specialization along lines of comparative advantage." Any "changes in commercial policy indicated by such studies should be urged upon the governments involved." While the ACTA report obviously saw technical assistance as a "stick" to be used (through its withholding) to "urge" changes in certain nations' economic policies, a State Department memorandum of 1953 also indicated that such assistance also had potential as a "carrot." Noting that there was "a growing body of opinion in Latin America which questions the benefit to Latin America of close cooperation with the United States," it concluded that "we must demonstrate that we are interested in helping to raise the status of the masses in Latin America who are determined that their material lot can and should be improved." Technical assistance would be one visible means of doing this.[31]

The efficacy of Point Four as both an economic and political tool would depend, of course, on its ability to convince significant numbers of Latin Americans that the program satisfied their demands for economic development and progress. This would be difficult to do. Many Latin Americans (not just "extreme nationalists") believed that development meant moving beyond the period of relying on the exportation of extractable materials. Point Four, however, had as its primary function the *increase* of materials development in Latin America. Indeed, its main goal was to contribute to the realization of a more efficient system of international specialization and comparative advantage. Fundamentally, the question at hand was whether U.S. efforts at economic inter-dependence could simultaneously meet the demands of both the United States and Latin America. The answer arrived at, after involved investigation and debate, was yes. . .and no.

One Man's Gain by Another Man's Loss

Explaining that programs such as Point Four—which sought to increase the output of raw materials from Latin America—would, in the end, work to the favor of the Latin nations was not an easy undertaking. After all, much the same message had been sent during World War II, when the United States, desperate for raw materials, pushed for increased production of strategic resources from Latin America. The experience had been a disappointment for the nations of that region for, as David Green has noted, even U.S. policymakers realized that "the wartime program of inter-American economic 'cooperation' had not resulted in equal and reciprocal benefits for both Americans and Latin Americans."[32]

It was not a very good example, and U.S. officials seemed to realize this. They therefore embarked during the years after the announcement of Point Four on an effort to construct a reasonable rationale for the continuation, indeed, the *increase*, of Latin America's traditional role as provider of raw materials. The two basic notions were, first, that industrial development in Latin America was not all it was cracked up to be; and, second, should Latin America still desire to develop and diversify its economic bases along industrial lines, the continued and intensified production of exportable raw materials was the best hope in achieving those ends.

During the months following Truman's announcement of his "bold" program of technical assistance, decidedly cold water was thrown on Latin American ideas that rapid industrialization was possible, or even desirable. Willard Barber, a special assistant to Edward Miller in the State Department, examined the issue in two letters in early 1949. In the first, he drew attention to a section of a draft statement that had urged "building up a sound industrial production" in Latin America. He advised "caution and care" in expressing that kind of thinking. Many people felt that "Latin America's basic economy is and will remain agrarian." Perhaps "diversification" could come in the agricultural field, instead of industrialization. In any event, "sound" industrialization should "not include hot-house industry protected by tariffs, quotas, subsidies and other artificial devices." In his second letter two months later, he was even more negative in his views, claiming that "there seem to be some false prophets who may mislead a number of people interested in inter-American trade by putting too much emphasis on the need for rapid industrialization. To anticipate the millennium by means of rapid industrialization is, of course, a fatal mistake." He even noted that, "Industrialization has its evils," and mentioned "unemployment cycles" and the artificial subsidization of local industries tending to "diminish the total wealth of the national economy."[33]

Four years later, Milton Eisenhower noted his first-hand views on the deleterious effects "indiscriminate industrialization" could have on Latin America. He claimed that in nations such as Brazil and Chile, "industrialization has outstripped production of food and fibers and the fundamental services of transportation, communication, and power"; this was a "roadblock in the way of balanced economic development." All in all, it appeared to him that "there is even danger of industrialization for its own sake rather than for a sound contribution to economic progress."[34]

Despite all the obvious drawbacks, even Milton Eisenhower was forced to admit that the "Latin American countries desire through industrialization and diversification to relieve themselves from imported goods."[35] Apparently, there would be no convincing the Latin Americans that industrialization could bring as many "evils" as blessings. It would, therefore, be necessary to convince them that industrialization had to be approached carefully and slowly—*very* slowly. And the best way to go about that process was by accelerating, not deemphasizing, Latin American raw material production.

In 1954, a State Department intelligence report stated that "natural resources in Latin America are generally adequate to support continued economic growth even if the population maintains the present high rate of increase."[36] This idea was given fuller expression in a 1951 report by economist Raymond Mikesell, prepared for the PMPC. "It is our firm belief," he announced, ". . .that the development of the material resources of the under-developed countries is not only compatible with their programs of general economic development, but that such development will be a key factor in the realization of higher standards of economic welfare." There was, he concluded, "a reciprocal and complimentary relationship between materials development and general or diversified economic development."[37]

First and foremost, U.S. observers noted, the expansion of raw material output for export resulted in what Latin America needed for development and diversification—capital. Mikesell pointed out that the proceeds from the sale of raw materials was "the major source of foreign exchange for the purchase of equipment and supplies needed for both industrialization and social capital of all kinds." "For most of the newly developed countries of the world," he concluded, "it has been the rapid expansion of the raw materials production which has been the basis for their rising standards of living and the means of financing and of providing markets and economic support for their industrial and social capital development."[38]

Economists Norman Buchanan and Howard Ellis, in a long study prepared for the Randall Commission in 1953, went to the heart of the matter, asking, "Should the United States seek to develop the presently underdeveloped countries as sources of supply for its consumers and industries, or should it subordinate such considerations to a policy of helping those countries attain a broad and diversified basis of development? Is this a clear choice between selfish and altruistic motives? Does primary production serve the interests of the industrial West, but retard the economic growth of the other three quarters of the earth? These are real issues. . . ." Indeed, these were *the* issues, and so they looked to find answers to those troubling questions.

Simple logic, they claimed, dictated that to attain *"balanced development"* the underdeveloped nations would have to "earn the material basis of economic growth by large exports of primary products." Therefore, "The United States is not confronted by a dilemma in furthering the development of foreign sources of supply or foreign markets for its own exports, and in furthering the development of the economic potential of low-income countries." Having dispensed with that sticky question, they then posited, in a section entitled "Charity Begins at Home," that, "The economic, political and humane interests of Western nations in the progress of the underdeveloped world should impress these countries with the truth that stability of domestic employment in the great industrial countries is the *first* ingredient of stability elsewhere." As they concluded in a synopsis of their study prepared a week later, "our own continued economic vitality, the progress of underdeveloped countries, and the survival of the Western European industrial nations depends upon a free and expanding system of world trade. As against tariffs, subsidies, quotas and other government interferences with private enterprise, this system does not purchase one man's gain by another man's loss."[39]

It was an impressive display of logic and humanitarianism. Certainly, the United States would benefit from such an arrangement; but, so would the underdeveloped nations. If it was industrialization and diversification they desired, then so be it. The two goals were not contradictory, after all. In fact, Latin American goals could best be served by fulfilling the U.S. goal of accelerated natural resource production. In this equation, everyone gained; no one lost. If achieved, it would be the crowning glory of economic interdependence. That it was not achieved was striking testimony to the contradictions inherent in the very pursuit of such ends by the United States.

Maintaining the Balance Now Existing

The idea that continued and expanded raw material production from underdeveloped regions such as Latin America would eventually result in the industrialization and development they desired was predicated on the assumption that the prices for those materials would increase (or, at the least, remain stable) and that demand would remain constant. Yet, as many U.S. officials and interested observers recognized, neither prices nor demand were likely to work in the favor of natural resource producers.

Milton Eisenhower recalled that one of the "serious problems" for that region was that it was forced to "buy from us industrial goods whose prices are fixed, and we buy from them the primary commodities whose prices fluctuate as much as 50 percent a year." The result was that "they have no basis on which to do reasonable planning, and this upsets their credit-worthiness and everything else."[40] Secretary Dulles, writing to the president in 1953, admitted that the problem was perplexing. The problem for Latin American nations was that "these countries are essentially raw material and not industrial countries." The relationship with the industrialized United States was therefore one of "'feast or famine.'" When the U.S. needed their products, they had a "feverish prosperity"; when demand dropped, they went into "economic decline with unemployment which, nowadays, the Communists organize against us." This brought into question the entire economic relationship between the United States and Latin America. "Only when we have the answer is it possible to develop a really sound permanent relationship of good will."[41]

The answer arrived at was that Latin America needed to expand its raw material production. Mikesell, in his 1951 report, noted the harsh impact economic changes could have on monoresource economies, and suggested that diversification might be one answer. This did not mean, however, "a reduction of, or even slackening of the expansion of, the production of primary commodities to be sold on world markets." A report on the MSP in 1953 reached the same conclusion. "The immediate prospects of maintaining Latin American export prices do not appear bright." The best solution the report could offer was that "principal reliance for overcoming these difficulties must be placed on increased productivity and on the institution of effective monetary and credit policies." Increased production of raw materials would only help, of course, if the United States kept its demand high, and here most U.S. observers were in agreement that this was the best thing their nation could do to alleviate the situation. As Mikesell stated, "The greatest protection to these countries from cyclical movements will be achieved through a continuation of the full employment policies of the United States and other important material importing countries."[42]

It was, all in all, an interesting argument. The "feast or famine" relationship between the United States and Latin America did not need to be fundamentally altered. Instead, both partners needed to take additional steps to make sure that it was a continuous feast. Latin America needed to increase its production of raw materials; the United States needed to keep its own economy in full-employment mode in order to absorb those materials. It was also an argument that, when the verbiage was chopped away, held out little hope that Latin America would see much advantage (comparative or otherwise) from the plan.

It has been previously noted that nationalistic economic policies by the Latin American governments were some of the problems that faced the United States; problems that might effectively "weaken our domestic economy" by denying markets and sources of raw materials. Indeed, as a CIA report of 1952 pointed out, government-supported industrialization in Latin America would be detrimental to U.S. interests, since the "[d]evelopment of new domestic industries and the basic transportation and energy services will probably involve the diversion of capital and other resources from development of the raw material export sector of the economy."[43] The report was not making an earth-shattering observation.

It was obvious that if Latin America wished to industrialize, it would mean diverting capital and "other resources" (manpower, government resources, etc.) from the production of natural resources. Yet, this simple conclusion went to the heart of the matter, and a State Department document from 1950 zeroed in on the problem. How could the "continuance of economic development in Latin America" be reconciled with the fact that "we are expanding our plant facilities in the United States."[44] Francis Adams Truslow, in a 1951 letter to Edward Miller, doubted that the United States could really answer such a question. "We seem willing to declare a national policy of international development," he wrote, "and thereby raise everyone's hopes; but I am not sure how deep-rooted our intention is to back up this policy with equipment and material that we need at home or to furnish real financial aid to move the equipment we can supply. I think this is particularly true of our public attitude toward South America."[45]

A Study Group meeting of the CFR in early 1952 dispensed with diplomatic niceties, and got down to brass tacks. Edward Mason, dean of the Graduate School of Public Administration at Harvard, set out the parameters of the problem:

> Changing the relationships now existing between manufacturing nations and raw material producing nations would cause economic difficulties for some of the manufacturing nations. . . .Therefore, it might be beneficial to consider the validity of the thesis that the balance now existing between manufacturing and raw material producing nations contributes more to the economic strength of the free world than some other arrangement.

General Consul of the CIO Arthur Goldberg chimed in with his agreement: "the strengthening of the economies of underdeveloped nations by creating a better balance between raw material production and manufacturing might well create serious maladjustments in many sectors of the economy of the highly developed nations."[46]

The essential point had finally been made. The economic interdependence between the United States and Latin America demanded that the "proper" roles be played by both parties. Any changes in that relationship would "create serious maladjustments" for the U.S. economy; and, after all, wasn't the health of the U.S. economy necessary for the health of all free world nations? For everyone's benefit, therefore, the "balance now existing" should be continued indefinitely. In that regard, any U.S. assistance program—such as Point Four—should always keep in mind, as an ACTA report put it, that "a prime yardstick should be the consistency of the proposed undertaking with the international specialization objective." While it might at times be difficult to adequately assess the issues involved in such a determination, "they must be attempted if the developments which result from our assistance program are not to imperil our international trade objective."[47] Through a brief examination of technical assistance to Central America during the years 1945–1954, we can more clearly see that in terms of its economic (and political) goals, Point Four would "imperil" nothing.

Pretty Small Potatoes

John Ohly, who served as special assistant for Mutual Security Affairs for the Department of State from 1951 to 1952, aptly summarized the magnitude of the Point Four program as a whole when he recalled that "at this early stage the technical assistance program was pretty small potatoes." It never got much beyond that stage. In 1954, Point Four funding was about 2 percent of total MSP spending ($140 million out of $5.8 billion).[48]

In addition, Point Four assistance to Latin America paled in comparison to that given elsewhere. In 1953, the nineteen participating nations of that region received about one-third the funds allocated to South and Southeast Asia, and about two-fifths of the assistance given to the Near East and Africa. Burma was the recipient of twice as much Point Four assistance as the leading Latin American nation, Brazil. Iran received $23.3 million; all of Latin America received $21.6 million. Only Brazil, Peru, and Paraguay received more than Liberia. Central American nations ranked low on the list for Point Four funds: Costa Rica was ninth; Honduras, tenth; El Salvador, twelfth; Nicaragua, thirteenth; and Guatemala, eighteenth.[49]

The small amount of aid doled out to Latin America should not, however, be reason to dismiss the program as simply an economic "bone" that was thrown to the region following the war. From the strictly economic point of view, U.S. officials did not really see the need for a heavy monetary investment in the technical assistance program. After all, the basis for the program was that through the sharing of U.S. know-how and technology, the Latin Americans could more efficiently use what was at hand. Its purpose was not to construct or rebuild; it was designed to sharpen and focus the resources already present in Latin America.

Such was particularly the case in regards to Central America. Here, the purpose of U.S. assistance was clearly defined. An NIE of 1954 summed up the situation. The predominant "industry" in Central America was agriculture—particularly the export crops of bananas, coffee, and sugar. With the exception of coffee, most of the export crop industries were controlled by foreign interests. On the whole, however, "Economic development has been retarded by lack of capital and of technical skill and by the inadequacy of transportation and power facilities of of other basic services." Except for the export crops, "agricultural methods are generally primitive." Foreign trade was vital to the area's economic growth, but the monoresource economies were subject to "fluctuations in the terms of trade." The lack of "technical skills" was a big roadblock to further economic development.[50]

According to a 1953 MSP report, the dual objectives of U.S. technical assistance in Central America therefore, were: "(1) to increase the productivity per worker and the number of skilled workers by carefully planned programs in health, nutrition, housing, and education; and (2) to increase total production by selected programs in agriculture and industry, public administration, natural resources, power, and transportation."[51]

If such economic considerations could determine the aim of technical assistance, they could, when combined with political considerations, also determine the amount of assistance granted to a particular Central American nation. This is what a fascinating 1952 study by the State Department attempted to do, using an impressive array of statistics to support its conclusions. In three separate charts, this study used material provided by the U.S. diplomatic posts in the various nations to determine "Overall Political Importance of the Country to the United States," "Need for Point 4 Assistance," and, finally, "Level of Point 4 Assistance." In these assessments, it was determined that of the nineteen nations rated, the five Central American republics would rank among the bottom six countries in terms of Point Four allocations. "Political Importance" was the most important factor in such low ratings. When such variables as "Subversive Pressures," "Trade Controls," and "Source for U.S. of Materials & Supplies," were considered, the Central American nations did not stand out. Thus, except for Guatemala which scored high in "Subversive Pressures," the other republics were at the absolute bottom of the list. In terms of their "Need for Point 4 Assistance," they did somewhat better. Here, however, need was weighted with population, so that the lightly populated Central American nations were at a disadvantage competing against more heavily populated countries such as Brazil or Mexico.[52]

All of this might suggest that since the Central American nations were small, did not export uranium, iron ore, or tin, and were not (with the exception of Guatemala) seen as being perilously threatened by "subversive pressures," the Point Four aid allocated was small and pro forma during the postwar years. This was not the case. The funds distributed *were* small, though it should be noted that on a per capita basis, Central American allocations of technical assistance ranked relatively high (rates for the five republics were much higher than those for Republic of China, South Vietnam, India, and Brazil during the period 1946–1962).[53] And, the distribution of these funds was never pro forma; a variety of factors could act together to increase or decrease the aid, or change its direction.

This was certainly true in the case of El Salvador. Between 1951 and 1954, the amount of technical aid never rose above $628,000. A glance at the figures, however, provokes some questions about why such a level of aid prevailed and where such aid went. For example, why did U.S. technical aid to El Salvador rise so dramatically from 1951 ($99,000) to 1953 ($628,000)? Among Central American nations, only Costa Rica received a higher yearly grant during that time. Why did U.S. aid for "Industry, Mining, Labor" projects in El Salvador rise from $4,000 in 1952 to $130,000 in 1953, and then back to $14,000 in 1954? No other Central American nation got more than $20,000 for such purposes in any of those years. Why, considering these fairly impressive numbers, did El Salvador receive less per capita technical assistance than any other Central American country prior to 1962?[54] To answer those questions, we must briefly examine the political development of El Salvador after World War II, analyze the U.S. reaction to that development, and consider the overall Central American backdrop to all this.

After a dozen years of his brutal rule, discontented Salvadorans, coupled with a coup arising from the Army, finally forced the dictator Maximiliano Hernández Martínez to step down in May of 1944. The next four years was a time of military rule and inefficient leadership from the "elected" president, General Salvador Castaneda Castro. In 1948, he was in his turn overthrown by another military coup, this one led by Major Oscar Osorio.[55]

The post–1948 regime in El Salvador has been characterized by some historians as "reformist" or "developmentalist" in nature. In the social and political realms, this translated into new legislation establishing a social security system and the adoption of a new constitution in 1950 that called for programs in public health, women's suffrage, new laws for labor, and land reform. In economic terms, as Cynthia Arnson describes it, "the government increased taxes on landowners and channeled resources into infrastructure projects—dams, hydroelectric plants, and ports—as well as agricultural and industrial ventures. The number of state institutions devoted to fostering industrialization expanded rapidly, as did the size of the government bureaucracy. Industrialization appeared to be the wave of the Salvadoran future."[56]

Whether the efforts of Osorio and the Salvadoran government were sincere in their attempts to bring about a more liberal political and modernized economic atmosphere is debatable, with many scholars agreeing with James Dunkerley's assessment that many of the "reforms" written during that time "never saw the light of day; what mattered was that things were proclaimed, not that they were realised." "Its [the Osorio regime] wafer-thin populist guise enabled a degree of cooptation of the urban masses, but without impeding repression of militant opposition."[57]

In the early months of its existence, the new Salvadoran government (which Osorio soon came to dominate) developed smooth relations with the United States. By mid-1949, U.S. Ambassador Albert Nufer sent along a request from the Salvadoran government that the U.S. Army Mission to that nation be expanded from one officer to three. Nufer felt that this was a good idea, and to support his position enclosed a memorandum prepared by the the the U.S. military attaché, Lieutenant Colonel Alva R. Fitch. Fitch first pointed out that the military was the chief source of stability in El Salvador and was "the principal barrier to Communist in-roads." He noted approvingly that the current regime was "substantially more democratic than any recent regime here and probably more democratic than any other regime in Central America." However, that "same democracy renders it that much more susceptible to Communist penetration." Aid should therefore be given to the Salvadoran armed forces in order to "spread American tactical doctrine, American technical methods and esteem for the United States."[58]

By late 1949, however, disturbing reports began to be filed by the new U.S. ambassador, George P. Shaw. While admitting that it was unlikely that El Salvador would "change its policy of generally supporting United States objectives in the international field," he cautioned his superiors that "there is in the offing one important element which may cause trouble." The "element" was a preliminary draft of a new Salvadoran constitution. It contained "a concept of excessive nationalism and would undoubtedly promote anti-foreign sentiment." Without divulging particulars, Shaw then proceeded to examine recent political events in El Salvador. Osorio was being criticized "for playing with the leftists and becoming involved with communists and fellow travelers"; support from the "wealthy class" for his upcoming presidential campaign (elections would be held in 1950) was shaky. Given these problems, especially the "extreme nationalism" in the draft constitution, Shaw suggested that the standard State Department policy of trying to meet Salvadoran requests for economic aid "should be considered in light of. . .the effect of the proposed constitution on investment of private American capital and discrimination against American interests." In a later report, Shaw returned to the question of nationalism in El Salvador, stating that, "New American capital certainly would not receive a warm welcome in El Salvador and existing American investments would be endangered by a basic national charter such as envisaged. The country's present financial situation is good and this may be a part of the reason why a spirit of independence and excessive nationalism has become so apparent."[59]

Worries about a proposed constitution, however, soon paled in comparison to concerns about the upcoming 1950 elections, which centered on the influence of communists in El Salvador. Throughout the first months of 1950, U.S. officials in El Salvador kept the State Department up to date concerning the machinations of communists in that nation. Shaw reported in February that there was an "intense campaign of public agitation principally against the Government and the Army." This campaign, taking place mainly among the lower classes, "seems to bear a strong Communist imprint." In response, Salvadoran "capitalists" had thrown their support behind Osorio. As one of these men put it, "'Better Osorio in our hands than against us.'" Other reports focused on communist infiltration into Salvadoran labor unions. William Bennett, writing a month earlier, stated that, "Communism is not strong in El Salvador, but is ceaseless in its attempts to gain control of the labor movement." According to a State Department study prepared a few days later, the communists had already established themselves in the existing unions. Two of the three unions discussed in the study were classified as "communist led" and were "similar to" or "influenced by" Guatemalan labor unions. Sounding a note of warning, the report claimed that "Osorio has courted labor's favor."[60]

Guatemala's role in these developments was emphasized by U.S. officials. Already by early 1950 the United States was having serious doubts about the political direction of the Arevalo administration. Chargé William A. Wieland reported in January 1950 that a political exile, operating out of Guatemala, was "looming as a rival to Osorio" and was reputed to be "under the direct leadership of the Communist Party." Shaw, commenting on the just completed election in April, noted that "Guatemalan Communists" had snuck over the border to vote against Osorio.[61]

It was little wonder, then, that Shaw was happy to report after the election of Osorio that the people of El Salvador seemed "relieved." The nation, he exclaimed, was "on its way back to constitutional and representative government" for the first time since 1948. Apparently, the ambassador was himself so "relieved" that he overlooked the fact that, as an earlier State Department memo had concluded, Osorio's election had never been in doubt. His nomination by the Partido Revolucionario de Unificación Democrática [PRUD] practically guaranteed that end "because the government and PRUD have so fixed the electoral machinery that his election could be assured."[62]

For the next four years, the U.S. relationship with El Salvador would be determined by a complex mix of issues and events. Osorio's first four years in power coincided with a growing uneasiness on the part of U.S. officials about El Salvador's neighbor Guatemala. Fearful that communism was establishing a beachhead in the Western Hemisphere, U.S. policymakers saw as a first step the isolating of that wayward nation by establishing closer and friendlier relations with its neighbors. This, of course, included El Salvador. However, while Osorio's government gave every indication of being strongly anti-communist, it also staked out certain economic positions with a decidedly nationalistic bent. In addition, high coffee prices during those years meant that El Salvador was not as reliant on U.S. foreign assistance as some other underdeveloped nations. These circumstances worked to focus U.S. attention on Point Four and how it might be used to obtain U.S. objectives in El Salvador. Since this program involved technical aid, it was assumed that El Salvador might look more approvingly on this assistance—the nation needed the aid, and it did not appear to have as many "strings" attached as might be the case with other types of assistance. The program could be used to bolster the Osorio regime, increase friendliness between the United States and El Salvador, and simultaneously decrease any possible Guatemalan influence in El Salvador. It might even help alleviate the disturbing nationalism in that nation.

In mid-1950, however, it appeared that the issue of nationalism in El Salvador would have to be immediately confronted. A long report from Shaw indicated that the new constitution being debated contained several troubling clauses. Particularly cited as signs of a "definite tendency towards ultra-nationalism" were Articles 40 and 41, both limiting future foreign ownership of land in El Salvador and also requiring that such lands presently owned by foreigners would have to be sold within a stated amount of time. Shaw advised that the best way to attack these articles would be to explain how they would "result in a gratuitous and serious damage to the economy of El Salvador, an economy which at the moment is comparatively healthy and is progressing." Foreign investments would dry up, U.S. interests would probably pull out, and these actions "could seriously hinder any industrialization." A State Department analysis reached the same conclusions. Adoption of the articles would "undermine the present credit structure and future economic growth of El Salvador." Shaw should "informally" meet with "appropriate Salvadoran figures." In the event that "a wave of superheated nationalism" in El Salvador might push through their adoption anyway, the department should request a legal opinion on their constitutionality.[63]

These "nationalistic" components of the Salvadoran constitution (which was enacted, with minor changes, later in 1950) were to remain of concern to U.S. policymakers throughout the period of Osorio's regime. It was clear by 1951, however, that other issues would push that concern into the background (for the time being) and, simultaneously, push U.S. technical assistance to the fore. Shaw raised the alarm in November 1951, when he noted that despite good coffee prices, there was "little improvement" in the living standard of most Salvadorans. Giving a brief history lesson, he explained how the revolt of 1931 had "shown that such a population can prove extremely responsive to the agitation of subverting elements." The "subverting elements," of course, were but a veiled reference to Guatemalan efforts. For now, "It is in the best interests of the United States that a stable democratic government should be maintained in El Salvador." One of the best methods would be through technical aid, especially in the areas of agriculture, education, and health and sanitation. Shaw followed this up with a lengthier report one day later. He expanded his analysis of El Salvador's role in the battle against communist subversion by putting it in a global context. Like the other

Central American nations, El Salvador could never be built up to an effective military power; nevertheless, it was "highly desirable to assist El Salvador in maintaining internal security." This could be done by providing limited military assistance. Just as important, however, would be U.S. efforts in helping Salvadoran officials to "provide more effectively for the needs of the population. . . . The importance of building up the capacity of El Salvador to support itself cannot be overemphasized." This is where technical assistance could have an impact, "increasing the volume of production of coffee and cotton and, more particularly, foodstuffs on the land already under cultivation." El Salvador "has traditionally supported the United States in most international situations and the present policy being followed [in terms of economic, technical, and military aid] is believed to be effective in strengthening this attitude." While the present situation in El Salvador was "satisfactorily stable," there was always the threat of "subversive activity."[64]

Shaw's analysis revealed some of the troubling questions concerning the use of technical assistance. The main purpose of the program was to increase the production of materials needed by the United States. In the case of El Salvador, this essentially meant coffee and, to a lesser degree, cotton and sugar. Since increasing coffee, cotton, and sugar production would mean increasing the labor force and land under cultivation for those crops, it was difficult to see how foodstuff production could simultaneously be increased. Indeed, as Liisa North points out, the two goals were not compatible. Coffee, cotton, and sugar production did increase dramatically after 1950. But basic foodstuff crops—such as rice and maize—increased only incrementally; production of beans actually dropped. And the expansion of land under cultivation of the export crops meant a displacing of tenant farmers.[65] Furthermore, the political aims of the program should also have raised some questions. "Stabilizing" the Salvadoran government and increasing its allegiance to the international aims of the United States did not necessarily translate into "democratic government." Even Shaw recognized that the Osorio government was "power grabbing," and had remarked skeptically on the government's claim in early 1951 that a recent crackdown on civil liberties was done to thwart plots by rightists *and* communists.[66]

Ignoring these issues, U.S. policymakers between 1950 and 1954 pursued even more vigorously the policy of using technical assistance to get what they wanted out of El Salvador. In 1951, technical assistance to El

Salvador totaled a mere $99 thousand, all of that amount in the areas of education and health and sanitation. Only four U.S. technical personnel were working in the country. By 1952, the total amount of aid had increased to $425,000. While education and health and sanitation received continued funding, and minor amounts were given to public administration and industrial and labor programs, over half of the assistance went into agriculture. The number of U.S. technicians increased to twenty. In 1953, the United States sent $628,000 in aid. The largest increase was in the area of industrial and labor programs, from $4,000 to $130,000. Twenty-seven U.S. technicians now served in the nation.[67]

These investments were to be used to achieve goals which combined economic and political aims. In terms of the former, the United States wished to bring a higher standard of living to the people of El Salvador through economic growth. Primarily, the focus would be on agriculture and the "basic necessities"—health and education, for example. Economic growth would be stimulated by increasing agricultural production and diversification. When events so dictated, there would also be assistance in the area of industrial development. The results would bring not only a closer economic link between the United States and El Salvador, but would also help achieve political goals. El Salvador would be more stable, and less prone to 1931-like convulsions. Of more pressing concern, that nation would be less susceptible to the extremely nationalistic, and possibly communistic, policies emanating from its neighbor, Guatemala. Indeed, perhaps the results in El Salvador would serve notice to Guatemala's rulers that greater rewards might be found in following other pathways to economic development.

The major focus of the U.S. technical assistance program in El Salvador had always been agriculture. A 1949 report from the U.S. embassy in that nation hammered that point home: "at the present time El Salvador could derive the greatest benefit from the President's program [Truman's Point Four] through technical assistance for its agriculture." And in line with the thought that healthy workers are better workers, programs in health and sanitation were also called for.[68]

In terms of Salvadoran agriculture, coffee was king. Coffee made up nearly 80 percent of the nation's exports; cotton was a distant second, accounting for 4.4 percent of total exports. Most of that went to the United States, which purchased 77 percent of El Salvador's exports. It was, therefore, to the advantage of both El Salvador and the United States that coffee production be kept high. As Ambassador Shaw explained in 1951, coffee was "an important item in the economy of the United States" and provided "most of the dollar exchange of the Republic." (Those dollars were important, since 73 percent of El Salvador's $41.5 million worth of imports came from the United States.) He concluded that, "If the coffee market should be cut off, it would ruin the economy of El Salvador." In his opinion, U.S. economic aid should be aimed at "increasing the volume of production of coffee and cotton."[69]

The U.S. focus on increasing coffee (and cotton) production in El Salvador as a key to economic development is not surprising. It fit in well with the prevailing view that had developed, in which the increased production of exportable raw materials resulted in more capital, which could then be invested in "infrastructure." "So long as the coffee prices hold up," wrote State Department official Gordon Reid in 1953, "it is to be expected that Salvador will have a favorable balance of payments and will have a continuation of the present prosperity."[70]

As tensions increased between the United States and Guatemala, however, the focus of Point Four assistance to El Salvador changed. Issues of "balanced development" and "industrialization," which had earlier been discounted or passed off as manifestations of economic nationalism, were now taken seriously by U.S. officials, who sought to not only "protect" El Salvador from the Guatemalan menace, but also to demonstrate the rewards of working *with* the United States, instead of against it.

United States officials were quick to come to the conclusion that the moderate social reforms of the Osorio regime needed, at least for the time being, to be cultivated and assisted to provide an alternative to Guatemalan communism. By early 1954, the Osorio government had, according to the State Department, "become the principal bulwark in Central America against Communist pressures from Guatemala." Even the very conservative large landowners in El Salvador supported his "enlightened social objectives" since they regarded them as "much less evil than the dreaded Guatemala variety of reform." While noting the "growing nationalistic spirit" of the Osorio government, "The U.S. desires to cooperate to the fullest in the Salvadoran Government's efforts to establish sound political and economic conditions."[71]

As early as January 1953, it was clear that Point Four was seen as an important part of U.S. support for the Osorio government. The U.S. embassy in San Salvador stated that the "ultimate goal of the joint program [referring to MSP programs] is the emergence of a nation which will cooperate in building a strong, peaceful and free world." In this quest, "the most positive and effective instrument is the Point IV Program." A major push should come in "Productivity and Vocational Education," in order to achieve a "balanced, integrated program, comprising the four basic elements of food supply, health, productivity and education." "With the development of the Point IV program," it went on, "a major force toward internal political stability and security is being created." Another hint of how important Point Four could be is found in a mid-1953 State Department assessment of Salvadoran statesmen. In sum, it seemed a mediocre group, at best. Osorio was "limited in his mental and educational background," though he was a "strong opponent of communism." The Foreign Minister was "volatile, immoral, and untrustworthy"; the Minister of War, a "robust Indian," who was "extremely ambitious and cold-blooded"; the Minister of Labor, "an ambitious, dialectical bore"; the Minister of Finance was "one of the most stubborn and dull human beings found in El Salvador." In contrast was Minister of Economy Jorge Sol, cited as the "most intelligent and interesting personality in the Cabinet." Labeling him a "new-deal type liberal," the report went on to note that "American businessmen find Sol intelligent, helpful and understanding." He was also "the prime backer of the Point Four Program now underway in that country."[72]

Michael McDermott, who became U.S. ambassador to El Salvador in 1953, was high on the use of technical assistance in forging closer ties between the two nations. The needs in El Salvador were greater efficiency and "sound development of local industry." To that end, a technical assistance agreement for a Productivity Center, designed to increase the efficiency of local industries, had been signed. He was certain that U.S. assistance "contribute[d] materially to internal political stability, particularly in its role of improving rural living standards." "The traditionally close political, social and economic ties with the United States have been strengthened by U.S. interest as manifested through technical assistance." The Department's response to McDermott's assessment was positive. Claiming that "part of the problem created by Communist influence in Guatemala is the need to strengthen other Central American countries economically," it concluded that it was "natural to think of TCA as the existing organization to carry out these objectives." There was no reference to aid to agriculture; instead, it was argued that "substantial economic assistance to El Salvador could be channeled into (1) industrial development, and (2) road construction." McDermott was to prepare a list of "possible projects" for technical assistance in El Salvador which would be "useful" and would "produce results not only economically beneficial but of such significance and tangible proportions as to be noteworthy by El Salvador's neighbor."[73]

McDermott was quick to respond. He and his staff had formulated several programs for technical assistance in El Salvador. "While all," he claimed, "can be justified purely on economic grounds, they are advanced, nevertheless, in part for the possible psychological effect which might be felt elsewhere should any or all of them be carried out with substantial assistance from us." They would "give graphic proof of the effective results of democratic countries actively cooperating in contrast to the emotional appeals and empty promises of the communists." He then proceeded to call for more support of the Productivity Center (which the United States had already given $50,000), aid to the Salvadoran fishing industry, "establishment of an ammonium sulphate industry," building of warehouses and cold storage plants, and "construction of a lime plant."[74]

As noted earlier, United States technical assistance to El Salvador rose from $99,000 in 1951, to $425,000 in 1952, to $628,000 in 1953; assistance to "Industry, Mining, Labor" rose from $4,000 to $130,000. The desire to promote pro-U.S. stability in El Salvador, and the goal of impressing the Guatemalan government with the wisdom of working with the United States, were obvious impetuses for both the increase and direction of U.S. aid. As one State Department official concluded in mid-1953, "during the next several years the primary job in El Salvador will be to encourage the Salvadorans to defend themselves against the Guatemalan onslaught." In achieving that goal, military aid, together with technical assistance and economic aid, would be needed. In addition, "we should endeavor to bolster the part of the Cabinet most friendly to the United States."[75]

Yet, once the Guatemalan crisis had passed, U.S. perceptions changed rapidly. A State Department report from 1953 had made the observation that should the Guatemalan threat recede, "it would almost seem axiomatic that Salvador's present government would be endangered." The logic was that Osorio's support among the conservative elements of Salvadoran society was based on their fear of the "Guatemalan variety" of reform. Once that threat evaporated, so would their support. That analysis applied equally well to U.S. support of Osorio. Just a short while after the successful U.S.-organized counterrevolution in Guatemala in July

1954, a meeting was held at the State Department between Assistant Secretary Holland, Ambassador McDermott, and other officials on the subject of El Salvador. The change in their attitude was striking. First on the agenda was a discussion of Osorio. McDermott claimed that one of his "principal problems" was in dealing with the president and his officials. Osorio, he claimed, "was to be treated as an Indian, but a very sagacious one who had acquired considerable political knowledge during the past year." He would "do nothing which will make him appear as a satellite of the United States." In contrast to a 1952 State Department report in which it was stated that "U.S.-Salvadoran relations [have] historically been excellent," McDermott took a different view of the historical record, pointing to an anti-U.S. declaration made by the Salvadoran delegate at the Sixth Inter-American Conference in 1928. "The seeds planted there," he concluded, "have flourished throughout Latin America." The ambassador also chided Osorio for his "careful neutrality during the Castillo Armas rebellion" (Armas was the Guatemalan leader of the 1954 counterrevolution). In El Salvador, the communist problem was minimal, but might develop since "the rich are becoming richer, the poor are getting poorer." In terms of matters pending between the United States and El Salvador, McDermott was deeply dissatisfied. A proposed U.S. Army Mission to that nation was still being "held up by certain Salvadoran nationalistic feelings relating to our article on exclusive functioning in the military advisor field." Military assistance was also on hold; Salvadoran desires for an agreement in order to secure a loan for the purchase of arms was "unfeasible." A U.S.-proposed "Friendship Commerce and Navigation treaty" was also in limbo, having secured no response from the Salvadoran government. El Salvador had been "slow to take up and match the proffer of $500,000 to continue work on the Inter-American Highway." The country had "worked up very little interest in our desire to pave the 50 miles at the eastern end of the highway." For future reference, the ambassador claimed that El Salvador's position at the upcoming Rio Conference would center on a floor for coffee prices. Holland interjected that "the United States could obviously accept no such proposition." Most striking was the short shrift given technical assistance. The U.S. effort was summed up in one, terse sentence: "The agricultural program has been concluded and the industrial productivity agreement is progressing toward conclusion."[76]

Salvadoran "neutrality" and nationalism were overlooked as long as the Guatemalan menace loomed. Once that was dispelled, however, many of the main supports for continued technical assistance to El Salvador were knocked out. While U.S. technical assistance was never entirely severed, between 1955 and 1962 El Salvador received the lowest per capita assistance in Central America. This was due, John McCamant concludes, to El Salvador's "attitude of self-sufficiency," which was sustained, at least until 1958, by high coffee prices. When prices crashed in that year (continuing to a 1960 low), the Salvadoran government reacted with repression in meeting public demands for action. In 1960, a coup deposed the elected government, which was, in turn, itself overthrown in January 1961. The new regime declared itself "anti-Cuban, anti-Castro, and anti-communist." That was enough for the new Kennedy administration, which promptly tripled U.S. economic assistance to El Salvador to $2.8 million; by 1963, aid had risen to $19.3 million.[77]

We Could Have Done So Much More Together

By nearly any measurement, the economies of the Central American nations remain depressed. While exhibiting some growth during the 1960s and 1970s, the 1980s brought to the fore the fragile state of those economies. By 1982, every Central American nation had a negative growth rate. Between 1978 and 1981, public debt increased by nearly 100 percent or more in each of the five republics. In 1978, in-flation was running anywhere from 9.2 percent (Costa Rica) to 48.1 percent (Nicaragua); it was double-digit in Honduras, Guatemala, and El Salvador.[78]

Given the hundreds of millions of dollars of U.S. aid, and the ringing rhetoric that has accompanied each successive program of "economic development" for Latin America—Point Four, the Alliance for Progress, the Caribbean Basin Initiative—it is natural that many have criticized U.S. assistance programs as failures. An early response to such criticism came in a 1954 State Department report, which claimed that U.S. "assistance to Latin American has been substantial." While "much remains to be done, we do not need to apologize for our record in the other American Republics." And, in fact, there *was* no "need to apologize." Such assistance programs could not fairly be condemned for failing to bring "economic development" to areas such as Central America. They were never really designed to do that. A 1956 study by the President's Citizen Advisors on the Mutual Security Program bluntly stated that, "Economic aid will promote long-term American interests and should not be supported on any other ground."[79]

Those "long-term" interests, as we have seen, generally dictated that economic development in Latin America would have to proceed along carefully defined pathways. Partially, this was due to the U.S. belief that the Latin Americans were inept in dealing with economic matters. More important was the fact that in purely economic terms, development of the Latin American economies beyond their natural resource production and export stage was not compatible with U.S. interests. Economic interdependence required of the Latin American nations that they do what they were best suited to do—export raw materials to the consumer-goods-producing nations, specifically the United States. Specialization and comparative advantage were the terms used to describe such a system, and U.S. economic assistance programs were designed to keep it running smoothly and efficiently. In the economic realm, these programs aimed at ensuring continued, and even expanded, raw material production from Latin America. Politically, the programs operated to stabilize certain governments, serve as examples to regimes going off in radical directions, or punish other governments that refused to follow U.S. prescriptions.

By the mid-1950s, this more "pragmatic" or "realistic" approach to U.S. foreign aid had definitely taken hold. The rhetoric about economic development still popped up, especially during times of crisis. For some, however, there was a feeling of an opportunity missed. Arthur Burnes, who served as a consultant to the International Cooperation Administration (ICA) during the first Eisenhower administration, recalled that one of his specific recommendations concerning the Technical Cooperation Program was that it should have been more of a "sharing arrangement." He reflected that, "The foreigners had much to contribute to us, and if we had drawn upon their people. . .we would have benefited to a good deal—instead of taking the attitude that only we had something to give to them." This, referred to by Burnes as "reverse technical assistance," "simply didn't get anywhere."[80] Certainly some Latin Americans had seen the opportunity. Stanley Andrews recalled a trip to Peru during the mid-1950s:

> I landed in Peru and went around to see the Minister of Agriculture. And I said, "What is your view of the Americans, particularly the agriculture and educational field, and how they worked here and in your country?" "Well," he said, "you Americans are wonderful people. You're generous, you've given us all kinds of money, but," he says, "you never listen. You come into our country here and treat us

as second-class citizens as if we know nothing and you brush us aside and go ahead and make damned fool mistakes." And he said, "If you would just listen and work along with us, together you'd—we'd save us a lot of trouble. We appreciate, and you've done wonderful things for us, but we could have done so much more together."[81]

Perhaps, perhaps not. In any case, the U.S. perspective did not allow it. It was an irony of economic interdependence that its very workings required the maintenance of a system which was viewed by many Latin Americans as inequitable, at best, and exploitative, at worst. This fact was not, apparently, realized by U.S. policymakers, as evidenced by a 1954 NSC memorandum dealing with Soviet "colonialism or imperialism." Apparently to counter communist accusations of colonialism against Western nations, it was suggested that an investigation of the relationship between the Soviet Union and its satellites "might demonstrate that the relation between these countries is the same as that which exists between a metropole and its colonies." It concluded that, "In dealing with the issue of economic exploitation we are on safe ideological grounds, for we can expose the contradiction between the Soviet theory of the unity of the working class and Soviet practice of exacting contributions from foreign lands to the building up of the 'Communist motherland.'"[82] The contradictions of their own theory of economic interdependence never seemed as obvious.

Notes

1.   See David A. Baldwin, *Economic Development and American Foreign Policy, 1943–1962* (Chicago, 1966), 8–71; Baily, *The United States and the Development of South America*, 54–61; Kaufman, *Trade and Aid*, 1–7.

2.   David Lloyd to Dawson, 5 Dec. 1950, Truman Papers, OF 20–U, International Development Advisory Board (Folder 1), HSTL.

3.   Green, *Containment of Latin America*, 169–208, 283–90, and "The Cold War Comes to Latin America," in *Politics and Policies of the Truman Administration*, ed. Barton Bernstein (Chicago, 1970):149–195; Stephen Rabe, "The Elusive Conference: United States Economic Relations with Latin America, 1945–1952," *Diplomatic History* 2 (1978):279–94; Jesse H. Stiller, *George S. Messersmith: Diplomat of Democracy* (Chapel Hill, NC, 1987),   214–17; Baily, *The United States and the Development of South America*, 40–48, 60–61; Dick Steward, *Money, Marines and Mission: Recent U.S.-Latin American Policy* (Lanham, MD, 1980), 87–92, 104–111; LaFeber, *Inevitable Revolutions*, 85–98; and John E. Findling, *Close Neighbors, Distant Friends: United States–Central*

American Relations (New York, 1987), 107–108. For a good recent overview of what the author refers to as the "discovery of underdevelopment in Latin America" by U.S. officials, see James William Park, *Latin American Underdevelopment: A History of Perspectives in the United States, 1870–1965* (Baton Rouge, 1995), Ch. 6. Marshall quote is cited in Baily, *The United States and the Development of South America*, 61.

4.   Tancer, *Economic Nationalism in Latin America*, 22–23.

5.   Hussey to Butler, 23 Aug. 1946, RG 59, Records of OARA, Box 16, NA.

6.   Clark to Woodward and Daniels, 1 Feb. 1949, RG 59, 710.11/2–149, NA.

7.   Ray to Barber and Miller, 30 Sept. 1949, RG 59, 710.11/9–3049; CIA, "Review of the World Situation," 14 July 1948, NSC Documents, 3rd supplement, reel 1.

8.   Truman, draft of speech, 8 Apr. 1948; Truman to Rockefeller, 9 Mar. 1951, Truman Papers, OF 27–B, Box 157, Export-Import Bank of Washington (1945–49) folder; OF 20–U, Box 20, Folder 1, HSTL; Acheson to Savage, 8 Apr. 1947, RG 59, 710.11/4–847, NA.

9.   Draft, General Regional Statement, 1951, RG 59, MSP Files, Box 1, NA.

10.   For the best study, see Hogan, *The Marshall Plan*.

11.   Clark to Woodward and Daniels, 1 Feb. 1949, RG 59, 710.11/2–149, NA; Marshall quote from Baily, *The United States and the Development of South America*, 61.

12.   George Elsey, Oral History, 17 July 1969, 376–77, HSTL.

13.   See endnote 9.

14.   Truslow to Miller, 12 Mar. 1951, RG 59, Miller Files, Box 4, NA.

15.   Schaetzel, "Analysis of Latin American Proposals. . . ," Mar. 1948, RG 353, Records of IAEAC, Box 2, NA.

16.   Dennis FitzGerald, Oral History, 26 May 1976, 8–9, DDEL.

17.   Ellis Briggs, Oral History, 19 June 1970 and 15 Oct. 1972, 3, DDEL.

18.   White to Miller, 12 Mar. 1951, RG 59, Miller Files, Box 4, NA.

19.   "Summary of Remarks at Conference on U.S. Foreign Policy, June 4 and 5, 1953," p. 54, Dulles Papers, Box 75, Mudd Library.

20.   For good overviews of the establishment of the Point Four program, see Thomas G. Paterson, "Foreign Aid Under Wraps: The Point Four Program," *Wisconsin Magazine of History* 56 (Winter 1972–73):119–26, as well as Paterson, *Meeting the Communist Threat: Truman to Reagan* (New York, 1988), Ch. 8. A good outline of the legislative history of Point Four, and its relation to other economic assistance programs of the postwar period, is found in Robert Macy to W. F. Finan, 30 Dec. 1954, Records of CFEP, Chairman, Dodge Series: Subject Subseries, Box 2, Foreign Aid–Factual Data from Bureau of Budget file, DDEL. A good starting place for understanding the Point Four

program's place in U.S. economic foreign policy after the war is Baldwin, *Economic Development and American Foreign Policy*, especially Chs. II and III. See also Walter M. Daniels, ed., *The Point Four Program* (New York, 1951).

21.   Cited in Paterson, "Foreign Aid Under Wraps," 120.

22.   Stanley Andrews, Oral History, 31 Oct. 1970, 4, HSTL.

23.   Executive Committee on Economic Foreign Policy, "Objectives and Nature of the Point IV Program," 1 March 1949, Papers of Benjamin Hardy, Box 1, Point IV file, folder 1, HSTL; Cabot, "Summary of Remarks at Conference on U.S. Foreign Policy, June 4 and 5, 1953," Dulles Papers, Box 75, Mudd Library. For an insider's account of the development and workings of the Point Four program, see Jonathan B. Bingham, *Shirt-Sleeve Diplomacy: Point 4 in Action* (New York, 1953). An important article by Claude C. Erb, "Prelude to Point Four: The Institute of Inter-American Affairs," *Diplomatic History* 9 (1985):249–69, makes the argument that Point Four was not really a "new" idea, and that the work of the Institute of Inter-American Affairs, established during World War II, preceded and presaged Point Four.

24.   Paterson, *Meeting the Communist Threat*, 156.

25.   Philip M. Glick, *The Administration of Technical Assistance: Growth in the Americas* (Chicago, 1957), is an excellent survey of the nuts and bolts of the Point Four program in action in Latin America.

26.   Office of the Assistant Secretary of the Army, "Strategic and Critical Materials in Latin America," 18 Feb. 1948, RG 218, GF, 1946–1947, CCS 401.1 Latin America (2–18–48), NA; "Regional Conference of United States Chiefs of Mission, Rio de Janeiro, Brazil, March 6– 9, 1950," RG 59, Miller Papers, Box 5, NA; FOA, "Materials Development and Allied Programs," 18 Dec. 1953, Papers of Albert Huntington, Box 5, FOA–Materials Development TCA Programs, Aug. 1953 file, HSTL. Gerald K. Haines, *The Americanization of Brazil: A Study of U.S. Cold War Diplomacy in the Third World, 1945–1954* (Wilmington, DE, 1989), Ch. Six, is a good illustration of how U.S. policymakers used the Point Four program in Latin America.

27.   Bennett to Coombs, 26 June 1951, Records of PMPC, box 125, Projects–TCA–Explanation file, HSTL; ACTA, "Objectives and Nature of the Point IV Program," 2 May 1949, RG 353, Records of ID/ID Committees, box 86, Presentation Book on Pt. 4 Program file, NA.

28.   PMPC, "Chapter VIII: Technical and Financial Assistance in Support of Foreign Materials Development," 4 Sept. 1951, Records of PMPC, Box 14, First Draft–For. Resources, Chapter VIII file, HSTL.

29.   "NSC Staff Study on Proposed Transfer of the Point IV Program from the Department of State to the Economic Cooperation Administration," 1951, Truman Papers, PSF, SF, Box 198, National Security Council: Senior NSC Staff–Point IV file, HSTL; "The Mutual Security Program for Fiscal Year 1952," 1951, RG 353, Records of ID/ID Committees, Box 82, 5.32 MSP 1951: c. MSP Committee Prints, Annexes, President's Message file, NA.

30. "Discussion at Special Meeting of the National Security Council, March 31, 1953," 7 Apr. 1953, Eisenhower Papers, Whitman File, NSC Series, Box 4, Special Meeting of the NSC, Mar. 31, 1953 file, DDEL. For a more on Point Four as an anti-communist device, see Paterson, *Meeting the Communist Threat*, Ch. 8.

31. ACTA, "Objectives and Nature of the Point IV Program," 2 May 1949, RG 353, Records of ID/ID Committees, Box 86, Presentation Book on Pt. 4 Program file; Cale to Woodward, 24 June 1953, RG 59, Records of Deputy for I–A Affairs, Box 3, Economic and Financial Aid, 1953–54 file, NA.

32. Green, *Containment of Latin America*, Ch. IV (quote taken from p. 111).

33. Barber to Woodward and Daniels, 15 Mar. 1949; Barber to Daniels, 18 May 1949, RG 59, Records of OMAA, Subject File, 1947–1956, Box 2, CPA–General–1949: Policy file (hereafter, Records of OMAA, Subject file, box number and file designation); Ray to Barber and Miller, 30 Sept. 1949, RG 59, 710.11/9–3049, NA.

34. "Summary of Milton Eisenhower's Report. . . ," 1953, Eisenhower Papers, WHCF, CF: Subject Series, Box 25, Eisenhower, Milton, Trip to South America (3) file, DDEL.

35. Ibid.

36. OIR, *Intelligence Report*, no. 6718, 8 Oct. 1954, Records of United States Participation in International Conferences, Commissions, and Expositions, Record Group 43, Records of the Organization of American States, 1949–1960, Box 23 (hereafter RG 43, Records of OAS, with box number), NA.

37. Mikesell, "Foreign Interests and Attitudes Toward the Development of Their Material Resources," 4 July 1951, Records of PMPC, Box 10, HSTL.

38. Ibid.

39. Ellis and Buchanan, "The United States and the Economic Progress of Underdeveloped Countries," 15 Nov. 1953, Records of Randall Commission, Box 56, Studies–Economic Development file (emphasis in original); Ellis and Buchanan, "The United States and the Economic Progress of Underdeveloped Countries," 19 November 1953, enclosed in Alfred Neal to Members of the Commission on Foreign Economic Policy, 19 Nov. 1953, Records of Randall Commission, Box 41, Drafts of Report–Drafts Concerning Foreign Investment file, DDEL.

40. Milton Eisenhower, Oral History, 106, DDEL.

41. Dulles to Eisenhower, 3 Sept. 1953, Dulles Papers, White House Memo Series, Box 1, White House Correspondence 1953 (2) file, DDEL.

42. Mikesell, "Foreign Interests and Attitudes. . . ," 4 July 1951, Records of PMPC, Box 10, HSTL; "Statement in Support of the Mutual Security Program for FY 1954," 23 April 1953, RG 59, MSP Files, Box 1, NA.

43. CIA, "Conditions and Trends in Latin America. . . ," 12 December 1952, Truman Papers, PSF, IF, Box 254, Central Intelligence Reports, NIE 67–75 file, HSTL.

44. "Briefing Book," 1951, Truman Papers, PSF, SF, Box 177, Foreign Ministers of American Republics–Meetings file, HSTL.

45. Truslow to Miller, 12 Mar. 1951, RG 59, Miller Files, Box 4, NA.

46. Study Group on Political Implications of Economic Development, 1953, Study Group Report on 1st Meeting, Feb. 26, 1952, Records of Groups, Vol. 43, CFR Archives.

47. ACTA, "Objective and Nature of the Point IV Program," 2 May 1949, RG 353, Records of ID/ID Committees, Box 86, Presentation on Pt. 4 Program file, NA.

48. John Ohly, Oral History, 30 Nov. 1971, 50, HSTL; MSP information attached to Rand to Eisenhower, 11 May 1953, Whitman File, Box 34, Stassen, Harold, 1952–53 (2) file, DDEL.

49. TCA, "Point 4 Program Costs for Fiscal Year 1953," 21 July 1953, Andrews Papers, Box 10, Govt. Service File, 1942–1957: 1953 Status of Point IV, HSTL.

50. "The Caribbean Republics," 24 Aug. 1954, *FRUS, 1952–1954*, 4:379–399.

51. "Report to Congress on the Mutual Security Program for the six months ended December 31, 1953," Eisenhower Papers, WHCF, OF, Box 665, 133–L 1954 (1) file, DDEL.

52. Tables contained in Hoover to Cook, 28 Apr. 1952, RG 59, 720.5–MSP/4–2852, NA. For more on this, see Michael L. Krenn, "By the Numbers: The Use of Statistics in U.S. Policy Toward Latin America During the 1950s," *The SHAFR Newsletter* 21, No. 1 (March 1991):7 –17.

53. John F. McCamant, *Development Assistance in Central America* (New York, 1968), 29.

54. For relevant figures, see National Planning Association, *Technical Assistance in Latin America: Recommendations for the Future* (Washington, 1956), 149–158; McCamant, *Development Assistance*, 29. The National Planning Association, formed in 1934, was a broadly based group of leaders in the fields of business, agriculture, etc., interested in studying topics of national interest. Its membership included Walter Reuther, William C. Ford, and Luther Gulick.

55. Some good introductions to El Salvadoran politics during the period 1931–1948 are found in Patricia Parkman, *Nonviolent Insurrection in El Salvador: The Fall of Maximiliano Hernández Martínez* (Tucson, 1988); Tommie C. Montgomery, "El Salvador: The Roots of Revolution," in Steve C. Ropp and James A. Morris, *Central America: Crisis and Adaptation* (Albuquerque, 1984), 75–80; Enrique A. Baloyra, *El Salvador in Transition* (Chapel Hill, NC, 1982), 8–17; Cynthia Arnson, *El Salvador: A Revolution Confronts the United States* (Washington, D.C., 1982), 13–16; Robert Armstrong and Janet Shenk, *El Salvador: The Face of Revolution* (Boston, 1982), 21–38; and James Dunkerley, *The Long War: Dictatorship and Revolution in El Salvador* (London, 1985), 15–35. Liisa North, *Bitter Grounds: Roots of Revolt in El Salvador*, 2nd ed.

(Westport, CT, 1985), 29–60, also covers political developments, but focuses more thoroughly on economic developments in El Salvador. The best single volume on the *matanza* of 1932 is Thomas P. Anderson, *Matanza: El Salvador's Communist Revolt of 1932* (Lincoln, NE, 1971).

56. Arnson, *El Salvador: A Revolution*, 17. The following analysis of El Salvadoran economic and political development from 1948 to the early 1960s is based on Dunkerley, *The Long War*, 35–71; North, *Bitter Grounds*, 43–60; Montgomery, "El Salvador: The Roots," 80–83; Baloyra, *El Salvador in Transition*, 34–40; Hector Perez-Brignoli, *A Brief History of Central America*, trans. by Ricardo B. Sawrey A. and Susana Stettri de Sawrey (Berkeley, 1989), 131–143; John Martz, *Central America: The Crisis and the Challenge* (Chapel Hill, NC, 1959), 83–111; and Victor Bulmer-Thomas, *The Political Economy of Central America Since 1920* (Cambridge, 1987), Chapters 6–8, passim.

57. Dunkerley, *The Long War*, 35–36. Bulmer-Thomas, *Political Economy of Central America*, 105–129 passim, is more favorably impressed with El Salvador's performance, claiming that the policies followed did lead to modernization of the nation's economy. He points out, however, that the nation's efforts failed in two crucial areas: national economic integration and attention to rural development problems. Martz, *Central America*, 83–91, contends that, at least from the perspective of 1959, the economic reforms had a positive impact on the nation.

58. Nufer to DS, 15 July 1949, RG 59, 816.20M/7–1549, NA.

59. Shaw to Acheson, 10 Dec. 1949, RG 59, Miller Files, Box 6, NA.

60. Shaw to DS, 12 Feb. 1950, RG 59, 716.00/2–1250; Bennett to Barber, 4 Jan. 1950, RG 59, 713.00/1–450; Clark, "El Salvador Notes," 6 Jan. 1950, RG 59, Records of OMAA, Subject File, Box 6, El Salvador–1950–General file, NA.

61. Wieland to DS, 6 Jan. 1950, RG 59, 716.00/1–650; Shaw to DS, 2 Apr. 1950, RG 59, 716.00/4–250, NA.

62. Shaw to DS, 23 Apr., May 5, 1950, RG 59, 716.00/4–2350; /5–50, NA.

63. Shaw to DS, 12 July 1950, RG 59, 716.00/7–1250; Siracusa to Bennett, 18 July 1950, RG 59, Records of OMAA, Subject File, Box 6, El Salvador–1950–General file, NA.

64. Shaw to DS, 1 Nov. 1951, RG 59, 816.00TA/11–151; Shaw to DS, 2 Nov. 1951, RG 59, 816.00–FA/11–251, NA.

65. North, *Bitter Grounds*, 44–50.

66. Shaw to DS, 24 Aug. 1950, RG 59, 716.03/3–2450; Shaw to DS, 16 Mar. 1951, RG 59, 716.00/3–1651, NA.

67. National Planning Association, *Technical Assistance*, 153.

68. Report from U.S. embassy, 22 Mar. 1949, contained in ACTA, "Objectives and Nature of the Point IV Program," 2 May 1949, RG 353, Records of ID/ID Committees, Box 86, Presentation Book on Pt. 4 Program file, NA.

69.　Figures for exports and imports are from "El Salvador Notes," 6 Jan. 1950, RG 59, Records of OMAA, Subject File, Box 6, El Salvador–1950–General file; Shaw to DS, 2 Nov. 1951, RG 59, 816.00–FA/11–251, NA.

70.　Reid to Leddy, et al., 18 June 1953, RG 59, 716.00/6–1853, NA.

71.　Fisher to Holland, 23 Apr. 1954, RG 59, 716.00/4–2354, NA.

72.　Angier Biddle Duke to DS, 9 Jan. 1953, RG 59, 716.5–MSP/1–953; Reid to Leddy, et al., 18 June 1953, RG 59, 716.00/6–1853, NA.

73.　McDermott to DS, 14 July 1953, RG 59, 716.5–MSP/7–1453; Leddy to McDermott, 30 Dec. 1953, RG 59, 816.00–TA/12–3053, NA.

74.　McDermott to Leddy, 13 Jan. 1954, RG 59, 816.00–TA/1–1354, NA.

75.　Reid to Leddy, et al., 18 June 1953, RG 59, 716.00/6–1853, NA.

76.　Reid to Leddy, et al., 18 June 1953, RG 59, 716.00/6–1853; "Minutes of Meeting Held August 13, 1954," RG 59, Holland Records, Box 3, NA. The 1952 evaluation is found in RG 59, F.W. 720.5–MSP/10–352, NA.

77.　McCamant, *Development Assistance*, 30. For analyses of Salvadoran political development between 1955 and 1963, see Dunkerley, *The Long War*, 40–49, and Arnson, *El Salvador: A Revolution*, 17–23. Figures for U.S. assistance are found in Agency for International Development, "U.S. Economic Assistance Programs, April 3, 1948–June 30, 1971," Huntington Papers, Box 5, AID: U.S. Economic Assistance Programs, 1948–1971 file, HSTL.

78.　Figures found in Richard Feinberg and Robert A. Pastor, "Far from Hopeless: An Economic Program for Post-War Central America," in *Central America: Anatomy of Conflict*, ed. Robert S. Leiken (New York, 1984), 201; and Bulmer-Thomas, *Political Economy of Central America*, 202, 243.

79.　Edward Sparks to Undersecretary of State, 13 Nov. 1954, RG 59, Records of OMAA, Misc. Records, Box 1, Aid to Latin America, 1954–1955 file, NA; "Comments on United States Foreign Economic Aid Policy," 5 Sept. 1956, Records of U.S. President's Citizen Advisors on the Mutual Security Program (Fairless Committee), 1956–1957, Box 1, Advisers' Conference—Oct. 11, 12, 13, 1956 file, DDEL (hereafter Records of Fairless Committee, box number, and file designation).

80.　Arthur Burnes, Oral History, 8 Mar. 1967, 7, DDEL.

81.　Andrews, Oral History, 74–75, HSTL.

82.　Taquey to Craig, 30 Aug. 1954, WHO, Papers of NSC, OCB CF, Box 58, OCB 091.3 (File #1) (8), DDEL.

5

Life with Somoza

One of the most troublesome postwar problems to confront U.S. policymakers in regards to their political relations with Central America and the rest of Latin America was the question of what stance should be taken toward dictatorial governments. The answer seemed obvious. One of the avowed purposes of the war was to free the world's peoples from despotism and allow them to choose their own destinies. How, then, could the United States recognize and even support dictators in its own hemisphere?

The ideals of political interdependence also seemed to exclude any notion of finding a "working arrangement" with Latin American dictators. Since it was assumed that the world's peoples desired basically the same cornerstones upon which rested the U.S. system of government, it would hardly be appropriate for the United States to lend even tacit support to the maintenance of Latin American despots. The battle against communism made such a stance even more necessary. People suffering under the heavy hand of dictatorial oppression were hardly likely to be reliable allies in case of global confrontations with the Soviets. It did not make very effective propaganda to condemn communist totalitarianism while at the same time condoning dictatorship.

Yet, perhaps the issue was not as clear-cut as it seemed. Ideally, the cement of political interdependence should be composed of roughly equal portions of prodemocracy and anticommunist elements. It was not enough to support the ideals of democracy, if one was not willing to sacrifice and slug it out with the communists. Nor, of course, was it sufficient to take a hard anticommunist line without at least a tacit recognition of the desirability of democratic goals. On the other hand, the battle against communism might sometimes require that less than democratic means be used in the fight. Indeed, there might even be such a thing as *too much* democracy. Especially might this be true in the less developed nations where democracy had never really had a sure grip to begin with. Could it be the case that the United States would find it necessary to support dictators in order to defend the "Free World" from communism?

To understand how U.S. policymakers handled these rather delicate questions, this chapter will focus on the roller-coaster relationship between the United States and the Somoza dictatorship in Nicaragua during the postwar years. That relationship symbolized the uneasiness and uncertainty of U.S. officials as they confronted the issue of reconciling the not always complementary goals of democracy, anticommunism, and political interdependence.

Dictatorships and Disreputable Governments

The end of World War II once more brought into focus the sticky issue of U.S. relations with dictatorial governments in Latin America. The matter was one that had plagued U.S.–Latin American relations during most of the twentieth century. During that time, the United States had been instrumental in helping dictators such as Somoza in Nicaragua and Trujillo in the Dominican Republic gain and maintain power. The announcement of the Good Neighbor Policy had seemed to indicate a decided change in U.S. policy in favor of prodemocratic governments in Latin America. As World War II unfolded, however, the United States adopted a policy which saw the better part of valor as working with any regime that would aid the war effort, regardless of its nature.[1]

As the war drew to a close, it seemed a propitious time to once again reconsider the U.S. policy toward dictatorship in Latin America. The war solidified the notion that dictatorship was an odious form of governance, and it was also evident that democracy seemed on the upswing in Latin America. In Central America, Martínez in El Salvador and Ubico in Guatemala had been toppled in 1944. It was in this atmosphere that a lengthy debate began in the State Department over what the U.S. stance should be in these circumstances.

A department report, prepared in October 1945, summarized the cogent points of that discussion.[2] The opening round was a January dispatch from the U.S. ambassador to Cuba, Spruille Braden, entitled "Policy re Dictatorships and Disreputable Governments." At the urging of Assistant Secretary of State Nelson Rockefeller, he had refined his early ideas on that subject in a longer note in April. That note had then been sent to each of the U.S. missions in Latin America for their comments; by October, twelve replies had been received. The department report began by summarizing the main thrust of Braden's proposal:

> [I]t should be the policy of the United States Government to encourage democracy by demonstrating a warm friendship for the democratic and reputable governments and to discourage dictatorships and disreputable governments by treating them as something less than friends and equals, i.e., by maintaining with them a relationship courteous and proper, but at the same time aloof and formal.

By "courteous and proper" treatment, Braden meant that the United States should refrain from intervening in Latin America's internal affairs, but should give every indication possible that Washington did not support dictatorships. No "favors" should be offered. Recognition of governments that come to power through extralegal means should be based not only on the ability of the new government to maintain internal order and carry out its international obligations, but also on the issue of "whether the new government enjoys general popular support without active opposition." The report concluded that, "He believes that 'a careless tolerance of evil institutions' within the Hemisphere may 'endanger our future self-preservation by leaving receptive media open for infection and employment by the Nazis, who are now going underground, and by others opposed to Democracy." In a dramatic flourish, Braden declared that, "'If. . .we fail to sustain and augment the enthusiasm for the practice of democratic ideals, the void will be filled by pernicious "isms" imperiling our way of life. . . .the modern world of multiplied speed can no more live half free—half slave than could our nation in Lincoln's time.'"

Following this, the report summarized the replies received from the U.S. missions. Seven responses expressed support for a new policy toward dictatorships in Latin America, although three did contain some reservations. From Chile, Ambassador Claude Bowers voiced strongest support, arguing that "because of the effectiveness of its Good Neighbor policy and the impressiveness of its achievements in the war, now is the appropriate time for the United States to take a strong position." Orme

Wilson, responding from Haiti, agreed with the general idea, but wondered whether, in practice, the policy would have to be modified to fit special cases—such as Haiti, where "'the deplorable lack of political education, the very widespread ignorance and great poverty, and. . .the fact that an aggressive and ill willed dictator holds sway just across the boundary [Trujillo in the Dominican Republic]'" would have to be taken into account.

In general, the report expressed the view that only Bowers offered anything in the way of new arguments to bolster Braden's position; the rest simply chimed in with agreement, or suggested that they had certain reservations. This was certainly not the case in examining the five negative replies. These replies were broken down into thirteen different categories, representing factors that had led the various missions to disagree with Braden's assessment. Some of the most important were that such a policy would be a "violation of non-intervention," would "provoke non-cooperation," and, in the end, would be "unproductive." Other objections included the argument that the proposed policy was "unprecise," and that the "suggested means of implementing [non-recognition, withholding economic assistance, etc.] are objectionable."

A number of other objections centered on the question of whether the region was really ready for democracy. Four of the responses, for instance, suggested that the policy exhibited "unfairness to backward countries." Focusing on the nations of the Caribbean and Central America, the argument made was that such a stance "might result in the penalizing not only of a very good friend of the United States but also of the most progressive government which the country has any prospect of having." Ambassador Erwin, writing from Honduras, expressed his belief that a "free press and radio are not unmitigated goods in backward countries." To sum up, the report cited a long passage from the response from Guatemala:

> [R]eal democracy does not depend as fundamentally upon laws or leadership from above as it does upon the will and capacity of the great mass of average citizens. All of the efforts made in this direction by enlightened Latin American leaders and by dozens of United States Ambassadors and Ministers throughout the years—to say nothing of the more drastic Wilsonian technique which has recently been revived, of not recognizing certain governments—have not yet created the basis for practical democracy in most of the American nations.

Finally, the report drew the following conclusions. First, while the replies had been fairly evenly divided, they did "indicate a widely held belief that the policy of the United States had frequently been inconsistent with the professed ideals of the American people." A new policy seemed to be called for. Second, the "arguments presented so far have not demonstrated an urgency great enough to warrant the adoption of the proposal in its present form, i.e. in a form which might cause the United States to run serious risk of alienating some of its 'good neighbors.'" Third, if the policy was adopted, it would need to be used with "considerable caution and with due consideration for the. . .political immaturity prevailing in a number of the other American republics." Fourth, and finally, it suggested that Braden's policy be modified to "eliminate its most serious defects." Some sort of "inter-American agreement providing for a system which would work toward the same objective on an international basis" held appeal, as did the notion that a "positive policy of assistance" should be given to nations trying to "improve basic conditions in order to achieve and maintain liberal democratic government."

It was a significant document, and very likely the most important produced dealing with the subject of Latin American dictatorships and U.S. policy after World War II. Much of its significance stemmed from the fact that it revealed the extremely ambivalent position of U.S. policymakers. While some, like Braden and Bowers, seemed to unequivocally take a stand in support of an anti-dictator policy, most of the other replies backed away from its *application*, primarily because of fears of damaging relations with "good" allies and the belief that the Latin Americans were unprepared for democracy. In the decade following the war, the debate would continue.

The Lines Are Becoming More Clearly Defined

Considering the rather tepid support for Braden's proposal in the State Department, it was hardly surprising that the specifics of the ambassador's suggestions were never put into action. This did not mean, however, that the issue of U.S. relations with dictatorial governments had been settled. Throughout the postwar years, analysis and discussion continued. By the late 1940s and early 1950s, however, the outcome of those analyses was not in doubt: the United States would collaborate with Latin American dictators who supported U.S. policies and opposed communist expansion.

U.S. officials were well aware of the changing political and social makeup of Latin America. The traditional ruling elements were being challenged by the developing middle and working classes, as well as intellectuals and students. As a 1946 State Department reported noted, "In the ideological struggle between those who believe that governments exist for the welfare of individuals and those who hold that individuals exist only to serve the state the lines are becoming more clearly defined."[3] A few years later, another department official wondered what the United States might do to help the situation, since "when we realize the number of dictators now existing in the American republics, the frequent violent changes in Government, the little progress made in raising the standard of living and the slowness of progress towards democracy, it should lead us to wonder whether there is not something more we could do for our neighbors—not as Santa Claus but in our own interest."[4]

As was the case during the 1945 debate over Braden's proposal, however, U.S. officials began to perceive that the issue was not so simple; it was not merely a question of democracy versus dictatorship or of prodemocracy versus anticommunism. They argued that in the case of Latin America one had to consider a number of other factors.

One argument used to chip away at a strict antidictator stance by the United States was that dictatorship in Latin America had a long history and was "different" from other types of dictatorship. This view was perhaps best summed up in a 1949 State Department problem paper which stated that, "It is important to determine if a dictatorial regime is of the traditional Latin American military or authoritarian type, or if it is of Communist, Nazist, or other police state type." Focusing specifically on the Caribbean and Central American nations, a 1954 study also noted the long history of dictatorial government in the region: "Traditionally, politics have revolved around persons rather than public issues; the continued or shifting favor of the army has been the decisive political factor; and rule by military 'strong men' has been normal." In discussing the issues of democracy or dictatorship, those two terms were always in parentheses—"democracy" or "dictatorship"—as if to alert the reader to the fact that they meant different things in relation to Latin America. Democracy, of course, rarely existed among the "illiterate, poverty—stricken, and socially and politically inert" population. Those elements pushing for social and political change had "no common program," and were not above using "extremist doctrines and demagogic tactics" to gain support. In this political vacuum, dictatorship flourished, but this did make for a certain amount of stability. Political power was usually transferred by means of "military *pronunciamiento*, with minimal public disturbance. Really bloody civil conflicts are rare."[5]

This rather even-handed evaluation of dictatorship in Latin America was combined with a belief that, like any good thing, too much democracy in that region was dangerous. In the political realm, the primary goals of the United States were to increase stability and support governments which shared its anticommunist outlook. Too often, U.S. officials believed, democracy ran directly counter to those aims. As noted in chapters 1 and 2, U.S. policymakers, while supporting the general idea of democracy in Latin America, also believed that the groups likely to spearhead democratic movements—students, labor, the middle class—were unstable, and prime targets for both anti-U.S. nationalists and communist agitators. As a December 1952 State Department report stated:

> It is not expected that Latin American democracies will ever adhere strictly to anglo-saxon forms or that they will have standards identical with ours. Furthermore, we recognize that while dictatorships set in motion violent forces and invite instability, in the present state of world affairs revolutionary governments are apt, like Peron and Arevalo, to observe the form in order to destroy the substance of democratic processes. As already observed they sometimes invite irresponsibility which not only makes it difficult for us to obtain the cooperation which we need but precipitate economic crises which in turn produce more unrest and instability.[6]

Such analysis raised some crucial questions about the relationship between dictatorship, democracy, and U.S. aims in Latin America. What it strongly suggested was that, in terms of stability and cooperation in the battle against communism, dictatorship, while odious, was perhaps preferable to unreliable and irresponsible democracy.

A significant debate among State Department officials had preceded the aforementioned report and, undoubtedly, established some of the notions it contained. In many ways, this 1950 discussion was just as important as the 1945 exchanges over Braden's proposal. The reader will note, however, that a harder edge has taken the place of much of the somewhat more moralistically-tinged rhetoric of 1945. The setting was a conference held in March 1950 at the American embassy in Rio de Janeiro. The participants included the U.S. chiefs of mission from the various Latin

American nations, as well as Assistant Secretary Edward Miller, Louis
Halle, a member of the Policy Planning Staff, and George Kennan, who
was then serving as department counselor.[7]

The first few days of the conference were taken up in discussing economic relations with Latin America. By the last day of the meetings,
Kennan, showing obvious impatience, claimed that he was worried about
the "possible danger of neglecting political problems in Latin America
because of our being faced with so many serious economic problems."
Dismayed over the possibility that the Soviets were gaining influence in
the region, Kennan concluded that "we must roll up our sleeves and get
into the political argument of Communism versus Western liberalism."
The discussion that followed, however, focused more on the question of
communism and dictatorship than on economics.

Leaping directly into his own analysis, Kennan posed the question of
what should be done if communists began to gain strength in a particular
Latin American nation. Answering his own question, he stated that "the
final answer might be an unpleasant one, but that we should not hesitate
before police repression by the local government. This is not shameful
since the Communists are essentially traitors." He continued:

> Moreover, one cannot ignore the effectiveness of police action, and the
> cases of Turkey and Portugal are examples of nations which, although
> not invulnerable to Communism, have been successful in repressing it.
> It is better to have a strong regime in power than a liberal government
> if it is indulgent and relaxed and penetrated by Communists.

Halle agreed with the general principle that the United States should not
"indulge in denunciation of other governments, or pass judgment on
domestic affairs." Yet, he also believed that the nation should "keep alive
certain basic ideals and aims for the reason that these ideals and aims
constituted one of the indispensable elements in inter-American
solidarity." Kennan's response was to wonder out loud "just what our
common ideals were." Latin America had "an unfortunate political history stemming from the imposition of Spanish authoritarianism on peculiar
geographic and climatic conditions." Backing down somewhat, Halle
stated that "common ideals were only one indispensable ingredient of the
inter-American cement." Most nations in the region, he believed, were
moving towards democratic government. That being the case, he "attached importance to lip service" from the U.S. supporting that

movement. Even a dictator such as Ubico in Guatemala had "kept alive the ideal of democracy and actually steered the country in that direction." That was certainly preferable to "a country under Fascist or Communist control which is going the other way."

Even this analysis left Kennan unconvinced. He "admitted that tyranny was bad but wondered what to do about a benevolent authoritarian rule." Democracy was a familiar concept in this country, but he feared that we were "on less certain grounds when dealing with foreign countries." Furthermore, he was "bothered by the fuzziness of words" such as "democracy" and "ideals." Another participant came to Halle's defense, pointing to the "usefulness of lip-service to democratic ideals." "Latin Americans," he continued, "enjoy the use of idealistic statements" in treaties and the like. Again showing impatience, Kennan stated that he "would go along with" a "general agreement on the desirability of stressing democracy," though his own experience in Latin America suggested that some people in that region had a "fear of genuine democracy."

With the debate bogging down, Ambassador Willard Beaulac tried to find common ground. No one, he explained, "seriously suggested the abandoning of our expressions concerning democracy and individual rights in our statements on Latin America." On the other hand, "if they are repeated too often they lose their meaning." In respect to handling the communist problem, "he was not recommending tolerance toward governments adopting a flabby approach to Communism and said that police repression should be faced if necessary." That seemed to satisfy the group, and discussion veered off into the economic field. It was not long, however, before the issue of U.S. relations with dictatorial regimes again came up, this time raised by Ambassador Fletcher Warren. The political and idealistic matters did not seem to concern him, but he was worried that a nation that uses police repression might one day be overthrown and that the "opposition would have a ready-made system at hand to use in a way possibly inimical to us." It was problematic, admitted Kennan, who "conceded that the best assurance against Communism was a working democratic system but pointed out that this cannot always exist."

Halle, who had remained quiet for some time, now expressed dismay that whereas earlier sessions of the conference had "emphasized the need for demonstrating the viability of our system to the noncommunist world . . .here the emphasis appeared to be on the negative aspect of combatting

Communism rather than developing a positive approach." He asked what should be done to "go about demonstrating that the system does work." Kennan's answer was that "nothing succeeds like success." He wondered "whether we have a theory or philosophy of doing things, saying that the United States is primarily a pragmatic nation." Ambassador Herschel Johnson agreed, saying that "we should be guided by ethical precepts but have a readiness to compromise with the devil if that were necessary to achieve our aims and by making our principles clear we could gain respect."

This 1950 debate thus ended on much the same note as the earlier discussion concerning Braden's proposal. All seemed to agree that the espousal of democratic precepts was a worthy activity; even Kennan would "go along" with that. Yet, the rather tenuous argument used to support that position—that "lip service" to democratic ideals was somehow "useful"—did not exactly echo Braden's dramatic language of 1945. By 1950, it was the other side of the argument—that a harsh stance against dictatorships in Latin America was unworkable and would hurt allies in the battle against communism—that had begun to prevail. In that battle, "police repression" might be needed; if so, the United States should not back away from supporting governments that resorted to such techniques. "Democracy," after all, was a "fuzzy" notion, fuzzier still when applied to Latin America, which did not seem to have either the background or disposition to support that particular form of governance. It seemed to be the "pragmatic" thing to "compromise with the devil" if that was what it took to hold communism at bay in the region. In this rather roundabout way, they had gotten to the crux of the dilemma imposed by U.S. theories of political interdependence. That interdependence was based on an allegiance to shared ideals. Yet, it was also based on the necessity of alliance in battling international communism. Which was the more important part of the equation? Was democracy desirable, even if it was "flabby" in prosecuting the war against communism? Was dictatorship allowable, if that was deemed the best insurance against communism infiltration and subversion? Fundamentally, the biggest question was whether the nations and peoples of Latin America could encourage and sustain democratic principles and practices while simultaneously serving as trustworthy allies in the fight against communism. As a 1954 NIE on the Caribbean and Central America revealed, the United States could not arrive at a satisfactory answer. "The conflict between 'democracy' and 'dictatorship'. . .confronts the United States with a dilemma, for both sides feel entitled to active US support." Dictatorships in the region "present themselves as guarantors of stability and order and of cooperation with the United States." On the other side, "reformists, by definition, are an unsettling influence, but they contend that the United States, as a progressive democracy dominant in the area, has a moral obligation to foster social and political development."[8] There was no suggestion offered as to which of these sides the United States should support.

During the period 1945–1954, however, the United States found that faced with that "dilemma" it would have to make a choice. Dictatorships in Central America, most notably the Somoza regime in Nicaragua, were not mere hypothetical examples that might be referred to in the intellectual discussions going on about the relative merits of democracy versus dictatorship. They had to be confronted.

Too Bad He Can't Crumble Right There

The story of the U.S. relationship with Anastasio Somoza during the late 1920s and early 1930s has been covered in numerous monographs, and therefore need not be recounted in detail here.[9] Following the end of the U.S. military intervention in Nicaragua in 1933, Somoza had rapidly consolidated his own power, using the U.S.-created Nicaraguan National Guard as his base. In 1936, he deposed the elected head of state, Juan Bautista Sacasa, and took direct control of the government. By 1939, he had pushed through the Nicaraguan congress a new constitution that allowed Somoza to serve an eight-year "term" as president, with no reelection. U.S. officials were not entirely thrilled over the prospect of Somoza serving as commander-in-chief of Nicaragua, but made the best of the situation.

During World War II, Somoza proved to be a willing ally.[10] Despite this unabashed support, by 1944 Somoza's regime—and its relationship with the United States—seemed to be in serious trouble. In mid-1944, large demonstrations broke out against the dictator, symptomatic, perhaps, of the Central American–wide revolt against repressive regimes (Martínez in El Salvador and Ubico in Guatemala). More problematic for U.S. officials was the apparent desire of Somoza to continue in power beyond the scheduled 1947 elections. By early 1945, members of the State Department were convinced of Somoza's "determination to continue in control" of Nicaragua.[11]

From that point onward, the U.S. relationship with Somoza deteriorated rapidly. The notable exception to this trend was Ambassador Fletcher Warren, who continued to be favorably impressed with the dictator, seeing him as a bulwark of pro-U.S. stability. In June 1945, he recalled a recent trip with Somoza which had "left no doubt in my mind as to the ability of the President as a politician and as a man able to handle his people." The department obviously disagreed; the words, "Oh! What a dupe he's proved," were written in the margin of the message.[12] The author of that derogatory remark might possibly have been William Cochran, Chief of the Division of Caribbean and Central American Affairs. During the next few years, Cochran, taking up Braden's anti-dictator cudgel, would lead the attack on Somoza's regime, while Warren would serve as a pipeline for pro-Somoza analyses.

Cochran began the war of words against Somoza's decision to retain power after the 1947 election with a long analysis of political conditions in Nicaragua in July 1945. The dictator had now officially announced his intention to run in the upcoming election. This meant, of course, that he would win, since "he retains the support of the Guardia Nacional." Public response in Nicaragua would "reach fever heat," but this would not deter Somoza. A "clean democratic wind is sweeping the world," Cochran claimed, and therefore "Somoza's action seems to me ill-timed historically as well as locally." His recommendation was to get word to Somoza that the United States would look unfavorably upon his bid for reelection. While this risked provoking the charge of intervention in Nicaragua's internal affairs, he predicted that the United States would be hit with that charge no matter what it did: "We cannot avoid the *charge* of intervention; and if we are to play a part (and we cannot avoid doing so), let it be on behalf of democratic processes." He ended with an impassioned argument for his position:

> It will also be argued that Somoza is the only man who can maintain order in Nicaragua—which boils down to the old distrust of the people, and the feeling that order, rather than freedom, is the ultimate good of man. Possibly, conditions under a new President might be unstable. Possibly the Leftists—and it is highly fashionable in certain countries to term any opposition "Communist"—will exercise much influence. But it seems to me that we can neither look on with disinterest while the people of Central America are kept in a state of economic and political peonage, nor fight real Communism with a passive attitude. On the

contrary, the United States wears the mantle of greatness, willingly or not, and I should like to see it stand forth in the world proudly and positively for the principles which made it great.[13]

Ambassador Warren, while agreeing with some of Cochran's analysis, nevertheless continually tried to put the best face on Somoza's decision to run for reelection. He admitted that it might be true that "a majority [of Nicaraguans] do not wish him to continue in the Presidency." And it was true that this might mean revolution. For all that, Warren was convinced that Somoza was "the most capable, the most intelligent and the most personable man in sight." If he would give up his business interests and allow free elections, these actions would "write General Somoza down as the greatest of his country's Chief Executives." In another message, Warren commented on the opposition to Somoza in Nicaragua. It was not reason for encouragement. "The Embassy does not feel that the cause of democratic government will be essentially advanced in Nicaragua or abroad should the opposition take over the Government of Nicaragua."[14]

Throughout late 1945 and 1946, the general themes laid out by Cochran and Warren were repeated many times. Continuing his anti-Somoza crusade, Cochran referred to the Somoza regime as a "clear-cut case of what has recently been discussed within the Department as a 'dictatorial and disreputable' government." With Cochran in the lead, the State Department strained hard to discourage Somoza in his political plans. When Somoza hinted that he might visit the United States in 1946 to see his son graduate from West Point, the reaction was sharp. Secretary of State James Byrnes informed Warren that if the dictator wished to visit, that was within his rights, but an official visit to Washington "might prove embarrassing to him." Cochran was more blunt. He told Warren that the department was trying to make sure that "his reception will be quite different from what he anticipates. I hope we succeed. If we do, he is going to be furious." And Ellis Briggs, in a memorandum to Braden, declared that a visit by Somoza to the White House would be "unthinkable." "He is," Briggs lamented, "of course, a problem for Nicaragua to solve; but we must avoid letting him 'use' us to bolster his campaign, or a continuance of dictatorship and shameless exploitation."[15]

The same response greeted Warren's analysis of economics in Nicaragua. What the country needed, he reported in early 1946, was "political tranquility," markets for its export products, and a "quiet labor front." Cochran thought this was nonsense. Nicaragua's financial difficulties were "due primarily to Somoza's political campaign" and the fact that he had given the National Guard two salary increases in the past two years. When word reached the department that Nicaragua would be seeking a $3 million Export-Import Bank loan, Braden was quick to react. State had "reservations concerning a loan on political grounds. Somoza is a dictator." A large U.S. loan at this time "may be interpreted (or misinterpreted) locally as support for the Somoza regime or a Somoza presidential candidate."[16]

Through all of this, Warren stuck to his guns. He was under no illusion about Somoza's objectives, or methods. In a report filed in early 1946, he described a train derailment in which two people had been killed and many others injured. Faulty equipment was probably to blame, but Somoza was charging that members of the opposition had sabotaged the tracks. Warren took this as an action in preparation for taking "future dramatic action to stifle his political opponents." Somoza's position was such that "recourse to force might appear as the only means of retaining power."[17] In other words, Warren was hardly the "dupe" that officials such as Cochran believed him to be. Nevertheless, he did continue to remind the department that Somoza continued to prove a willing ally. Recounting a February 1946 meeting with the dictator, the ambassador stated that Somoza was eager to "cooperate fully" with the United States at the upcoming conference in Rio de Janiero. According to Warren, Somoza "said that the United States had been able and should be able to use Nicaraguan representatives to do certain things which our own representatives could not easily carry out." Given this stance, Somoza felt let down by the recent U.S. attitude toward his regime. In addition, Warren pointed out that Somoza was a solid anticommunist. The ambassador concluded that "the President is sincerely concerned with the growth of communistic or extreme leftwing activity and thinking in Nicaragua."[18]

Warren's concerns made little impact on the State Department. When Warren cabled in July 1946 that Somoza was ill and sought medical treatment in U.S. medical facilities in Panama, he dramatically concluded that a lesser man might have "crumbled before this." An unsigned memo attached to the cable at the department reluctantly agreed that the United States could not refuse such a request, but sarcastically noted, "Too bad he can't 'crumble' right there in Managua." A handwritten message said simply, "Agree, WPC"—William P. Cochran.[19]

Handling Somoza

During the years 1947–1949, Nicaraguan politics acquired a surreal aspect. Three presidents served during that time: one "elected" with Somoza's backing, and then promptly overthrown by the dictator; one "appointed" by Somoza, and then tossed aside; and another one, again "appointed" by Somoza, who almost immediately schemed to take his place.[20] Through it all, Somoza undoubtedly remained the most powerful force in Nicaraguan politics. It was during this period that the United States policy toward the dictator began to subtly change. The ringing rhetoric that denounced dictatorship in Latin America was still present, and often made an appearance; Somoza himself was still as unsavory as ever for most U.S. officials. Nevertheless, by the end of Somoza's political machinations, many members of the State Department had come to accept the conclusion that some sort of "working arrangement" with the despot needed to be hammered out.

By late 1946, Somoza had apparently become convinced that to placate the United States, the scheduled 1947 presidential elections would proceed without his running as a candidate. Warren reported from Nicaragua that this did not necessarily mean that Somoza was going to quietly slip off the stage of the nation's politics. His hand-picked candidate, Dr. Leonardo Argüello, was expected to win the February election. Almost immediately, the plot took a bizarre twist. By December 1946, Warren noted tension between Somoza and Argüello. The State Department noted this development with interest; a memorandum on the subject declared that the "political pot has begun to boil." Apparently, Somoza was infuriated with Argüello over the latter's refusal to sign a commission to continue his tenure as head of the National Guard. "It begins to look as though if the elections are held as scheduled, Somoza will lose whoever wins." A note in the memorandum's margin translated as "God Grant!"[21]

The election went off as planned in February. Warren was certain that the Somoza regime had "made effective use of its control over the ballot boxes to have Argüello declared victor." The State Department concurred: while the elections were "'reasonably' free from coercion," it was obvious that fraud was widespread. And while the United States extended recognition to the new government, it made its displeasure known. When Nicaragua requested a special U.S. mission to attend the inauguration, Under Secretary of State Dean Acheson advised President Truman that, "in light of the character of the Nicaraguan Government and our doubts concerning the methods employed by President Somoza in bringing about the election of his successor," he would reject the proposal. In the end, only the ambassador, his second secretary, and the army and navy attachés attended the function.[22]

If Somoza was dismayed by these actions, he did not show it, but proceeded to go on the attack. In a talk with Warren a month after the election, he complained long and vigorously about the U.S. failure to complete construction on the Inter-American Highway through Nicaragua and to equip the National Guard. He concluded that such U.S. policies were "causing a growth of anti-American feeling and that we were working against our friends." He felt compelled to stay in charge of the National Guard, "to protect the nation from the advance of Communism."[23]

Warren departed from his post as ambassador to Nicaragua in mid-May and thus missed the fun as Somoza proceeded to throw that nation's politics into another uproar. On May 25–26, Somoza took power from Argüello, holding the now ex-president "incommunicado." The State Department viewed this development with deep concern. Maurice Bernbaum, acting head of the American embassy until a new ambassador could be appointed, talked to Somoza shortly after the coup. "He realized the bad international effect of his coup but felt that the country's welfare demanded his sacrifice." Secretary of State George Marshall informed Bernbaum of the "bad effect" it was having in Washington. Marshall expressed disbelief that after just one month, Somoza would be "snatching power away from Pres whose candidacy he himself sponsored. Allegation Somoza took this action because he was QUOTE forced to take drastic measures to protect his life ENDQUOTE hardly impressive." His use of the National Guard in the coup was "deplored."[24]

In Nicaragua, meanwhile, Somoza continued the political merry-go-round by having the national congress name Benjamin Lacayo Sacasa as interim president. Again, this resulted in negative reaction from the State Department, but confusion about how to handle the problem began to appear. Ellis Briggs complained that the avenues of possible U.S. action were limited. Unilateral intervention in Nicaragua was unthinkable; multilateral intervention with other Latin American republics seemed doubtful because of lack of support from those quarters. He lamely recommended that the U.S. confer with the Latin American nations and defer appointing a new ambassador.[25]

While Washington continued its nonrecognition of the Lacayo government, by mid-1947 that policy was beginning to fall apart. The longer the regime lasted, the harder it was to keep the other Latin American governments from recognizing it. Argentina, for example, extended formal diplomatic relations in July. Questions were also raised about exactly how effective nonrecognition was in achieving U.S. goals. This was especially true following more political maneuvering by Somoza in August, which resulted in a Constituent Assembly appointing Dr. Victor Román y Reyes as the new president. There was little doubt in the State Department that the election had been a "fraud."[26] Despite this feeling, a definite weakening of the U.S. position began to become evident.

Under Secretary of State Robert Lovett expressed his doubts about the U.S. stance toward the "constitutional" Román y Reyes administration less than a week after it was established. "In all honesty," he informed the U.S. embassy in Managua, "we must take into account fact that, like it or not, present regime in Nicaragua has all attributes and qualities of stable *de facto* Govt." State Department veteran Dana Munro observed that the policy of nonrecognition was causing Washington to lose its leverage over Managua; recognition, on the other hand, might help to clear up the mess in Nicaragua. On the "basis of his experience with Somoza," he was confident that an "American Ambassador, if firm and experienced, would 'handle' Somoza, i.e., stop his bossing of the Government and persuade him to step out of the picture." Gordon Reid, still trying to hold the line against Somoza, succinctly responded: "Fletcher Warren was firm and experienced and was totally unsuccessful in 'handling' Somoza."[27]

It was clear that no one was going to "handle" the dictator. While Bernbaum continued to press on the department the case for non-recognition, other events rapidly undercut his position. Argüello's death in December 1947, as Thomas Leonard explains, "reopened the recognition question. His absence removed the last obstacle to the legitimacy of the Sacasa regime." As Leonard also notes, the non-recognition coalition among the Latin American nations began to disintegrate at about that time. Costa Rica became the first nation to recognize Sacasa. By early 1948, the Dominican Republic and a number of other Latin American nations had followed suit. At the Bogotá Conference, which began in March, Robert Pastor describes what occurred: "[T]he foreign ministers of the American states adopted a resolution urging the continuity of diplomatic relations among OAS. . .nations as a general principle. As a result of that resolution, the United States extended recognition to the government of Victor Manuel Román y Reyes."[28]

From Nicaragua, Bernbaum could barely contain his frustration and disappointment. On the very day that a new U.S. ambassador was appointed—May 22—he expressed the opinion that the "departure of General Somoza is extremely unlikely." U.S. recognition had "elated the Nicaraguan Government and disappointed the opposition." He concluded that there would be no peaceful political settlement in Nicaragua until Somoza was removed; open revolution "looms on the horizon as a possibility." It was a strongly worded message, but it was essentially Bernbaum's last salvo; he would be gone in a few months, and most of the reports on the new situation in Nicaragua would be the work of the new ambassador, George Shaw, and his team of advisors.[29]

While Shaw was not blind to what kind of man Somoza was and the kind of regime he had established in Nicaragua, it seems safe to say that he took—as Kennan might have referred to it—a more "pragmatic" approach to the situation. A few months after arriving at his new post, Shaw noted that some groups in Nicaragua were asking Somoza to run for president in 1951. He opined that there was a "feeling of resignation to the inevitability of Somoza's continuance in power." The opposition had been sapped of its morale, and the danger of popular revolt was "not great." In early 1949 the new ambassador passed along to the department a long report prepared by Third Secretary Robert Blake dealing with politics in Nicaragua. It was, Shaw stated, an "excellent report. . .and I am in general agreement with its content." It deserves to be looked at in depth, as it was symptomatic of a basic change taking place in the U.S. attitude toward Somoza and the whole issue of dictatorship and democracy in Latin America.[30]

When "the Nicaraguan looks at politics," Blake claimed, they did so through very different eyes from their U.S. counterparts. The focus was not on "plans and programs" but rather on "a leader"—a "man on a white horse." "General Somoza," he believed, "to a great extent fills this bill even today." The term "democracy" was not the same to the average Nicaraguan as to the typical U.S. citizen. The "institutions" of democracy—elections, and so forth—held little attraction for most Nicaraguans. Parties were vacant entities. The people did not "participate directly in the political life of the country; they have never done so and have little understanding of or interest in the problems involved." The nation suffered from "political defeatism"—a "national inferiority complex."

The people themselves were not capable of serving as the basis for representative government. As Blake noted, "Centuries of living in a hot and unhealthful climate have tended to create a group of people necessarily physically listless and to a certain extent less aware of their surroundings." This factor was one which had worked to "limit influx of the European elements which in other Central American countries have mixed with the native white families to form progressive elements within the society." The Nicaraguan upper class considered politics mainly a way to "lead an exciting and profitable life." The lower classes, subjected to a brutal standard of living, formed a sullen mass. "[E]xploitation of this feeling by Communist or other extremist groups must always be considered a possibility."

The most powerful political force in 1949 Nicaragua was the National Guard, which retained Somoza in his commanding position. Political, social, and economic change was incremental, at best. Somoza had "given the country fourteen years of peace at the expense of civil liberties and popular participation in representative government." Yet, before decrying that situation too loudly, Blake suggested it be considered within the context of Nicaraguan history and present realities. The Nicaraguan masses had not participated in politics before 1949, and there was little indication that they avidly sought this. Leaders of the anti-Somoza opposition did "not basically hate authoritarian government; they merely hate Somoza." All things considered, "it would be foolish if we expected a millennium with the overthrow of Somoza." There were, to be sure, reasons for optimism: "Democracy is an ideal that the majority of the Nicaraguans would be very proud to achieve. In the long run, however, the Nicaraguans will get the kind of government they want, deserve, and understand."

As further reports from Shaw seemed to indicate, the kind of government Nicaraguans would get in the near future revolved around Somoza. By May 1949, the general was complaining about Román y Reyes; the president was "allowing the country to go to the dogs." What was needed was, not surprisingly, a "strong man." A few days later, Shaw reported that Somoza had been "proclaimed" as the next presidential candidate of the National Liberal Party. "Somoza gracefully admitted he could not oppose the wishes of the people or the demands of the National Liberal Party."[31]

Gordon Reid, wrapping up three years as head of the Nicaraguan–Honduran desk in the State Department, was struck by the change in U.S. policy. "Our policy toward Nicaragua, when I assumed my duties, was one of toughness toward dictators and friendship for those in the good neighborhood with democratic tendencies. This was followed by a period of treating dictators and democracies alike. At the present time, I am not aware of our arms policy toward Somoza, our financial policy toward Somoza or our general attitude toward the dictators." Like Bernbaum, he believed that Somoza caused most of the troubles of Nicaragua and Central America, but believed there were few alternatives. In any case, Somoza was there to stay; "vanity, delight in power and position and avarice"—and a wife who had expressed that she "would rather be the widow of Dictator Somoza than the wife of Sr. Somoza retired to the United States"—were all factors that kept him hanging on.[32]

Reid's tone of resignation echoed the "political defeatism" noted by Blake in his description of the Nicaraguan electorate. The rhetoric of antidictatorship lingered, but it had certainly lost its momentum. In the specific case of Somoza, the despot had simply outlasted U.S. efforts to encourage his departure from the Nicaraguan political scene. Yet, as Reid seemed to ask, did this mean a change in the U.S. policy toward dictatorship in Latin America? He probably knew the answer. In a rough chronological breakdown, the years 1945–1947 had been ones in which the United States had exhibited "toughness" toward the Somoza regime. From 1947 to 1949, subtle changes had taken place; yes, Somoza was odious and repressive, but he maintained order, was no worse (if no better) than opposition elements in his nation, and was probably the kind of leader the Nicaraguans "deserved." After this period of ambivalence, however, U.S. policy from 1950 to 1954 would move toward active support of the Somoza dictatorship.

Life with Somoza

There was a change in the U.S. relationship with the Somoza government after 1949. From 1950 onward Nicaragua found itself the recipient of large amounts of economic assistance, as well as military aid, particularly in the form of a 1954 bilateral military assistance agreement. Somoza himself began to be looked upon much more approvingly.

The primary factor in this change was the view that developed among U.S. policymakers that Somoza was a trusted bulwark in the fight against international communism, particularly in Central America. That anticommunism would begin to replace prodemocracy as the foundation of U.S. policy at that time is not entirely surprising. The latter part of 1949 had not been a good one for the U.S. in its Cold War struggle against the

Soviet Union. The Soviets broke the Americans' atomic monopoly. China was "lost" to the communist bloc. As 1950 dawned, more bad news arrived. Senator Joseph McCarthy leveled serious charges against the Truman administration, accusing it of harboring known communists in the State Department. The outbreak of the Korean War a few months later drove the Cold War to a fever pitch.

In Latin America, as we have seen, the years 1948–1950 were viewed as critical ones, in which tremendous political, economic, and social changes were taking place. In such a crisis situation, communism was finding a more and more receptive audience for its message. In Central America, in particular, the United States was faced with some worrisome problems. The government of Guatemala, led by President Arévalo, seemed to be taking a turn to the left. Figueres, who had taken power in Costa Rica in 1948 (substantially aided by Arévalo), was a wild card; as LaFeber puts it, "neither a fish such as Arévalo nor a fowl such as Somoza. He fit no easy ideological categories." The inability to pigeon-hole Figueres troubled U.S. officials who preferred to have their choices black or white.[33] Somoza, on the other hand, presented a clear, if not particularly appealing, choice. He was a dictatorial "fowl" but his unrelenting stand against leftist "fish" led U.S. policymakers to conclude that it was better to live with Somoza than without him.

By July 1949, the State Department replaced Ambassador Shaw with Capus Waynick, who was equally aware of the repressive nature of Somoza's Nicaragua. Yet, Waynick accepted the need for a strong ruler in the nation, primarily because he saw communism as a far greater danger in Nicaragua than did his predecessors.

Waynick was quick to point out the dubious political maneuverings undertaken by Somoza in preparation for the 1952 election. He reasoned in February of 1950 that since Somoza was campaigning so hard for an election that was two years away, he was probably going to try and see to it that a constituent assembly, instead of the general electorate, put him into office. Somoza "wants to avoid a general election for the presidency. He much prefers the quiet efficiency of a *constitugente* [sic] of stooges with a pre-determined vote." The election, when it was held, would in no recognized sense be free: "The leopard does not change his spots."[34]

The State Department also realized that the upcoming "election" did not indicate that democracy had arrived in Nicaragua. A memorandum recounting a conversation with Nicaraguan Ambassador Guillermo Sevilla Sacasa was labeled with the sarcastic heading, "Subject: The Happy

People." Sevilla Sacasa had been full of stories of the "happy faces" in his country since the election had been announced. The department's attitude toward Somoza was still one that sought to keep the dictator at arm's length. When informed by Waynick that, once again, Somoza desired to visit the United States for medical care, Secretary of State Acheson responded that he hoped Somoza would avoid Washington and would travel "incognito." Gordon Reid, now handling Middle American Affairs in the department, chimed in that, "I believe the storm warnings should be hoisted."[35]

More and more, however, the issue of communism began to dominate the discussion and analysis of the Somoza regime. In early 1950, Waynick approved that Somoza "had his foot firmly on the spark of Communism here." A few months later, he notified the department that some in Nicaragua were praising the general for keeping the peace and standing against communists. "In the main," Waynick explained, "he does preserve order. The mechanics of discipline are obvious and tyrannical." Nevertheless, "Somoza has a pleasant personality, he is insistently 'Americanista,' and the United States can get from him as President or as strong man of the country any wanted cooperation or concession that does not interfere importantly or practically with his own purposes."[36]

Waynick also emphasized that radicals and communists from Guatemala and Costa Rica were interfering in the internal affairs of Nicaragua. The ambassador was aware, through "respectable" sources in Washington, that "President Arévalo would not go out of office in Guatemala before he had helped the enemies of Somoza 'liberate' Nicaragua." Figueres also would "like to see something not trivial happen to Somoza." Despite these threats, Waynick was impressed with Somoza's composure: "He is not a fearful man, having right considerable animal courage."[37]

Notwithstanding Somoza's courage, Waynick, by early 1951, was more concerned than ever with communist intrigues in Nicaragua. In analyzing the Nicaraguan response to the emergency caused by the Korean War, the ambassador reported that, "We sense some increase of Communist activity. It appears that efforts are being exerted on the 'party line' to spread the belief that the United States is in deep trouble and is looking to Latin Americans to protect our 'imperial' interests." Among Nicaraguan officials, there was some "definite concern" about the situation, though the "danger that we see in the United States seems very remote to the average Nicaraguan." He was worried that the masses, through the use of propaganda, could be convinced that the United States was trying to "use" the Latin Americans to defend its own interests, instead of clearly seeing that the United States was "the great force" standing between communism and Latin America. The economic situation was bad, making the people even more susceptible to communist propaganda.[38]

Such analyses prompted quick action by the State Department. In May of 1951, the question of military aid to Nicaragua began to receive support from many quarters. Oddly enough, one of the first to raise the issue was Gordon Reid. In a memo to several other department officials, he explained that during the immediate postwar years, while Braden served as assistant secretary of state, the policy of the State Department had been to veto any military assistance for the Somoza dictatorship. Indeed, "During those years General Somoza was turned down so many times on every request that he made that he stopped making requests and, as Colonel Somoza [Anastasio, Jr.] put it to me in 1949, 'If we don't ask, we don't get slapped down.'" He commented on a recent note from the Department of Defense which indicated that no Nicaraguan trainees would be brought to the United States in 1952: "I can see no valid reason for this omission. I believe that the Nicaraguans should be included in any training program and that consideration should be given to the reestablishment of the military mission in that country." He recommended that Defense be told that State had "no objection to the inclusion of Nicaragua under all phases of the military program."[39]

As if on cue, General Maxwell Taylor, Army assistant chief of staff, queried State less than a week later about whether Nicaragua would be interested in receiving a U.S. Army Mission. "Unsolicited comments made to U.S. Army officers by Nicaraguan officers attending U.S. Army schools in Panama indicate that such a mission would be highly desirable." Forwarded to the embassy in Nicaragua, Waynick was supportive, but warned that it might intensify criticism of the United States as Somoza's "keeper." This was the "sole political objection. . . . I do not regard it as particularly important." He had already asked Somoza for a battalion for the war in Korea; if he agreed, the mission should be sent "immediately." Waynick concluded, "In *any event* the net of my opinion is that the Department of the Army should be encouraged to assign the mission to Nicaragua."[40]

A 1951 policy statement from the State Department was positively impressed with U.S. efforts in Nicaragua. "We have achieved," it concluded, "our immediate objective of enlisting and keeping the support of the Somoza regime for our foreign, economic, and political policies."

Nicaragua had "solidly aligned itself with the United States in demonstrating an awareness of the threat of international Communism and the necessity to resist it both internally and internationally." Democracy, unfortunately, had been slow to develop since the war. This, however, was a "long term" goal, and it would be wise to "guard against wishful endeavors too rapidly to emplant democracy where the ground is not yet fertile."[41] The statement skirted the question of whether those "long term" and "immediate" objectives might clash; could communism be fought by democratic means in a country that had no "fertile ground" for such means? If the answer was "yes," what would that mean for relations with Somoza? And if the answer was "no," what would that mean for the ideal of political interdependence?

U.S. policy was indeed changing and, coincidentally, so was the ambassadorship (again). Three men had served as U.S. ambassador to Nicaragua since 1945; in 1951, Thomas Whelan would begin a ten-year term as the highest ranking U.S. official in Nicaragua. In congratulating Whelan on his new post, Edward Miller gushed, "I can assure you that you will find in Nicaragua people who are strongly pro-United States and possibilities of development, particularly in the field of agriculture, which are very great. The Embassy residence is one of our finest, with a swimming pool which you will find very enjoyable. In President Somoza, you will find a most convivial and delightful character."[42] Aside from the fact that Somoza apparently ranked below the embassy swimming pool in terms of interest, Miller's letter is evidence of a definite warming of relations with the dictator. In many ways, policy under Whelan mirrored that begun by Waynick. There were two important changes, however. First, the issue of communism in Nicaragua and Central America—and Somoza's role in containing and combating it—became much more significant. Second, in addition to military assistance (which was continued and expanded), economic aid also began to pour into Nicaragua at the prompting of the U.S. embassy.

Throughout late 1951 through 1954—especially as U.S.–Guatemalan relations worsened—the anticommunist stance of Somoza came to be the main focus of Whelan and other U.S. policymakers. As it did, the general view and evaluation of Somoza as both man and leader began to change drastically. Where in the immediate postwar period he had been castigated as a viciously repressive tyrant, and in the late 1940s seen as an unpleasant, but perhaps inevitable, institution in Nicaragua, by the mid-1950s Somoza emerged as a necessary, even desirable, force.

According to a January 1952 review of Nicaraguan politics by Gordon Reid, however, it was not so much that U.S. policy had changed; the important changes had occurred in Nicaragua and Somoza. Entitled "Life with Somoza," the report bluntly noted, "Somoza is Nicaragua." Any of the changes in that nation, therefore, were "directly tied to the personality of this one man." Some of the most notable were that Somoza now "believed that Nicaragua's future was in the economic field." There was a "determination on Somoza's part to put his [economic] house in order." There was a greater understanding between the United States and Nicaragua in terms of international affairs: "the Nicaraguan today appears to be giving his support out of belief and not as a hopeful supplicant for favors." "All of the foregoing," Reid stated, "might lead one to believe that Nicaragua is fast becoming an ideal country. That pleasant aspect is far from realization, but a start has been made." The biggest problem now was what would happen when Somoza left office or died. "Somoza today is still the most interesting figure in Central America, and for my money, the smartest." That could hardly be said of his most likely successors—members of his own family. "A larger and more vigorous collection of leeches would be hard to find." In sum, Somoza's departure from the Nicaraguan political scene would lead to "chaos [that] would ensue for an indefinite period."[43]

As a sign of the new acceptance of Somoza and his brand of rule, during a mid-1952 visit to the United States he was actually welcomed into the White House. A letter from Secretary of State Acheson informed President Truman that his lunch guest was "an able man with an engaging personality. He is informal, genial, energetic, persuasive and politically astute. He is also impulsive, vain and egocentric. His drive for personal gain is very great." He had ruled Nicaragua "largely as a one man show." Often criticized, he had, nevertheless, "restored order to Nicaragua and in recent years has been less repressive." A final point to consider was that "Nicaragua has consistently supported United States foreign policy."[44] No "storm warnings" this time; no necessity for the dictator to travel "incognito." The "new" Somoza was welcome at Truman's table.

The main themes of both Reid's memo and Acheson's letter were often repeated during the next few years. John Ohmans, of the Nicaraguan Desk in the State Department, wrote the U.S. chargé in Managua in June 1952, reassuring him that "we believe as you do that he [Somoza] has mellowed, and has leadership, and that he is in general good for the country in its present stage of development." A 1953 review of

Nicaraguan politics, economics, and society stated that, "General Somoza is in firm control of the government and, in fact, enjoys wide-spread popularity among his people." The next presidential election was scheduled for 1957 and although there were plots afoot in Nicaragua to keep Somoza from running, he had, "in typical Nicaraguan fashion and in his usual friendly way," informed Whelan that "he will be glad to make the sacrifice if the United States wants him to do so." The report added, "A basic factor in President Somoza's actions is his sincere admiration of the United States." As for U.S.–Nicaraguan problems, "There are none." Relations were "excellent" and Nicaragua had proved itself to be a "loyal and friendly collaborator with the United States in the Organization of Central American States and the United Nations. In nearly every case the Nicaraguan Government can be counted on to follow the lead of the United States in any international matter."[45]

The fear of what would become of post-Somoza Nicaragua also continued to plague U.S. officials. John Ohmans, writing to Chargé Rolland Welch in Nicaragua, posed a troubling scenario: "The death of Stalin has set me to think (it happens at times). What happens when Somoza dies, as he must some day?" In response, Welch tried to find the silver lining in such a dire assumption. He noted that personalismo dominated Nicaraguan politics, and would for some time to come. "In the past we have thrown up our hands at the horror of it all. We have been particularly pained because one leader—Somoza—has topped all the rest—has greedily grabbed off wealth for himself and family. We have failed to realize that any other 'leader' would do as much, if not more. It might be worse. We can work with Somoza." Since no amount of U.S. pressure was "going to change the situation," Welch recommended that the U.S. simply "accept it and work with it. We can turn it to our own advantage, if we try harder." And when the old dictator died? In Welch's opinion, accept the fact that politics in Nicaragua was a "barnyard hierarchy." When the present "cock of the roost" died, another one would take his place—maybe "it is some little known rooster who at this moment is just putting out pin feathers and learning to crow." More problematic at the moment was what would happen at the end of Somoza's term of office (after the death of Román y Reyes in 1950, Somoza served the rest of his term and then finagled another "election"). There was no lack of candidates: "Here everybody wants to be President. Why not—it's a good paying job." For now, Somoza was healthy and safe; "Nicaraguans have never gone in for assassinations."[46]

The issue of Somoza and his rule in Nicaragua even penetrated into the discussions of the CFR. Meeting in late 1952, a discussion group dealing with political unrest in Latin America mulled over the dictator. The general assessment was that Somoza, warts and all, was good for Nicaragua. Douglas Allen, of the Otis Astoria Corporation, noted that although Somoza was "a real rogue, he has maintained stability." Charles Cumberland from Rutgers University, echoing Ohmans' fears, stated that "the really frightening thing is what will occur when Somoza leaves." Even Spruille Braden admitted that "it is to Somoza's credit that he has been consistently anti-communist through the years." And Frederick Hasler of the Continental Bank and Trust Company capped the discussion by saying, "If every Latin American country had a Somoza, there would be no need for a discussion of political unrest in these countries. It must be remembered that few Latin American countries are ready for democracy."[47]

Also of note for U.S. officials was the increased awareness of communism by the Nicaraguan people and leadership, and Somoza's willingness to help in combating it. Second Secretary Robert Brewster reported the changing atmosphere in late 1951: "For the first time since the end of World War II, the press and public have become aware of the existence of organized communism in Nicaragua and discovered that it operates through the CGT [Confederación General del Trabajo de Nicaragua—the largest labor union in Nicaragua]." This "new awareness" was all the more conspicuous when compared to the situation developing in Guatemala. When a U.S. businessman queried the department about investment possibilities in Nicaragua, he was told that as long as Somoza stayed healthy, political stability was pretty well assured. As explained by one department official, "Conditions in Nicaragua for the type of investment. . .contemplated seemed to me to be as favorable—if not more favorable—than anywhere else in that region." The conversation then turned to Guatemala, where the entrepreneur already had investments in place. His opinion was that "things were going from bad to worse" in that nation. He wished that the United Fruit Company would just pull out, causing the present government to fall or, at least, a "change in attitude on the part of the present Government towards the communists whom he said would then be recognized as responsible for the deterioration of the Guatemalan economy."[48]

Somoza was also particularly helpful in the U.S. campaign against the Guatemalan government. In a September 1952 conversation with

Ambassador Whelan, Somoza had bluntly informed him that, "We will take care of Guatemala, but I have got to have more arms and it's costing us money." Even some U.S. officials back in Washington were somewhat taken aback at Somoza's willingness to do whatever it took to remove the Guatemalan menace. Thomas Mann recommended to Whelan that he quietly inform Somoza that the United States was not in a position to offer a "blank check" to support "any military adventure" against Guatemala. The U.S. government "welcomed an awareness on the part of all American Republics of the dangers which Communism represents in Guatemala" but any action would have to be taken in a "responsible and legal way." Mann's proscriptions were undercut, however, by his rationale that if Somoza wanted weapons to "maintain internal order," then "Tacho can buy arms here. If he wants our help on priorities, licenses, etc., he has only to ask for it." A State Department analysis of early 1954 claimed that, "Next to Trujillo, General Somoza is the most articulate in his hatred of the present regime in Guatemala. . . . Somoza would relish the overthrow of the Guatemalan Government, and would probably help out if he could safely do so."[49]

For the U.S., however, actions spoke louder than words, and following up on their new, approving assessment of Somoza, they actively pushed programs of military and economic aid for Nicaragua after 1950. In the economic field, Point Four came to be the weapon of choice, while in the military arena, Army and Air Force missions were dispatched, capped by the signing in 1954 of a bilateral military assistance agreement.

As noted earlier, U.S. officials had become impressed with Somoza's "forward looking" economic development policies in Nicaragua; he was, in their words, "putting his house in order." In order to bolster that development, as well as draw Nicaragua more securely into the anti-communist camp, U.S. economic assistance—particularly Point Four aid—was pumped into Somoza's nation beginning in 1951. Analyzing the impact of Point Four in November of that year, Second Secretary John Topping stated that, "The purposes of the Technical Assistance Program in Nicaragua fall almost entirely within the three principles of increasing the capacity of the area to produce essential civilian goods, of strengthening the support for friendly governments, and of improving popular attitudes toward the free world and the United States." He was confident that if such aid were continued, stability in Nicaragua would be increased, "further orienting the Nicaraguan Government and people toward the United States."[50]

John K. Chattey, who was put in charge of the U.S. technical co-operation program in Nicaragua, could also see the advantages of this form of economic assistance, but was more cautious than Topping. In two messages during the summer of 1952, he explained that Nicaragua was a good candidate for such aid. It could be "unquestionably classified as underdeveloped"; the nation's economy was "'backward'" in every sense of the word. And, Nicaragua had great economic potential. Reflecting a widely held belief among U.S. officials, he believed, however, that the United States needed to move with "extreme caution." Nicaragua was not going to be "'modernized' overnight"; limitations in the nation's political, economic, and "sociological" character would narrow the amount of change that might be expected. "In many respects, these backward people are no more ready for technological changes than is the average American kindergarten student ready for the study of trigonometry."[51]

Chattey's reservations aside, U.S. officials could often get fairly dramatic when plugging for technical assistance for Nicaragua. Such was the case in October 1951 when Assistant Secretary Miller sent a pleading letter to George Wythe, Director of the American Republics Division, Office of International Trade in the Department of Commerce. Apparently Nicaragua was requesting thirteen Caterpillar tractors and two Caterpillar scrapers for work on the Inter-American Highway. The economic benefits, Miller explained, were self-evident. The technical assistance program in Nicaragua was trying to increase production of foodstuffs, and the improved transportation resulting from the acquisition of the tractors and scrapers would be quite beneficial in this regard. The political side of the question was just as important, however. Improving the economy of Nicaragua would "make Nicaragua less susceptible to communist propaganda." It was wise to remember that "communists have already gained a substantial foothold in Guatemala and that they are seeking every means and excuse to spread their influence elsewhere in the area." It would be a blow to this "strongly anti-communist country whose government and people have given full and consistent support to United States foreign policy" if renewed construction on the Inter-American Highway—which had been pushed by the United States—were allowed to lapse. For lack of a tractor or scraper, in other words, an ally might be lost. By 1952, Gordon Reid could state, "Thus Nicaragua today, in Central America, is the leading country in the Point Four sweepstakes."[52]

The International Bank for Reconstruction and Development (IBRD) loaned Nicaragua $4.7 million in 1951 for highway and agricultural projects. To those who might complain that loaning money to a dictatorship might be unseemly, IBRD Vice-President Robert Garner, at a 1952 CFR meeting, stated that Nicaragua under Somoza was an example of a country taking the economic bull by the horns: "Leadership that arises for the purpose of strengthening a country's economic system is very seldom democratic."[53]

Military aid was also lavished on Nicaragua during this period. An Air Force Mission was agreed to in 1952; an Army Mission was approved the next year.[54] Of greater significance was the push for a bilateral military assistance agreement in 1953. As noted in chapter 3, the idea for signing such agreements with the Central American nations of Honduras, El Salvador, and Nicaragua originated in early 1953, when U.S. officials became more concerned over the budding communist threat in Guatemala and Honduras. To ensure that Nicaragua got its share of the aid, Nicaraguan Ambassador Sevilla Sacasa visited the State Department in May 1953. He played to the concerns of his department hosts, claiming that Somoza was quite alarmed over the communist menace in Guatemala. Nicaragua needed arms to protect itself, and wanted to sign a bilateral military assistance agreement. Undersecretary of State Walter B. Smith informed the ambassador that he "shared" his "apprehensions" and that the possibility of such an agreement had already been raised. He suggested that Thomas Mann, also in attendance, "expedite a decision." Soon, the State Department was suggesting that even if the Defense Department turned down the requests for aid to El Salvador and Honduras, Nicaragua definitely needed it. Aid to all of those nations, of course, would "promote the attainment of political and psychological objectives related to the considerable communist penetration in Central America, especially Guatemala." If necessary, however, aid to Nicaragua alone would be requested.[55] The agreement with Nicaragua was signed in April 1954 (the first Central American nation to do so), and the first shipment of arms was expected to arrive the next month.[56]

The Only Possible Political Alignment

In June 1954, John Ohmans wrote to two of his State Department colleagues to counter criticisms of U.S. policy in Central America leveled by Nicaragua. The United States, according to Nicaragua, was too timid, too afraid of criticism, not frank enough, and did "not make best use of our Latin American friends." Finally, the list concluded, "We still think too much in terms of democracies vs. dictatorships, when the only possible political alignment today is Anti-Communism vs. Communism."[57] That conclusion must have been terribly surprising to U.S. policymakers. Since at least the late 1940s, the former antidictatorial stance of the State Department had been slowly eroded until by the 1950s a dictator such as Somoza was seen as a successful statesman, a useful friend for the United States, and a solid opponent of communist intrigue in Central America. By 1954, the political makeup of Latin American governments was of little concern to U.S. officials. Indeed, a certain amount of cynicism about the distinctions between dictatorship and democracy had permeated U.S. policy. In late 1954, Ohmans, once again writing to department co-workers, suggested the awarding of the Legion of Merit medal to Somoza. His rationale was that Nicaragua had been a good ally. Of course, opponents of Somoza would say that the "State Department is favoring the militarist dictator governments." Trujillo would want a medal; so might Perón. Ohmans suggested offering the medal to the leader of "one of the so-called liberal governments" in Latin America—Victor Paz Estenssoro of Bolivia, perhaps, or someone from Chile or Uruguay.[58] Ohmans' assumption seemed to be that one "liberal" cancelled out one "dictator" in political gamesmanship.

Relations between the United States and the dictatorship of Anastasio Somoza during the post-World War II decade were hardly consistent, and not always clear. From disparaging the dictator as a brutal despot, inimicable to U.S. ideals of democracy and freedom, U.S. officials had, by 1954, come to the point of bestowing high honors on their friend and ally. More important than medals, economic and military aid had flowed into Nicaragua after the late 1940s, bolstering Somoza's regime.

The decision to support Somoza was not arrived at easily. A gradual process led U.S. policymakers to the conclusion that the defense of the Free World might sometimes require dictatorial methods. Despite Nicaragua's criticisms, the United States by 1954 had for several years accepted the premise that the battle upon which hinged their dreams of a politically interdependent world was not between "democracies" and "dictatorships," but between "anti-communists" and "communists."

Notes

1.   For a summary of U.S.–Latin American relations from the late 1920s through World War II, see Green, *Containment of Latin America*.

2.   DRAR, "Ambassador Braden's Proposed Policy Respecting Dictatorships and Disreputable Governments in the Other American Republics," Oct. 1945, RG 59, Records of Deputy for I-A Affairs, Box 2, Dictatorships and Disreputable Governments file, NA.

3.   Hussey to Butler, 23 Aug. 1946, RG 59, Records of OARA, Box 16, NA.

4.   Ray to Barber and Miller, 30 Sept. 1949, RG 59, 710.11/9–3049, NA; "Briefing Book," 1951, Truman Papers, PSF, SF, Box 177, Foreign Ministers of American Republics–Meetings file, HSTL.

5.   Untitled problem paper, 29 Aug. 1949, RG 59, Miller Files, Box 10, NA; "The Caribbean Republics," 24 Aug. 1954, *FRUS, 1952–1954*, 4:380, 383.

6.   Report, 4 Dec. 1952, RG 59, 720.00/12–452, NA.

7.   "Regional Conference of United States Chiefs of Mission, Rio de Janiero, Brazil, March 6–9, 1950," 86–99, RG 59, Miller Files, Box 5, NA. For a good background to this document, see Roger Trask, "George Kennan's Report on Latin America (1950)," *Diplomatic History* 2 (1978):307–11.

8.   "The Caribbean Republics," 24 Aug. 1954, *FRUS, 1952–1954*, 4:397.

9.   See Richard Millett, *Guardians of the Dynasty* (Maryknoll, NY, 1977); William Kamman, *Search for Stability: United States Diplomacy Toward Nicaragua, 1925–1933* (Notre Dame, IN, 1968); Bernard Diederich, *Somoza and the Legacy of U.S. Involvement in Central America* (New York, 1981); Eduardo Crawley, *Dictators Never Die: A Portrait of Nicaragua and the Somoza Dynasty* (New York, 1979), 49–94; and Karl Bermann, *Under the Big Stick: Nicaragua and the United States Since 1848* (Boston, 1986), Chs. 10 and 11. Knut Walter, *The Regime of Anastasio Somoza, 1936–1956* (Chapel Hill, NC, 1993), presents a fairly positive appraisal of Somoza's rule arguing that, "The Somoza regime provided those things that the country's business and agricultural interests demanded: peace, social order, adequate government support and stimulus for economic expansion, and all of this at the lowest cost possible" (245).

10.   Bermann, *Under the Big Stick*, 231–234; Crawley, *Dictators Never Die*, 98–100.

11.   Cochran to Finley, 23 Feb. 1945, RG 59, 817.00/2–645, NA.

12.   Warren to DS, 20 June 1945, RG 59, 817.001 Somoza, Anastacio/6–2045, NA.

13.   Cochran to Rockefeller, 25 July 1945, RG 59, 817.00/7–2545, NA.

14.   Warren to DS, 25, 26 Sept., 1945, RG 59, 817.00/9–2545, /9–2645, NA.

15.   Cochran to Braden, 6 Nov. 1945, RG 59, 817.001 Somoza, Anastacio/11–645; Warren to DS, 22 Oct. 1945; Byrnes to Warren, 13 Mar. 1946; Cochran to Warren, 10 Apr. 1946; Briggs to Braden, 10 Apr. 1946, RG 59, 817.00/10–2245, /2 –2146, /4–346, /4–1046, NA.

16.   Warren to DS, 9 Feb. 1946, RG 59, 817.50/2–946; Cochran to Briggs and Braden, 21 Mar. 1946, RG 59, 817.51/3–2146; Braden to Clayton, 22 July 1946, RG 59, 811.516 Export-Import Bank/7–2246 (Secret File), NA.

17. Warren to DS, 11 Feb. 1946, RG 59, 817.00/2−1146, NA.

18. Warren to DS, 15 Feb. 1946, RG 59, 817.00/2−1546; Warren to DS, 15 Mar. 1946, RG 59, 817.00B/3−1546, NA.

19. Warren to DS, 10 July 1946, RG 59, 817.001 Somoza, Anastacio/7−1046, NA.

20. Crawley, *Dictators Never Die*, 101−108.

21. Warren to DS, 27 Nov., 5 Dec. 1946; Newbegin to Briggs and Braden, 29 Jan. 1947, RG 59, 817.00/11−2746, /12−546, /1−2247, NA.

22. Warren to DS, 3 Feb. 1947; Reid to Newbegin, et al, 19 Feb. 1947, RG 59, 817.00/2−347, FW817.00/2−547; Acheson to Truman, 3 Apr. 1947, RG 59, 817.001 Argüello, Leonardo/4−347, NA.

23. Reid to Newbegin, et al., 25 Mar. 1947, RG 59, FW817.00/3−647, NA.

24. Memo of phone conversation, Braden to Bernbaum, 26 May 1947; Bernbaum to DS, 26 May 1947; Marshall to American Embassy in Managua, 26 May 1947, RG 59, 817.00/5−2647, NA.

25. Bernbaum to DS, 27 May 1947; Briggs to Marshall, 27 May 1947, RG 59, 817.00/5−2747, NA.

26. Reid to Wise, et al., 14 Aug. 1947; Bernbaum to DS, 15 Aug. 1947, RG 59, 817.00/8−1447, /8−1547, NA.

27. Lovett to Managua, 21 Aug. 1947; Memcon, Dana Munro and Sandy M. Pringle, 5 Oct. 1947; Reid to Woodward, 21 Oct. 1947, RG 59, 817.01/8−2147, /10−547, NA.

28. Bernbaum to DS, 9 Oct. 1947, RG 59, 817.01/10−947, NA; Leonard, *United States and Central America*, 148; Robert Pastor, *Condemned to Repetition: The United States and Nicaragua* (Princeton, 1987), 29.

29. Bernbaum to DS, 22 May 1948, RG 59, 817.00/5−2248, NA.

30. Shaw to DS, 20 Oct. 1948, 2 Apr. 1949, RG 59, 817.00/10−2048, /4−249, NA.

31. Shaw to DS, 5, 18 May 1949, RG 59, 817.00/5−549, /5−1849, NA.

32. Reid to Wise and Reveley, 14 Oct. 1949, RG 59, Records of OMAA, Costa Rica and Nicaragua, Box 1, Nicaragua: The Pay Off file, NA.

33. LaFeber, *Inevitable Revolutions*, 98−106.

34. Waynick to DS, 18 Feb., 24 April 1950, RG 59, 717.00/2−1850, /4−2450, NA.

35. Memcon, 19 May 1950; Waynick to DS, 18 Feb. 1950; Acheson to Waynick, 11 Mar. 1950, RG 59, 717.00/5−1950, /2−1850; Reid to Bennett, et al., 23 Feb. 1950, RG 59, 717.11/2−2350, NA.

36. Waynick to DS, 18 Jan., 31 Mar. 1950, RG 59, 717.00/1−1850, /3−3150, NA.

37. Waynick to DS, 19 May 1950; Waynick to Reid, 30 Jan. 1951, RG 59, 717.00/5−1950, /1−3051, NA. For an interesting study of the Somoza−Figueres

feud, see Charles D. Ameringer, *The Democratic Left in Exile: The Anti-dictatorial Struggle in the Caribbean, 1945–1959* (Coral Gables, FL, 1974).

38.   Waynick to DS, 13 Feb. 1951, RG 59, 717.00/2–1351, NA.

39.   Reid to various department officials, 9 May 1951, RG 59, Records of OMAA, Subject File, Box 6, Nicaragua–1950–General, NA.

40.   Taylor to DS, 16 May 1951; Waynick to DS, 19 June 1951, RG 59, 717.58/5–1651, /6–1951, NA.

41.   "Nicaragua: Policy Statement," 1951, RG 59, Records of OMAA, Costa Rica and Nicaragua, Box 3, Nicaragua 1955 [?] Policy Statement file, NA.

42.   Miller to Whelan, 31 July 1951, RG 59, Miller Files, Box 8, NA.

43.   Reid to Nufer and Siracusa, 3 Jan. 1952, RG 59, 717.00/1–352, NA.

44.   Acheson to Truman, 1 May 1952, RG 59, 717.11/5–152, NA.

45.   Ohmans to Welch, 16 June 1952; "Nicaragua," 1953, RG 59, Records of OMAA, Costa Rica and Nicaragua, Box 2, Nicaragua 1952: General Somoza file; Box 1, Nicaragua, 1953 General Information file, NA.

46.   Ohmans to Welch, 13 Mar. 1953; Welch to Ohmans, 16 Mar. 1953, RG 59, Records of OMAA, Costa Rica and Nicaragua, Box 2, Nicaragua 1952: General Somoza file, NA.

47.   "Second Meeting of Discussion Group on Political Unrest in Latin America," 18 Nov. 1952, Vol. XLV, Records of Groups, CFR Archives.

48.   Brewster to DS, 9 Sept. 1951, RG 59, 817.06/9–951; Memcon, 30 Jan. 1952, RG 59, 717.00/1–3052, NA.

49.   Statement of Whelan contained in Welch to DS, 3 Sept. 1952; Mann to Whelan, 20 Oct. 1952, RG 59, 717.00/9–352, /10–2052; Fisher to Col. Turner, 4 Jan. 1954, RG 59, Records of OMAA, El Salvador and Guatemala, Box 2, Guatemala 1954, Memos ID file, NA.

50.   Topping to DS, 6 Nov. 1951, RG 59, 817.00–TA/11–651, NA.

51.   Chattey to DS, 31 May, 18 Aug. 1952, RG 59, 817.00–TA/5–3152, /8–1852, NA.

52.   Miller to Wythe, 3 Oct. 1951, RG 59, Records of Deputy for I–A Affairs, Box 4, Nicaragua file; Reid to Nufer and Siracusa, 3 Jan. 1952, RG 59, 717.00/1–352, NA.

53.   Black to Steelman, 8 Aug. 1951, Truman Papers, OF, 212–A, Box 802, Foreign Debts–Foreign Loans (1951–1953) file, HSTL; Second Meeting, "Study Group on Political Implications of Economic Development, 1953," 7 Apr. 1952, Records of Groups, Vol. XLIII, CFR Archives.

54.   For both the Air Force and Army missions, see RG 59, 717.58 file for the years 1952–1953. See especially, Welch to DS, 2 June 1952; Acheson to Welch, 15 July 1952 for the Air Force Mission; for the Army Mission, see Welch to DS, 22 June 1953, RG 59, 717.58/6–252, /6–2253, NA.

55.   Memcon, 5 May 1953, RG 59, 717.5/5–553; Woodward to Dulles, 16 July 1953, RG 59, FW 717.5–MSP/7–2353, NA.

56.   Welch to DS, 23 Apr. 1954; Dulles to Managua, 21 May 1954, RG 59, 717.5–MSP/4–2354, /5–2154, NA.

57.   Ohmans to Leddy and Burrows, 4 June 1954, RG 59, Records of OMAA, Costa Rica and Nicaragua, Box 3, 1954—Relations with U.S. file, NA.

58.   Ohmans to Neal and Newbegin, 17 Nov. 1954, RG 59, Records of OMAA, Costa Rica and Nicaragua, Box 2, Nicaragua, 1954: Chronological–Interdepartmental Memos file, NA.

6

The Danger Zone

In terms of U.S. efforts at establishing the bases for interdependence with the republics of Central America following World War II, Guatemala was a constant sorespot. In Guatemala, U.S. policymakers saw manifestations of their worst fears: an unstable and chaotic political system; economic nationalism, with a decided anti-American tinge; and, especially during the early 1950s, a communist presence that threatened to slowly engulf the entire nation. In this chapter, therefore, it is appropriate to focus on the U.S.–Guatemalan relationship during the years 1944–1954, for in their efforts to "reorient" Guatemala toward the interdependent world system they sought to build, U.S. policymakers came face to face with all of the inherent contradictions of that system. With the U.S.-directed counterrevolution of 1954 and its relations with the post-revolutionary regime in Guatemala, we may witness the climactic and ultimate failure of interdependence.

In recent years, a number of excellent studies have examined U.S.-Guatemalan relations after World War II, particularly focusing on the U.S. role in the 1954 overthrow of the Arbenz government.[1] The purpose of this chapter, therefore, is not to retill adequately plowed historical soil. Instead, we will analyze U.S. perceptions of Guatemala, both before the events of 1954—when Guatemala was increasingly viewed as a hemispheric troublemaker and as a monkeywrench in the interdependent system—and after—when the United States attempted to "remake" Guatemala into a member of the international interdependent order.

A Danger Zone

In Guatemala, Jorge Ubico had ruled the nation since taking power in 1931. His regime was harsh and dictatorial but generally found U.S. support.[2] In 1944, however, a broadly-based coalition rose in revolt against Ubico's reign of terror and the dictator fled the country. A revolutionary junta ruled for a short while, until free elections were held in December. The winner was Dr. Juan José Arévalo Bermejo. The Arévalo administration, guided by what the new president referred to as "spiritual socialism," soon went to work. First, a new constitution was promulgated in 1945, expanding suffrage and enacting other political reforms. Health and education—major problems in the underdeveloped nation—were also addressed, with the building of sewer and water projects, the establishment of medical clinics, and more expenditures for education. The two most important reforms, however, were the Social Security Law, passed in 1946, and the 1947 Labor Code.[3]

Arévalo's successor, after 1950 elections, was Colonel Jacobo Arbenz Guzmán. His greatest contribution to the revolution in Guatemalan politics and society was the 1952 Agrarian Reform Law. This law provided for the expropriation (with compensation) of unused lands from large estates—both foreign- and domestic-owned. In the first year-and-a-half of its operation, the law distributed nearly one-and-a-half million acres to over 100,000 landless families.[4]

On the surface, developments in Guatemala may have seemed innocent enough. Indeed, perhaps this was one of the examples the United States often waxed eloquently about—a backward nation, throwing off the shackles of dictatorship and underdevelopment, struggling to build a strong economy and democracy. Yet, this was not what U.S. officials saw. In August 1951 Assistant Secretary Miller was recommending that as far as the anticommunist propaganda "Campaign of Truth" being waged by the United States in Latin America was concerned, Guatemala should be considered a "'danger zone.'"[5]

A problem paper prepared by Miller a year earlier explained that post-1944 Guatemala was an example of the worst problems facing the U.S. in Latin America:

> An excessive nationalism. . .a proclivity on the part of a weak President and others in the government for fuzzy economic and political philosophies and an upsurge of the influence of international

communism of the Latin American variety, which has taken full advantage of the first two factors, have combined to create this situation.[6]

Nationalism, communism, and a shaky political and economic system—in Guatemala, the three most perplexing problems facing U.S. policymakers existed side-by-side-by-side.

The most obvious linking of these problems in Guatemala was that between nationalism and communism. As a 1953 State Department memorandum explained, "While Guatemalan hostility toward and mistrust of United States interests derives largely from intense nationalism, this feeling has been deepened and aggravated by the communists." A 1952 CIA report agreed, noting that communists' success sprung from their ability to "identify themselves with the nationalist and social aspirations of the Revolution of 1944."[7]

A 1954 analysis detailed the spread of communist influence in the Guatemalan government. Moving from a solid base in the labor unions, communists and their sympathizers were present in those government departments concerned with agrarian reform, education, social security, and the media. Communists were influential in congress and the judiciary. And, although no known communists were reported in the Arbenz cabinet, another State Department study claimed that eleven cabinet members and other trusted Arbenz advisors were at least sympathetic to the "leftist" position.[8]

This unholy alliance between communism and nationalism was compounded by the fact that Guatemala's inherently unstable and backward political system seemed to provide little in the way of alternatives to the leftist pathway the nation was embarking upon. As Miller explained in his 1950 memorandum, Guatemala had a "turbulent and unstable" political history. Rule through "ruthless repression" had been the norm. Guatemalan society, "inherited from the Spaniards, has for centuries been feudal, with the white population regarding the Indians, who comprise two-thirds of the total population, as vastly inferior beings and treating them accordingly." Gross disparities in the distribution of wealth had left the legacy of a "low standard of living for the masses." Foreign interests had been able to secure "large concessions and special privileges." The overthrow of Ubico had ushered in what promised to be a new day. A popular government had been established "aimed at improving the standard of living of the masses, protecting them from the abuses of the old feudal system, and achieving freedom and democracy for the Guatemalan people." "This program," Miller stated, "was at its outset commendable." Unfortunately, the elimination of the old power bases from Guatemalan society and politics opened the door for many things Miller found far less than "commendable": an extreme nationalism and communist penetration.[9]

All of this went along with general U.S. thinking about the political changes taking place in Latin America. The overthrow of dictators and the breaking down of "feudal" structures did, in many ways, seem to presage a new democratic age in the region. Yet, U.S. officials viewed the situation with no little trepidation. The removal of the old sources of power in those nations obviously meant the rise of new sources—labor, the middle class, students, and intellectuals, for example. The problem with that scenario was that those were the exact elements in Latin American society most vulnerable to the sirens' song of nationalism and communism. In Guatemala, for example, the greatest success for communist subversives had been in penetrating and ultimately controlling the resurgent labor movement. In looking about for forces to control this upsurge in communist activity, U.S. policymakers were well aware that the best hopes—aside from the old, discredited sources of power such as the church, the military, and the large landowners—were the middle class, professional, intellectual urban elements who had also supported the 1944 revolution. The rub there, as reported in a 1954 State Department intelligence summary, was that although "the urban elements. . .are strongly anti-Communist, . . .they are also strongly nationalistic." As a 1953 State Department report to President Eisenhower bluntly warned, "The situation in Guatemala is indicative of underlying potentialities which might emerge in other Latin American countries if the present governing and propertied elements should lose their hold on government."[10]

What this all meant was that the Guatemalan revolution of 1944, "commendable" as it might have been in the beginning, was starting to spin out of control. The new elements in control in that country were far too nationalistic or communistic (and sometimes both) for there to exist a basis for amicable relations with the United States. Miller tried to make this clear in his 1950 memorandum, stating that the United States had "looked with favor upon its [Guatemala's] attempts to achieve a form of democratic government and to introduce needed social reforms." Nationalism and communism, however, were clouding the issues. The United States did not "oppose progressive social reforms as such," but it did "counsel caution and moderation." Guatemala's "nationalistic policies are not only contrary to United States interests but to the best interests of the Guatemalan Government and the Guatemalan people as well." He hoped that "nationalistic jingoism should be not be allowed to confuse the issue to the detriment of United States–Guatemalan relations." Assistant Secretary Cabot focused in on the communist angle, arguing, just as Miller had, that the United States had "no quarrel" with "any regime's purpose of social reform, insofar as it is sincere." In Guatemala, however, sincerity played no role in the government's policies. It was "openly playing the Communist game," and "despite its hypocritical appeals on behalf of the underprivileged, Communism does not give a snap of the fingers for the welfare of the masses. It will liquidate them or send them to slave labor camps by the millions to advance its tyrannical power."[11] Whatever "game" was being played—the nationalist, the communist, or some sort of ungodly mix—it did not bode well for U.S. interests.

Specifically, the situation in Guatemala was perceived as posing very direct threats to U.S. economic and political/military aims in that nation and in the Central American region as a whole. Guatemalan economic policies were completely unrealistic to U.S. officials. As Second Secretary Douglass K. Ballentine reported in 1951, "the Arbenz administration aspires toward extensive industrialization. . . .In Guatemala, as in other parts of Latin America, economic nationalism has made a fetish of industrialization." And, as another study claimed, in terms of the Guatemalan government's economic program, the "two major deficiencies. . .are the omission of private investment and the lack of plans for the development of natural resources." It obviously opposed private (especially foreign) investment, and, "With respect to natural resources, nationalism outweighs common sense. The Government's petroleum policy, for example, is keeping any oil Guatemala may have in the ground, where it can make no contribution to the improvement of the country." Or, the report might also have noted, to U.S. petroleum interests. (A 1947 Petroleum Law limited the development of mineral resources in Guatemala to Guatemalan nationals.) More threatening was the Guatemalan attitude toward U.S. investments and trading interests already in place. As a State Department memorandum of March 1954 noted, "American investments in Guatemala are valued in excess of $100 million. . . .The future of these American investments under the present Administration in Guatemala is extremely dark and the task of defending them extremely difficult." On top of that, the memorandum asked the reader to consider the fact that in 1953, the United States had imported over $63 million worth of goods from, and exported nearly $44.5 million in products to, Guatemala. "This export market," it warned, "will be seriously jeopardized by the accession of a Communist regime to power."[12]

As another State Department study pointed out, however, "Aside from its adverse effects on United States commercial interests, communist penetration is harmful to United States prestige in the area and affects adversely the presentation of a common hemispheric front. The situation in Guatemala is particularly important because it shows clearly that communist penetration can be successful in this hemisphere." A 1954 memorandum was even more specific:

> It has been asserted that Moscow cannot establish a satellite state save where the weight of the Red Army can be brought to bear directly or indirectly. Establishment of a satellite state in this hemisphere, and particularly so close to the United States, would enable Russia to claim throughout the world that the power of Communism lies in its appeal to men's minds and not in fear or force.[13]

Just as victory against the communist threat rested on the solid basis of interdependence, so too did defeat; the loss of one member of the Free World, even one so apparently insignificant, could have shattering effects. Assistant Secretary Cabot summed up the situation while recalling a recent conversation with Arbenz: "I did my best to convince him that he must choose which of two courses he was going to follow—that of cooperation with communism or that of cooperation with the United States."[14]

Guatemala was indeed a "danger zone." U.S. policymakers saw themselves as being whipsawed by not two, but three potentially destructive forces in that nation. The first was nationalism. Not only did this threaten U.S. investments and trade, but it was also being used by an even more frightening force in Guatemalan politics, the communists. Adopting their "typical" approach of working through nationalist revolutionary "fronts," the communists were slowly penetrating Guatemalan labor unions and the government. And who or what could stop them? The "traditional order," explained a 1954 NIE, "was shattered by the Revolution of 1944."[15] The new forces—labor, the middle class, intellectuals, and students—could hardly be counted on to stem the communist tide. All of this revolved around the third major problem—the inherently unstable and backward political Guatemalan political system. Certainly, it had been "commend-able" to attempt to bring democracy and economic development to Guatemala, but the revolution of 1944 had released uncontrollable forces that threatened to seriously impede, or even destroy, Guatemala's role in the interdependent world system. For U.S. policymakers, the problem now was to convince Guatemala that "cooperation with the United States" was in everyone's best interests.

A Policy of Judicious Discrimination

As relations with Guatemala deteriorated during the late 1940s and early 1950s, U.S. officials began to formulate policies designed to bring that nation back into the interdependent fold. First, economic policies were designed to punish Guatemala and demonstrate that working with the United States, instead of against it, would be profitable for everyone. Second, the United States made every effort possible to gain the favor of the Guatemalan military in the hope that it might serve as an anti-revolutionary force. And finally, political and diplomatic actions were taken to isolate Guatemala from the rest of the hemisphere. When none of these brought appreciable success, the United States relied on covert unilateral intervention to bring down the Arbenz government.

In attacking Guatemala at the economic level, the United States follow-ed what was referred to in a 1953 memorandum as "a policy of judicious discrimination": "We have withheld loan assistance, export priority assistance and greatly limited our technical cooperation." The purpose, explained Albert Nufer in 1951 (then stationed in Washington awaiting his next ambassadorial appointment), was that the United States "considered that withholding financial assistance. . .might have a persuasive effect on the Government and induce it to amend its policies." Following this line of thinking, the United States refused to assist Guatemala in obtaining a U.S. passenger service permit for Aviateca (the Guatemalan airline) or in building the Guatemalan section of the Inter-American Highway.[16]

By 1951, the lines had hardened even further. Albert Nufer, comment-ing on a Guatemalan request for an Exim Bank loan, suggested turning it down, but in such a way as to get maximum concessions. He did not believe that the U.S. should "flatly refuse" the request. Instead, he suggested that the Guatemalans be told that it would be "given every consideration and then stall them along indefinitely on technical grounds." His hope was that "eventually they will begin to understand that if action on their request is to be forthcoming it will be necessary first for them to correct certain of their past policies, particularly as they affect the U.S."[17] From 1948 through 1954, Guatemala received no Exim Bank—or IBRD—loans. In contrast, Nicaragua was granted $600,000 in Exim Bank funds and $9.2 million in IBRD loans, and El Salvador received $23.6 million from IBRD.[18]

Guatemala also faced "judicious discrimination" in terms of technical assistance funds. Here, the United States used the tactic of extending Point Four assistance without signing a formal agreement with the Guatemalan government. This assistance was principally in the form of an agricultural mission, a special mission to increase rubber production, and a health and sanitation mission. Secretary Acheson explained this approach: "On the one hand it did not wish to extend to Guatemala the full measure of cooperation that it was offering to more friendly nations; and, on the other hand, the existing state of affairs in Guatemala was recognized as being fluid and the Department did not deem it wise to terminate long-range programs which were doing good work (one of them on a commodity of strategic value to the United States) and which might be utilized to good purpose in its efforts to influence developments in Guatemala." This policy had been in effect for a year-and-a-half, however, and Acheson was beginning to have second thoughts. He informed the U.S. embassy in Guatemala that he was "increasingly doubtful that continuation our Tech Asst Progs in Guat served our best interest." While no decision had been made to terminate the program, it was the Department's belief that "termination Agric Mission will adversely affect economy thus increasing pressure on GOVT to modify present extremist, pro-commie course."[19]

No action was taken in terminating the programs, and as a 1953 report stated, the U.S. continued to keep a "toehold" in Guatemala through its technical assistance aid. The United States, however, would continue to snub Guatemalan proposals for a formal Point Four agreement. From 1952 through 1954, U.S. technical assistance remained constant at about $200,000 a year. During the same period, Costa Rica received $2.9 million; El Salvador, $1.8 million; Honduras, $2.4 million; and Nicaragua $1.7 million.[20]

The use of military assistance to achieve U.S. aims in Guatemala was also a tricky business. Most U.S. officials were of the opinion that the Guatemalan armed forces provided a possible source of anticommunist power in that nation. "The army," claimed a 1954 State Department intelligence report, "is the only organized element capable of rapidly and decisively altering the political situation." An earlier assessment by the CIA came to the same conclusion: the army "has shown some concern over the growth of Communist influence," and was "probably prepared to prevent a Communist accession to power."[21]

The problem, however, was that the Guatemalan armed forces did not seem predisposed to take action against Arbenz. As a 1953 State Department report rather reluctantly admitted, the army was "still loyal to Arbenz. . . . The Army considers itself to be apolitical but dedicated to the preservation of the Revolution of 1944." It did not appear to be "actively opposed to or even aware of the Communist infiltration of the Government." Yet, since it remained "free from any appreciable Communist taint itself, and since it is the only organization in the country which could by its own decision immediately unseat Arbenz or force him to reverse his policies, it remains a key factor in the situation." But how to get the key to work? The 1954 intelligence report judged that only if the armed forces "become convinced that their personal security and well-being are threatened by Communist domination of the government, or unless the policies of the government result in serious social disorders and economic deterioration" could they be expected to act against Arbenz.[22]

To aid in this, U.S. policymakers devised plans involving military assistance. The first plan was basically passive—simply keep the U.S. air force and army missions operating in Guatemala to maintain friendly links with the Guatemalan military. When, in 1951, it was proposed that Guatemala be eliminated from participation in the Inter-American Defense Board, Thomas Mann protested that such action might result in the "voluntary or involuntary withdrawal of our military missions in Guatemala which is also undesirable at this time." Barring Guatemala would "be hitting at the Guatemalan Army rather than at the communists." That would be foolish, since that body "represents our best hope of progress being made in Guatemala concerning communism and I do not think that we should take any action which would intend to drive the Army into the hands of Guatemalan nationalists and extremists."[23]

Another approach to the military situation in Guatemala, explained a 1953 State Department report, was the plan for "the military isolation of Guatemala through bilateral agreements with her neighbors under the Military Assistance Program." This was basically accomplished through the 1953–1954 negotiations that resulted in bilateral agreements being signed with Nicaragua, Honduras, and El Salvador.

In terms of economic and military aid, however, U.S. policy was basically one of inactivity. Economic aid was not taken away; it was simply denied or left at low levels. Military missions were not cancelled; on the other hand, Guatemalan military officials were shown in no uncertain terms that as long as the United States believed a communist threat to exist in their country no further aid would be forthcoming (unlike the case with the neighboring countries of El Salvador, Nicaragua, and Honduras). On one level, however, U.S. officials acted with great force and vigor: diplomatically isolating Guatemala from the rest of the Western Hemisphere. The climax of this effort was the Tenth Inter-American Conference held at Caracas in March 1954.[24]

A number of issues would be discussed at Caracas, but for the United States the primary topic was communism in the Western Hemisphere, especially in Guatemala. A State Department memorandum prepared the month before the meeting was to convene explained that, "The minimum United States objective at Caracas with respect to the Communist item is to achieve adoption of a resolution which will lay ground work for subsequent positive action against Guatemala by the Organization of American States. Our maximum objection would be the adoption, should conditions permit, of effective multilateral measures against Guatemala at Caracas."[25]

U.S. officials were of the opinion, however, that it would not be an easy task to achieve even their minimum objectives. Many of the problems with Latin America that they had noted since the end of the war—lack of understanding of U.S. aims, jealousy and/or fear of U.S. power, the shocking lack of concern over the communist threat—would, they believed, come home to roost at Caracas. A report by the OCB in March 1954 provided an overview of these assumptions.[26] At Caracas, the United States would confront "uncooperative attitudes among the Latin Americans on the main agenda items. Thus the prevalent disposition of the Latin Americans is not to face the issue of Communist intervention in the Hemisphere as manifested in Guatemala." The reason for this was "a failure by the respective Latin American states to feel an adequate sense of their own responsibility for the defense of the Hemisphere and of the free world to which it belongs. They represent a failure adequately to identify themselves and their own interest with the common cause of the free world, to connect the two in their own minds."

The solutions to these problems were relatively simple, and primarily involved a public relations campaign aimed at reorienting the Latin

American nations to their shared responsibilities. Public statements by high U.S. officials should accent "attention" to Latin America and an "appreciation of the importance of their contributions. . . .The indis-severable connection between Hemisphere defense and general free-world defense should be emphasized in public statements and magazine articles." Finally, the "concept of common responsibility for the common defense in all its aspects, which has lost some of its vividness since 1947, should be emphasized in public expression, especially by Latin Americans, as explicitly and frequently as possible."

Those suggestions were taken to heart by U.S. policymakers, who both during and immediately after the conference sought to identify the Guatemalan threat with the larger problem of communist penentration into the hemisphere. Further, this penetration was to be portrayed as a serious threat to *all* nations, not just the United States. The Latin Americans were to be convinced that in order to meet this situation, it would require the cooperation and effort of each member of the Western Hemisphere family. This is exactly what Secretary Dulles attempted to do in a March 4 speech to a plenary session at Caracas. He began by stating that "Soviet Communism stands for the liquidation of the values upon which our fraternal association is based." Then, without mentioning Guatemala by name, he solemnly warned the audience that "the Americas are not immune from that threat of Soviet Communism." Communists, the secretary claimed, were active in each nation in the hemisphere. Communism was the new threat of a new age: "In the past century battleships were the symbol of aggression against the hemisphere. Today the apparatus of an alien political party endangers the independence and solidarity of the Americas." In passing reference to the Monroe Doctrine (also not mentioned by name), he reminded his listeners that "we have all stood resolutely for the integrity of this hemisphere. . . .we stood resolutely against any enlargement here of the colonial domain of the European powers." The result—"a great danger has thus receded." It was time, Dulles exclaimed, "to make it clear with finality that we see that alien despotism is hostile to our ideals, that we unitedly deny it the right to prey upon our hemisphere and that if it does not heed our warnings and keep away we shall deal with it as a situation that might endanger the peace of America."[27]

In the more private confines of an NSC meeting following his return from Caracas, Dulles was a bit more open. In his mind, what he had sought to do at the conference was to use the idea of the Monroe Doctrine as the "background for the anti-Communist resolution which it had been his chief objective to see adopted by the Foreign Ministers." The goal was to extend the "Monroe Doctrine to include the concept of outlawing foreign ideologies in the American Republics." Despite his insistence on the hemispheric nature of the threat, Dulles made it clear to his fellow NSC members that such a resolution would mean that "the United States could operate more effectively to meet Communist subversion in the American Republics and at the same time avoid the charge of interference in the affairs of any other sovereign state."[28] A multilateral approach to the communist threat—which Latin Americans were to be convinced was absolutely necessary—obviously had its limitations.

So, too, did the persuasiveness of Dulles' appeal. True enough, a resolution condemning communist intrusion into the Western Hemisphere was approved, but not unanimously or easily. The vote on the resolution was seventeen for, one against (Guatemala—just as U.S. officials had hoped), and two important abstentions from Mexico and Argentina. Dulles, at the NSC meeting, could not hide his disappointment. He "admitted that it had not been easy to secure general acceptance of the anti-Communism resolution." There were a number of factors to explain this. The Latin Americans had their minds on other matters, specifically economic, and showed much "unhappiness and anxiety" with U.S. policy in their region. Others had insisted that the resolution was a thinly disguised effort "to permit American intervention in the internal affairs of the other republics of the hemisphere." It had taken two weeks of "very intensive work and almost daily meetings with the other Foreign Ministers" to get the resolution passed. Dulles was forced to admit that, "Even so, the resolution was certainly not adopted with genuine enthusiasm."[29]

Nor, U.S. officials felt, was the resolution particularly effective in assuaging the situation in Guatemala. A State Department report gloomily concluded that, "The action taken at Caracas with respect to Communism in the Western Hemisphere has not, at least for the present, weakened the Communists in Guatemala."[30] In the long run, this meant that the United States would have to keep at its efforts to convince the Latin Americans of the seriousness of the situation and of their role in settling it. In the short run, what this meant was that the United States would have to handle the Guatemalan problem alone. This was of little concern to U.S. officials; as Dulles had explained, the idea at Caracas had been to clear the path for "effective" unilateral action.

Unilateral action was taken, when the United States unleashed Operation PBSUCCESS.   This operation was the CIA-planned and -directed propaganda and paramilitary campaign carried out against the Guatemalan government.   Enough has been written concerning the planning and carrying out of this covert action; we need not rehash the details here.[31] Suffice it to say that, for the United States, PBSUCCESS was a smashing success.   The Arbenz government fell in late June, and was replaced by a revolutionary junta, eventually dominated by Colonel Carlos Castillo Armas.[32]   The "danger zone" had been nullified.

On the Whole, It's Quite a Challenge

The removal of the Arbenz government, however, was only half of the job.   U.S. officials believed that most of the problems in that nation that had allowed the situation to deteriorate so badly in the first place still remained.   Political instability, nationalism, and communism were still present.   The question now was how to keep a repeat of the 1944–1954 situation from developing again.   Not surprisingly, U.S. policymakers relied on answers that had already been developed elsewhere in Central America: military assistance to help enforce domestic stability and order; economic advice and assistance designed to tie Guatemala more closely to the U.S. economy; and support of dictators and dictatorial policies aimed at controlling the growth of communism.   As Assistant Secretary Holland wrote to his predecessor John Cabot in August 1954, "we still have a lot of problems in Guatemala.   However, they are problems of a constructive kind rather than the defensive ones with which we were wrestling.   We have a wonderful chance to find out about the Communist organization in this Hemisphere; to demonstrate that a Latin American people can aspire to better lives under a free government than under a Communist government; and to guide this new government into paths of democracy rather than of dictatorship.   On the whole, it's quite a challenge."[33]

With the fall of the Arbenz government and the rise of Castillo Armas to power, the United States embarked on a program of heavy and sustained military assistance for the new government.   By October 1954, the State Department was pushing for grant military assistance to Guatemala and the establishment of a bilateral military aid pact such as those signed with Nicaragua and Honduras.   (The pact with El Salvador was still being pursued).   Assistant Secretary Holland recommended to

Dulles that the Department of Defense be pressured to approve Guatemala for such assistance. The aid would "assist the present anti-communist government to remain in office and to prevent a possible re-emergence of communism." The new government "needs the support of the politically influential Guatemalan Army" and U.S. aid would help secure it. The U.S. would also gain the "friendship and cooperation of the Guatemalan Army and orient it toward the U.S. and its policies which is important because the Guatemalan Army not only influences the actions of the present Government but will probably determine the nature and orientation of any successor government."[34]

Dulles was convinced, and two days later wrote to Secretary of Defense Charles Wilson. He informed Wilson that U.S. military equipment had already been sold to Guatemala, and he was now requesting that Guatemala be deemed eligible for grant military assistance. The new government in that nation, Dulles explained, was "cooperating fully with the United States." Money and other aid had been sent, and that was helping the situation, "but they make no direct contribution to winning and maintaining the support of the Guatemalan military establishment, which probably will assert the determining influence in any political crisis in Guatemala." Due to the "special nature of Guatemala's case," Dulles pleaded with Wilson to find Guatemala eligible for grant military assistance immediately.[35] A bilateral military assistance agreement was signed with Guatemala in 1955.

Even before the 1955 military assistance agreement, however, State Department officials continued to press for additional military aid for Guatemala. Frederick Nolting, special assistant for mutual security affairs, wrote to FOA Director Harold Stassen in November 1954, notifying him that the U.S. ambassador in Guatemala had "urgently recommended" the sale of "certain military equipment" to be used in a military demonstration in Guatemala City in December. The demonstration would have the goal of "encouraging anti-communist elements and deterring communist conspiracy in Guatemala." The U.S. sale of the equipment would "emphasize to communist elements in the Central American area the firm intention and the capability of the present Guatemalan Government to resist communist subversion and conspiracy."[36] Such efforts were successful. While prior to 1954 Guatemala had been virtually excluded from U.S. military assistance programs, from 1954 until 1966 Guatemala was the recipient of $9.3 million in direct assistance, together with $756,000 of excess military equipment.[37] The "militarization" of Guatemala was complete. From 1954 on, the military would come to dominate Guatemalan politics, often through campaigns of brutal repression.[38]

Economic assistance was another way in which the United States attempted to put Guatemala back on the interdependent pathway. During the years 1944–1954 Guatemala did not find itself the recipient of much in the way of grants, loans, or technical assistance from the United States. U.S. officials had tried, without much success, to use the withholding of economic aid as a way to convince Guatemala not only to purge itself of the communist taint, but also of the extreme nationalism that threatened to interrupt interdependent economic relations. With the granting of massive amounts of aid following the 1954 revolt, however, the United States finally found the success that had previously eluded it.

Between 1954 and 1957, the United States awarded $46 million in direct emergency economic relief to Guatemala. This was supplemented with tremendous increases in technical assistance and Exim Bank and IBRD loans. Throughout the years 1948–1954, Guatemala had received but $600,000 in technical assistance. In 1955 alone, that nation was granted $6.7 million; that figure rose to $18.2 million the next year and continued (with but few exceptions) at extremely high levels well into the early 1960s. Exim Bank loans, which had been nonexistent during the Arbenz regime, suddenly became available—$500,000 in 1955, to $2.1 million in 1956. IBRD was even more generous: a huge loan of $18.2 million was granted in 1955. In all, between 1955 and 1960, United States loans and grants to Guatemala totaled $82 million; by 1971, the total was nearly $180 million.[39]

The price for such assistance, however, was the abandonment by the Guatemalan government of the most irritating of the nationalistic economic policies followed by the Arbenz regime. As a post-counter-revolution 1954 "Balance Sheet" prepared by the State Department bluntly explained, what Guatemala wanted was military and economic assistance; what the United States wanted was "Acceptance of United States advice in petroleum and agrarian reform legislation." At an August 1954 meeting between Assistant Secretary Holland, U.S. Ambassador to Guatemala John Peurifoy, and other department officials, it was noted that, "Petroleum, timber and mining legislation should be revised. Ambassador Peurifoy said this was high on his priority list, and agreed that interested investors should be encouraged to visit Guatemala. Mr. Holland will examine the petroleum law."[40]

U.S. efforts went far beyond "examination." As Jim Handy explains in his analysis of post-1954 economic developments in Guatemala, "American agencies came to control all major aspects of government and economic policy in Guatemala" and "assumed the operation of such crucial government departments as agriculture, finance and public works and developed policy in many others." As one U.S. economic planner put it, "'The U.S. dictated policies, Castillo Armas obeyed orders well.'" Whether Castillo Armas was merely a puppet or not, he obviously understood the new Guatemalan reality and he "embarked on a policy to impress the business-dominated Eisenhower administration and to promote investment." Through various pro-foreign investment strategies Castillo Armas sought to "impress" as many U.S. officials as he could.[41]

The most troublesome area, however, was that of agrarian reform. The 1952 Agrarian Reform Law had angered U.S. officials and, perhaps, had sealed the fate of the Arbenz regime. They were happy to see that the new Guatemalan government took a very different view of the question. A July 1954 summary of the political situation in Guatemala noted approvingly that, "As a replacement for the Agrarian Reform Law used as a political instrument by the Communists under the Arbenz regime, the Junta on July 26 issued a substantially more conservative transitional 'agrarian statute'. . . ." Looking back on the "new" agrarian reform in Guatemala, a 1957 ICA report lauded its achievements. While land reform under the communist government of Arbenz had "popular support," the report exclaimed that, "The new government's program included something better: ICA contracted for advisers to assist the Guatemalan government in planning a program of rural development which includes area planning, settlement of rural families on government lands, supervised credit, and an agricultural extension service to help settlers develop and use their new farms."[42]

In reality, as Handy explains, what happened was that, "In a remarkably quick time, over 99 per cent of the land affected by the agrarian reform was returned to previous owners, including the United Fruit Company, and many of the institutions established by the reform governments to meet the needs of highland peasants were disbanded or deprived of funds." While nearly 100,000 families had benefited from the 1952 law, most of these were stripped of their lands under the Castillo Armas regime. The Guatemalan ruler promised a new law, but under its conditions less than 16,000 families got land back by 1956. Between 1957 and 1963, only 2,451 families received land. By the mid-1960s "the agrarian program. . .ground to a halt." A further impact of this dispossession was that the national output of food crops began to drop. The corn harvest, for example, was so bad in 1955 that the U.S. had to export 30,000 tons of the grain to Guatemala.[43]

The problem, as Peter Calvert explains, was that the land policies of Castillo Armas—supported by U.S. aid—were "used to drive the peasants back off the land and to restore the old plantation system" based around the production of coffee. This, according to the State Department, was not an unfavorable development. As a September 1954 report observed, "The reconstitution of coffee plantations subdivided under the former agrarian law may help to restore government and private revenues." U.S. economic assistance was also aimed toward this end; most, claims Handy, was "almost exclusively directed to plantations producing crops for export, particularly the new export crops of cattle and cotton." Between 1950 and 1964, the amount of land given over to coffee production climbed by 85 percent, with a resulting 157 percent increase in output. There were also large increases in the production of three other export products: cotton, cattle, and sugarcane. All of this did little for the general Guatemalan population, which "saw their standard of living decline and the new opportunities for economic advancement that had opened for them during the Arbenz presidency closed off, [while] the economic and political power of the privileged landowning elite was strengthened."[44]

The United States also sought to point the new Guatemalan government in a more conservative, and decidedly anticommunist, direction. Its choice—though with some hesitation—for leading Guatemala through this turbulent time was Colonel Castillo Armas. It was not that U.S. policymakers thought that highly of the leader of the counterrevolution. The U.S. embassy in Guatemala complained in August that, "The political situation is tending to worsen because Col. Carlos CASTILLO Armas shows little political sense." Nevertheless, by September, Castillo Armas had secured election as president of Guatemala, after succeeding in pushing the other two members of the junta out. He ruled, according to a State Department analysis, under a "relatively conservative 'political statute' which has replaced the liberal 1945 constitution." The statute allowed Castillo Armas to take all executive and legislative powers, disenfranchised illiterates, and "stipulates that labor, social, and agrarian matters will be the subject of separate laws. . . .All political parties have been suspended." By October, one department official had concluded,

"The Castillo Government, which is struggling to establish a middle-of-the-road regime, is our best (and only) bet at the present time against the return of either leftist or rightist extremism in Guatemala."[45]

In this specific case, however, U.S. officials were willing to let Castillo Armas stray to the right side of the road, if that was what was required to keep communism under control. One of the first actions of the junta, for example, had been to disenfranchise illiterates. A July State Department study specifically noted this action as an indication that "the new regime showed a marked turn from its predecessor." The disenfranchisement law had cut nearly seventy-five percent of the Guatemalan population out of the electoral process. Nevertheless, this was "a move which has long been considered necessary by anti-Communists who saw the Arbenz regime manipulate this vote to install Communist elements."[46]

Castillo Armas took direct action against communism. As Stephen Rabe describes it, "Under the 'Preventive Penal Law Against Communism,' he suspended the writ of habeas corpus. He also returned the man who had been chief of secret police under the Ubico regime to his post." As Handy explains, Castillo Armas "abolished the General Confederation of Guatemalan Workers. . . , and the National Confederation of Peasants of Guatemala. . .and cancelled the legal registration of over 553 unions. He placed impossible restrictions on further union organization. Important sections of the 1947 Labour Code were annulled and by late 1955 union membership had declined from 100,000 in 1954 to 27,000."[47]

U.S. policymakers were, in general, extremely pleased with Castillo Armas's efforts. One example was the change in Guatemala's "Dependability Rating" as a source of strategic materials for the United States. This was a numerical rating based upon the following factors: "Political Orientation of the Government Toward the United States"; "Vulnerability of Raw Materials Production to Sabotage"; "Dependability of Labor"; and "Ability of the Economy to Continue Production in Wartime Conditions." In May 1954, Guatemala's "scores" had been absolutely abysmal—10, 30, 20, and 15 (its "final grade" was, taking the lowest grade, a "10"); hardly passing grades. In July, however, those figures were revised—80, 50, 50, and 80; not great, but passing, with an overall score of 70 (actually, the average is 65; apparently a new "curve" was being used). A September 1954 analysis of Guatemalan politics declared that, "There appears to be little chance of a resurgence of Communist leadership in the near future. All Communist organizations have been dissolved and a drastic anti-Communist decree of broad applicability has been enacted."[48]

Even with these successes, U.S. officials hoped and planned for more action on the anticommunist front. The United States Information Service (USIS) staff in that nation should develop an appropriate propaganda campaign, focusing especially on the "Communist and atrocity angle." Once documents on these topics were prepared, they should be released by the Guatemalan government, not USIS. A project was being developed whereby "Guatemalan anti-Communist speakers" would be "encouraged to circulate through the hemisphere." Communists who continued to serve in the Guatemalan Foreign Service and other government positions should be eliminated; "Ambassador Peurifoy will continue to press for their elimination." Finally, "More priests and ministers should go to Guatemala. Ambassador Peurifoy said that the new government had expressed desire for more American priests in preference to european [sic]." There was also a good indication of what would happen to Americans who questioned the anticommunist crusade in Guatemala. Two people had apparently approached the State Department complaining that the U.S.-owned railroad company in Guatemala was blacklisting "good union men." It was noted that the department would "get an FBI report" on one of the individuals.[49]

All in all, U.S. policymakers were quite satisfied with the new rule in Guatemala, evidenced not only by the flood of economic and military aid given to the Castillo Armas government, but by the words of praise they lavished on the Guatemalan leader. Stephen Rabe writes that U.S. officials believed that Castillo Armas was all that protected Guatemala from "'greater instability, a return of open communism, and a return of a more severe nationalistic, anti-American government.' Vice President Nixon toured Guatemala in early 1955, and in November 1955 President Eisenhower hosted Castillo Armas. Eisenhower was generous with his praise, writing to Castillo Armas that 'I count myself among those who deeply admire your achievements on behalf of the Guatemalan people and your determination to lead them steadily forward in freedom toward more secure peace and greater prosperity.' Eisenhower was shocked by the Guatemalan's assassination in 1957 and sent his son, John, to the funeral."[50]

It was hardly surprising that in praising Castillo Armas's accomplishments, U.S. officials would note his stance against instability, communism, and anti-American nationalism. Those were the problems plaguing the United States in terms of achieving its goals in Central America. The fact that Guatemala had been the site of some of the most threatening manifestations of those problems, but had—with a little help—reversed course and come to its senses, made it the success story of the postwar period for U.S. policy in Central America. By 1955, the Guatemalan military was well-prepared to keep internal order and was satisfactorily oriented toward the United States; nationalistic economic policies had been replaced by policies geared more to securing Guatemala's place in the larger interdependent economic picture; and communism had been routed.

Speaking just a few months before the counterrevolution, Assistant Secretary of State John Cabot had, in stirring language, defended U.S. actions toward Guatemala (and, by extension, all of Latin America):

> When we seek to defend the rights of our citizens under international law in Guatemala or elsewhere, we are often accused of opposition to any form of social progress. Such an argument is obviously absurd, so monstrous in the light of our entire history, that I find it difficult to know where to start refuting it. Am I to recite our Declaration of Independence or our Bill of Rights? Am I to invoke the shades of Jefferson, Lincoln, the two Roosevelts? Am I do [sic] describe the innumerable curbs which by law we have effectively placed on abuses of the power of wealth, or must I point out that our society is far less divided into classes than that of Soviet Russia? Need I remind our Latin friends of the freedom which we helped to win for Cuba and the Philippines and yielded to them spontaneously with our warm-hearted blessing? Is it for nothing that we have in the United States the highest standard of living in the world, that under wise laws the benefits of our material advancement are so widely spread throughout the community? . . .What selfish purpose are we supposed to be serving by the aid we have given millions of the underprivileged through our Point Four work? Over what people, territory or class does the Star Spangled Banner wave as a symbol of oppression or exploitation? No national record could show more clearly our sympathy for the weak, the stricken and oppressed, our desire for the greatest good of the greatest number.[51]

"The greatest good for the greatest number." It was a high-sounding phrase in a speech full of them. But was it merely so much verbiage, patriotic rhetoric as hollow as it was dramatic? Considering what the United States helped to bring about in Guatemala, it would be easy to answer that question in the affirmative. In that nation, U.S. policy ended up doing little for "the weak, the stricken and oppressed." Yet, it would also be misleading. For Cabot, and many other U.S. officials like him, what happened in Guatemala was not a necessary evil; it was simply necessary. In terms of the interdependent world they sought to construct, the "greatest good" was not to be found in nations determining their own political and economic orientations. Instead, for the benefit of the "greatest number," nations had to adhere to what U.S. officials had already defined as acceptable modes of political and economic behavior. Nations such as Guatemala that flaunted those norms threatened more than their own stability, prosperity, and safety. For the United States they represented ominous "danger zones." It would always be "quite a challenge" to keep them under control.

Notes

1.   Immerman, *CIA in Guatemala*; Schlesinger and Kinzer, *Bitter Fruit*; Rabe, *Eisenhower and Latin America*, 42–63; and Cook, *Declassified Eisenhower*, 217–292, all focus on the U.S. role in the 1954 counterrevolution. A new study, Gleijeses, *Shattered Hope*, goes into much more depth in analyzing the relationship between the United States and the revolutionary Guatemalan government after 1944.

2.   Gleijeses, *Shattered Hope*, Ch. 1. For the U.S. role in Ubico's rise to power, see Jim Handy, *Gift of the Devil: A History of Guatemala* (Boston, 1984), 77–102, and Kenneth Grieb, "American Involvement in the Rise of Jorge Ubico," *Caribbean Studies* 10:1 (April 1970):5–21. Grieb has also written the most complete study of Ubico's years in power: *Guatemalan Caudillo: The Regime of Jorge Ubico: Guatemala, 1931–1944* (Athens, 1979).

3.   Handy, *Gift of the Devil*, 104–113; Gleijeses, *Shattered Hope*, 30–49; Peter Calvert, *Guatemala: A Nation in Turmoil* (Boulder, CO, 1985), 73–77.

4.   Handy, *Gift of the Devil*, 123–133; Calvert, *Guatemala*, 77–79; and Gleijeses, *Shattered Hope*, 72–116. José M. Aybar, *The Guatemalan Agrarian Reform of 1952: An Abortive Challenge to United States Dominance and the Prelude to United States Intervention in 1954* (Ann Arbor, MI, 1978), 191–305, is the most detailed study of the agrarian reform and the U.S. response.

5.   Miller to Barrett, 16 Aug. 1951, RG 59, Miller Files, Box 7, NA.

6.   Miller to Webb, 16 May 1950, Papers of Richard C. Patterson, Jr., Box 5, Ambassador to Guatemala, 1948–51: Crisis file, HSTL.

7.   "Guatemala," 13 Mar. 1953, RG 59, Records of OMAA, El Salvador and Guatemala, box 1, Guatemala, 1954: Briefing Materials file, NA; "Present Political Situation in Guatemala and Possible Developments During 1952," 11 Mar. 1952, Truman Papers, PSF, IF, Box 254, Central Intelligence Reports, NIE 53–62 folder, HSTL.

8.   Untitled report, c. 1954, RG 59, Records of OMAA, El Salvador and Guatemala, Box 1, Guatemala, 1954: Briefing Materials file; "Guatemala," 9 Sept. 1953, RG 59, 714.00/9–953, NA.

9.   Miller to Webb, 16 May 1950, Patterson Papers, Box 5, Ambassador to Guatemala, 1948–51: Crisis file, HSTL.

10.   IR–6579, 1954, RG 59, 714.00/4–2254, NA; "Report for the President. Subject: Status of United States Relations with Other Free World Countries as of June 30, 1953," 1 Aug. 1953, Eisenhower Papers, Whitman File, Misc. Series, Box 2, Foreign Policy–Misc. Memoranda folder, DDEL.

11.   Miller to Webb, 16 May 1950, Patterson Papers, Box 5, Ambassador to Guatemala, 1948–51: Crisis file, HSTL; "Excerpts from Speech by Assistant Secretary of State Cabot of October 14, 1953," RG 59, Records of OMAA, El Salvador and Guatemala, Box 2, Guatemala, 1954: General file, NA.

12.   Ballentine to SD, 21 Mar. 1951, RG 59, 814.00/3–2151; "Guatemala," 9 Sept. 1953, RG 59, 714.00/9–953; Confidential Memoradum on Guatemala, 12 Mar. 1954, RG 59, Records of OMAA, El Salvador and Guatemala, Box 1, Guatemala, 1954: Briefing Materials file, NA.

13.   "Guatemala," 13 Mar. 1953, RG 59, Records of OMAA, El Salvador and Guatemala, Box 1, Guatemala, 1954: Briefing Materials file; "Excerpt from Memorandum," 14 May 1954, RG 59, Holland Records, Box 3, NA.

14.   Cabot to Major General R.C. Partridge, 21 May 1953, RG 59, 714.00/3–2053, NA.

15.   "The Caribbean Republics," 24 Aug. 1954, *FRUS, 1952–1954*, 4:384.

16.   "Guatemala," 13 Mar. 1953, RG 59, Records of OMAA, El Salvador and Guatemala, Box 1, Guatemala, 1954: Briefing Materials file; Nufer to Miller, 10 May 1951, RG 59, 814.053/5–1051; "Guatemala," 9 Sept. 1953, RG 59, 714.00/9–953, NA.

17.   Nufer to Miller, 10 May 1951, RG 59, 814.053/5–1051, NA.

18.   ICA, "Economic and Military Programs in MSP Countries," 20 June 1956, Records of Fairless Committee, Box 7, ICA (2) file, DDEL.

19.   Acheson to U.S. Embassy, Guatemala, 31 Dec. 1951, 29 Feb. 1952, RG 59, 814.00–TA/12–3151, /2–2952, NA.

20.   "Guatemala," 9 Sept. 1953, RG 59, 714.00/9–953, NA; "U.S. Economic Assistance Programs Administered by the Agency for International Development and Predecessor Agencies, April 3, 1948–June 30, 1971," 29 Feb. 1972, Huntington Papers, Box 5, AID: U.S. Economic Assistance Programs, 1948–1971 file, HSTL; ICA, "Economic and Military Programs in MSP Countries," 20 June 1956, Records of Fairless Committee, Box 7, ICA (2) file, DDEL.

21.   IR–6579, RG 59, 714.00/4–2254, NA; "Present Political Situation in Guatemala and Possible Developments During 1952," 11 March 1952, Truman Papers, PSF, IF, Box 254, Central Intelligence Reports, NIE 53–62 file, HSTL.

22.   "Guatemala," 9 Sept. 1953, RG 59, 714.00/9–953; IR–6579, 1954, RG 59, 714.00/4–2254, NA.

23.   Mann to Miller, 31 July 1951, RG 59, Records of Deputy for I–A Affairs, Box 3, Inter-American Defense Board file, NA.

24.   Gleijeses, *Shattered Hope*, Ch. 12, has a good discussion of the issues raised at Caracas.

25.   Attached to Burrows to Cabot, 10 Feb. 1954, RG 59, 714.00/2–1054, NA.

26.   OCB, "Recommendations for Dealing with Certain Basic Psychological Problems Confronting the U.S. at Caracas," 17 March 1954, WHO, Papers of NSC, OCB CF, Box 71, OCB 091.4 Latin America (File #1) (2), DDEL.

27.   "Address by The Honorable John Foster Dulles, Secretary of State and Head of the U.S. Delegation, Before a Plenary Session of the Tenth Inter-American Conference, Caracas, Venezuela, March 4, 1954," Dulles Papers, Box 79, Mudd Library.

28.   "Discussion at the 189th Meeting of the National Security Council, Thursday, March 18, 1954," 19 Mar. 1954, Whitman File, NSC Series, Box 5, 189th Meeting of the NSC, March 19, 1954 file, DDEL.

29.   Ibid.

30.   IR–6579, 1954, RG 59, 714.00/4–2254, NA.

31.   See the aforementioned books by Immerman, Schlesinger and Kinzer, Cook, Rabe, and Gleijeses, as well as Cole Blasier, *The Hovering Giant: U.S. Responses to Revolutionary Change in Latin America, 1910–1985* (Rev. ed.) (Pittsburgh, 1985), 151–177. Also see an interesting recent exchange by two scholars taking very different views of the U.S. involvement in the counter-revolution. Frederick Marks, III, "The CIA and Castillo Armas in Guatemala, 1954: New Clues to an Old Puzzle," *Diplomatic History* 14 (1990):67–86, and the rebuttal by Stephen Rabe, "The Clues Didn't Check Out: Commentary on 'The CIA and Castillo Armas,'" in the same issue, pp. 87–95.

32.   Gleijeses, *Shattered Hope*, 351–60.

33.   Holland to Cabot, 1 Aug. 1954, The Diplomatic Papers of John Moors Cabot, Part I: Latin America (microfilm), Reel II, Edward Ginn Library, The Fletcher School of Law and Diplomacy, Tufts University.

34.   Holland to Dulles, 25 Oct. 1954, RG 59, 714.5–MSP/10–2554, NA.

35.   Dulles to Wilson, 27 Oct. 1954, RG 59, 714.56/10–2754, NA.

36.   Nolting to Stassen, 26 Nov. 1954, RG 59, 714.56/11–2654, NA.

37.   Calvert, *Guatemala*, 44.

38.   Calvert, *Guatemala*, 40–45, 104–115; George Black, *Garrison Guatemala* (New York, 1984), passim; Handy, *Gift of the Devil*, 149–183.

39.   Rabe, *Eisenhower and Latin America*, 61–62; ICA, "Economic and Military Programs in MSP Countries," 20 June 1956, Records of Fairless Committee, Box 7, ICA (2) file, DDEL; "U.S. Economic Assistance Programs Administered by the Agency for International Development and Predecessor Agencies, April 3, 1948–June 30, 1971," 29 Feb. 1972, Huntington Papers, Box

5, AID: U.S. Economic Assistance Programs, 1948–1971 file, HSTL; Calvert, *Guatemala*, 141.

40.   Fisher, "Balance Sheet, November 1954," 1 Dec. 1954; "Minutes of Meeting Held August 12, 1954," RG 59, Records of OMAA, El Salvador and Guatemala, Box 2, Guatemala Memoranda–Interdepartmental file; Box 1, Check List file, NA.

41.   Handy, *Gift of the Devil*, 188–89.

42.   "Political Summary: Guatemala," 1954, RG 59, 714.00/8–454, NA; "The Achievements of U.S. Foreign Aid Programs," 16 Jan. 1957, Records of the Fairless Committee, Box 7, International Cooperation Administration (1) file, DDEL.

43.   Handy, *Gift of the Devil*, 187, 213.

44.   Calvert, *Guatemala*, 80; "Guatemala," 2 Sept. 1954, RG 59, 714.00/9–254, NA; Handy, *Gift of the Devil*, 187, 189, 197–200.

45.   "Memorandum for the Record," 24 Aug. 1954; "Guatemala," 2 Sept. 1954, RG 59, 714.00/8–2454, /9–254; Fisher to Holland, et al., 15 Oct. 1954, RG 59, Records of OMAA, El Salvador and Guatemala, Box 2, 1954–Memoranda–Inter-Departmental, NA.

46.   "Political Summary: Guatemala," 1954, RG 59, 714.00/8–454, NA.

47.   Rabe, *Eisenhower and Latin America*, 61; Handy, *Gift of the Devil*, 151, 186–87.

48.   Fisher to Mulliken, 29 July 1954, RG 59, Records of OMAA, El Salvador and Guatemala, Box 2, Guatemala, 1954 Economic file; "Guatemala," 2 Sept. 1954, RG 59, 714.00/9–254, NA.

49.   "Political Summary: Guatemala," 1954, RG 59, 714.00/8–454; "Minutes of Meeting Held August 12, 1954," RG 59, Records of OMAA, El Salvador and Guatemala, Box 1, Check List file, NA.

50.   Rabe, *Eisenhower and Latin America*, 62.

51.   "Excerpts from Speech by Assistant Secretary of State Cabot of October 14, 1953," RG 59, Records of OMAA, El Salvador and Guatemala, Box 2, Guatemala, 1954, General file, NA.

7

A Return to Normalcy

By the end of 1954, U.S. policymakers took pride in their achievements in Central America. Much of this had to do with the positive outcome of the Guatemalan counterrevolution. The fact that not only had the communist threat been blunted but had been almost entirely eradicated reassured officials of the power of the United States and the validity of its interdependent goals. From a hemispheric troublemaker, Guatemala had been reformed into a model citizen of the interdependent free world system.

Despite their tremendous success in Guatemala, U.S. officials were uneasy. After all, what had happened in that nation could conceivably happen anywhere in Central America. The internal instability in Guatemala had been the result of the rapid rise of new classes and groups in that country: the middle and working classes and students and intellectuals, for example. The challenge to the "old order" had undeniably made for a more "democratic" atmosphere; perhaps, though, it was *too* democratic. While U.S. policymakers hailed the development of democratic forces in Latin America, when those forces actually took power, officials of the State Department were often filled with uncertainty or even fear. Would these new forces adequately guarantee, as the old order had, the internal stability (and, hopefully, pro-U.S. orientation) of the underdeveloped and backward Central American nations? Could they withstand the organized force of communist subversives? And weren't these often the same groups that were the most heavily nationalistic and anti-American? The United States had its strategic interests in Central

America to protect, and needed reliable allies. Guatemala, undergoing a "democratic" revolution, had not been able to fulfill U.S. needs.

The economic nationalism displayed by Guatemala was also not an isolated phenomenon. Again, while U.S. officials publicly stated their support for economic development and growth in Latin America, they were often aghast at the methods heralded by their neighbors to the south. Statist economic policies, expropriations, and even nationalizations were viewed as constant threats to the interdependent economic relationship so valued by the United States. For the United States, increasingly supportive of theories of international specialization and comparative advantage, efforts by nations such as Guatemala to unilaterally redefine their place and roles in the world economic structure were unnerving, to say the least. The naive economic thinking that was behind those efforts would result in catastrophe; nations cutting themselves off from the world free market system would hurt not only themselves, but other nations as well. That had certainly been the case in Guatemala, where fuzzyheaded notions about economic independence had led to the stymieing of *real* economic development and undeserved attacks on private U.S. concerns in that nation.

The instability and extreme nationalism of Guatemala had provided ample opportunity for the development of the equally serious problem of communist penetration. Politically immature, the Guatemalans had not taken the communist threat seriously. Taking advantage of the political turmoil following the 1944 revolution, and using nationalism as a front for its insidious efforts, the communists, though few in number, had managed by the early 1950s to ingratiate themselves into important sectors of the Guatemalan economy and government. Guatemalan leaders and their people had neither the strength, will, or insight to adequately cope with the communist onslaught.

Eventually, of course, the United States had had to take matters into its own hands. It had been a close call, and U.S. officials recognized that fact. In a high-level meeting just a few weeks after the successful U.S.-directed counterrevolution, Secretary Dulles expressed his unease. Another outbreak of the violence which unfortunately had had to be used in settling the Guatemalan situation would "create very serious problems for the United States." In accordance with that view, it was "essential from the United States point of view that there be a period of peace and quiet in Central America." As Dulles put it, "we do feel that a return to normalcy is essential."[1]

Throughout the years 1945–1954, the United States had sought to secure that "peace and quiet" of which Dulles spoke. Of course, U.S. policy during that time had not simply been to hold the line or sustain the status quo. The belief in the advantages (and, by 1945, the sheer necessity) of constructing interdependent political, military, and economic systems had a strong hold on U.S. policymakers. A 1955 NSC publication stated, under the heading "U.S. and Latin American Interdependence," that, "The importance of Latin America to the United States in political, strategic, and economic terms should not require a great amount of documentation."[2] Nor, according to most officials, did it require a great deal of analysis. Military interdependence would secure protection and internal stability for the republics of Central America, while providing a necessary adjunct to U.S. strategic interests in that region, saving it from the necessity and cost of defending the area by itself. Economic interdependence would lead to growth and development for both. Finally, political interdependence—a sharing of the belief in and value of such ideals as democracy, freedom, and justice—would provide a sort of "safety in numbers" from the gravest threat to those ideals, communism. "Peace and quiet" were best accomplished through an intermeshing of interdependent political, military, and economic systems.

U.S. efforts at constructing those systems during the postwar years were very much in evidence in its dealings with Central America—and Latin America as a whole. Military assistance (under the MAP), designed to build reliable, pro-U.S. armed forces in Latin America, increased from just $200,000 in 1952 to $67 million in 1959. Economic assistance also rose, from $19 million in 1952 to $123 million in 1959.[3] The United States also sought to bolster regimes that evidenced the proper concern and attitude toward the communist threat.

In Central America there had been successes. Military assistance to Honduras, according to U.S. officials, had been instrumental in providing some much needed stability and internal order. Aid to the Honduran armed forces had played a role in stopping the spread of political and social instability in 1954, when strikes and political unrest threatened the "peace and quiet" of that nation. This "new" military would not be like that of years past. It would be modernized, imbued with the proper respect for order and stability (through U.S. training and indoctrination), and ready to take its place as a protector of the public good.

In the case of El Salvador, the withholding or granting of economic assistance had seemed to serve its purposes. Facing an increasingly nationalistic government in that nation, U.S. officials had used programs such as Point Four in an attempt to convince the Salvadorans that economic development could best be pursued through interdependent methods. The situation in neighboring Guatemala had forced U.S. policymakers, however reluctantly, to provide El Salvador with technical assistance for industrial development. While this did not correlate with direct U.S. economic interests in El Salvador, it had served the political purposes of showing Guatemala what it was missing by following its radical pathway and keeping Salvadoran nationalists quiet. Yet, once that threat was gone, U.S. aid was directed to where it would do the most good—the increased development of exportable agricultural products and natural resources. Economic interdependence—which relied on the theories of international specialization and comparative advantage—could only be sustained if both partners played their mutually beneficial roles. When El Salvador evidenced that it might want to revise the rules, U.S. aid was cut, and did not appreciably increase until the Salvadoran government embraced U.S. plans for development—under the auspices of the Alliance for Progress—during the early 1960s.

In the battle against communism, the success of U.S. policy was not always so clear. In Nicaragua, the United States acted to support one of the most virulently anticommunist rulers in the hemisphere, Somoza. The decision to work with the dictator, however, was not one easily arrived at. Could U.S. support of dictatorship really be justified? In the end, of course, U.S. officials answered in the affirmative. Somoza was not the best solution, but considering the history and culture of Latin America, and the fact that he did seem to sincerely desire to work with the United States in its Cold War goals, perhaps he was an inevitable compromise. The United States had already seen what "too much democracy" would do in Central America; it did not need another Guatemala.

All in all, by 1954, the United States had reason to be satisfied. The greatest threat to the Central American region—Guatemala—had been beaten, and then rebuilt in the proper image. The militaries of Central America were primarily supplied and trained by U.S. forces; their links to the United States seemed secure. The Central American economies were closely tied to the United States, which remained their best customer. And all of the republics, seeing the example of Guatemala, apparently now grasped the seriousness of the Cold War struggle. Perhaps "peace and quiet" had finally been achieved.

The Fallen Banners

In November 1954, C.D. Jackson—one of the Eisenhower administration's central figures in terms of propaganda and psychological warfare—wrote to Joseph Dodge, then chair of the Council on Foreign Economic Policy. He enclosed part of a study that had been done by Max Millikan and Walt Rostow of MIT concerning U.S. foreign economic programs. He was excited with what it said, and hoped that Dodge would see it as evidence that the Eisenhower administration was willing to "back a sense-making, courageous proposal to the hilt." It was not an entirely optimistic document, however. Written before the success of U.S. efforts in Guatemala and during the final death throes of the French effort in Vietnam, the report referred to the "crisis of 1954" as one that was of "political and psychological" making. The "roots of the crisis lie in the minds of men and women throughout the Free World. They have come to question whether the interests and objectives of the United States conform to their interests and objectives, whether the goals we are pursuing are their goals. This doubt of our purpose makes them hesitate to follow our lead." In sum:

> What increasing numbers of Free World citizens have come to believe is this: the United States regards the danger posed by the Soviet Bloc as a military danger to be dealt with primarily by military means and by repressive devices to secure the American base against Communism. They believe we are preparing to fight a war, with atomic weapons and probably on our initiative. They believe we are stubbornly maintaining hostility and tension and are neglecting possibilities for ameliorating the conflict with the Soviet Bloc by negotiation and diplomacy. They believe we no longer support economic and social advance for the benefit of the common man as the bulwark of democracy but rather seek alliance with any partner, however reactionary, who will pledge military opposition to Russia. In short, in their minds three banners of the Free World have dropped from our hands: the banner of positive faith in the viability of free societies, the banner of widely shared social progress, and the banner of peace itself.[4]

This rather sobering assessment hinted at the crux of the problem as far as U.S. efforts to construct an interdependent world went. While successes were evident and numerous, it seemed that the more the U.S. achieved its goals, the more its allies chafed and complained. Millikan and Rostow might conclude that, "The image, of course, is false," but some U.S. officials had begun to wonder. What they had to face was the fact that the achievement of the U.S. plans for interdependent political, military, and economic structures seemed to be internally contradictory. In essence, they confronted the reality that interdependence, as they defined it, did not always contain the elements of "mutual advantage" so central to its meaning.

The arming of Central American militaries might serve to protect U.S. interests and to maintain a certain stability, but did often repressive and well-armed military forces really bring security to the peoples of Central America, or ease a country's transition to democracy? At the core of the issue was whether the United States could allow "democratic" forces to work in that region if, by their very nature and actions, they threatened to erode the reliability and dependability the United States needed from its military allies.

In the economic realm, U.S. programs, such as Point Four, certainly aided in the U.S. goal of helping to maintain and enlarge the export economies of Central America. This was the primary economic aim of Point Four—to make the Central American region more efficient and effective in producing what the United States needed. Again, however, the mutually advantageous nature of this intercourse did not always become apparent. Could the republics of Central America really find development through increasing the volume of their exportable goods? Would they be able to earn the capital needed for modernization *beyond* the export economy stage? Even U.S. officials were doubtful about this; prices fluctuated wildly, some products were losing their appeal or were being challenged by cheaper products from elsewhere around the world, and the Central American economies did not seem to be growing in any appreciable way. The central issue, however, was whether the development of Central American economies beyond their export-oriented status was really in the best interests of the United States. If it was not, where was the mutually beneficial payoff of interdependence?

In the battle against communism in Central America, U.S. diplomats faced perhaps their most problematic situation. If, as many felt, the democratic forces in that region were not well equipped to battle communist subversion, then what did that leave as an alternative? In the postwar decade, it meant coming to terms with unsavory characters like Somoza. He was certainly anticommunist, his nation maintained a relatively admirable stability, and his professions of friendship and devotion to the

United States were numerous and seemingly sincere. By the early 1950s, there was little doubt among U.S. officials that he was an important factor in keeping the lid on communism's development in Nicaragua. And so there followed significant U.S. military and economic aid, as well as diplomatic pats on the head, such as honorary medals and visits with the president. There was no avoiding the conclusion, however, that Somoza's way of battling communism and maintaining internal stability was to rule through an unscrupulous and often repressive dictatorship. Were, as Millikan and Rostow noted, many of our free world allies right when they charged that the United States would "no longer support economic and social advance for the benefit of the common man as the bulwark of democracy but rather seek alliance with any partner, however reactionary, who will pledge military opposition to Russia"? Were the "banners" of anticommunism and prodemocracy really separate, and was it necessary to drop the latter to carry forward the former? Was the battle against communism of such magnitude that other Central American concerns and aspirations would simply have to wait?

As we have seen, U.S. officials were not oblivious to these apparent contradictions. Indeed, they often debated them at length. Unable or unwilling, however, to examine the issues in depth, they inevitably came to the conclusion that special circumstances in Central America meant that in discussing the mutually beneficial aspects of interdependence, that phrase could become a good deal more elastic than first thought. In essence, they sought to explain why interdependence did not necessarily bring all the benefits to Central America that, in ordinary circumstances, it would.

Normally, for example, military assistance to help modernize and professionalize a nation's armed forces would help that country along the pathway to orderly political development by providing a necessary, but nonpolitical, force for stability. But that was not the situation in Central America. Centuries of rule by incompetent, monarchical Spaniards had left a historical legacy of instability, political backwardness, and rule by force. Culturally, the people of that region seemed content to let a small group of individuals, centered around the church, the military, and the large estate owners, rule in whatever way that pleased them. It did not help, of course, that the peoples of the Central American republics were a bewildering mix of races—Indian, black, Latin, mestizo—that were difficult to assimilate and even more difficult to make into responsible citizens. Even under the most ideal conditions, the road to representative, responsible government was difficult; given the conditions existing in Central America, it would be an even more tortuous advance. What complicated matters, however, was that the postwar political ferment in Central America was bringing a greater and insistent demand for more democratic forms of government. U.S. officials applauded the commitment of the new groups leading these movements—labor, the middle classes, intellectuals—but wondered whether they were truly capable of carrying them to success. In the opinion of these policymakers, it was doubtful. Trying to make democracy grow in such inhospitable soil would only lead to the breakdown of traditional ruling institutions, without replacing them with reliable, sturdy new foundations. Anarchy and chaos might be the result, and in the muddle, nationalist and communist demagogues would have a field day. In this scenario, military assistance became a positive force for democracy. A well trained military would hold the forces of destruction in check, allowing time for the people of Central America to mature and shuck off their centuries of backwardness.

Economic assistance, too, took on a different meaning in Central America. In the language of interdependence, the interconnecting lines of trade and investment between industrialized and underdeveloped nations would rebound to the benefit of all. U.S. economic aid, especially in the war-ravaged world after 1945, would allow all nations to modernize and develop; to enjoy, as the United States did, the fruits of the free market system. Yet, what the United States found after the war was that, unhappy with the slow pace and relatively small investment of U.S. foreign aid, a number of Central American nations were turning to programs of economic nationalism. These were not programs of autarky, but they did demand a greater share and more direction of the foreign trade and investment in their nations. They claimed that their export economies made them dependent and incapable of long-range economic planning; some, like Guatemala, even complained that the economic relationship with the United States reduced them to a near-colonial status. Dismayed, U.S. officials once again reconsidered the meaning of interdependence. What they concluded was that the Central Americans did not really understand the complex economics that made up the world system. Their history preconditioned them to accept statist economic policies, and Spanish misrule had left them with backward and horribly underdeveloped economies. Culturally (and, as some U.S. officials believed, racially), the Central Americans were incapable of building and sustaining the economic systems they desired; real economic development, on the U.S. scale, was far in the future. Nevertheless, the Central Americans—because of their rising expectations, their jealousy over U.S. economic power, and their unwarranted sense of betrayal (as they saw more and more U.S. aid go to Europe and Asia) after the war—were demanding change.

Believing that the region could never rise to the level of the more industrialized powers, and also believing that the economic development of Central America, based on programs of economic nationalism, was not conducive to U.S. interests, the United States responded with programs such as Point Four, which sought to convince the Central Americans that development did not come from policies of economic independence, but rather from more efficiently and effectively performing their well-defined roles in the interdependent world system. In the case of Central America, this meant growing and mining what the U.S. market needed. Point Four would aid in developing healthier and better workers for the mines and plantations; would help in increasing the production of exportable agricultural goods and natural resources; and would seek to develop alternative resources needed by the U.S. market. And though U.S. officials, despite their rhetoric of modernization and growth, were skeptical about the prospects of sustained or equitable economic development in Central America based on such a system, their belief in the necessity of economic interdependence did not leave them much leeway to pursue alternative courses.

In the anticommunist field, U.S. officials faced their most distinct contradiction—supporting dictators such as Somoza in exchange for allegiance to their side in the Cold War. Those policymakers knew what Somoza was, and many decried his regime. Yet, by the early 1950s, again relying on the position that circumstances in Central American changed the framework of interdependence, a growing number of them had come to the conclusion that support of dictatorship in battling communist totalitarianism was not as contradictory as first supposed. Indeed, the support of individuals such as Somoza really did serve the interests of both the United States and Central America. The United States got a trusted ally. And Nicaragua? It got, according to many U.S. policymakers, about what it deserved and/or needed. The Central Americans, basically a politically inert lot, could not grasp the seriousness of the Cold War conflict. They seemed to have no idea that it had an impact on them and their societies; for them, it was just a battle between the United States and the Soviet Union, and they were willing to sit it out. They did not seem to realize that their countries—in political flux, filled with politically immature peoples, and with masses who groaned under horrible economic and social conditions—were fertile fields for the seeds of communist subversion.

Somoza, however, understood. Perhaps he didn't understand all of the political ramifications; perhaps he didn't even completely understand the issues involved in the battle between democracy and communism. What he did understand was that the United States feared the growth of communism in the Western Hemisphere and that its growth in his nation might seriously undermine his regime. He was, therefore, an anti-communist. And in a Central America where communism seemed to have already established a beachhead in Guatemala, that was enough for many U.S. officials. He was also, of course, a dictator. That bothered some, like Braden and others. As the years went by, however, more and more U.S. officials came to the conclusion that Somoza's rule was of a "traditional" Latin American type. He was Nicaragua's "man on a white horse"; there had been many in Nicaragua's past, and there would probably be more after Somoza's departure. This, in fact, was what most Nicaraguans desired—a strong man, who was only relatively corrupt, not overly repressive, and who would lead without bothering them too much. In a way, then, the support of Somoza was part and parcel of the interdependent anticommunist free world system: the United States got what it wanted, and so did Nicaragua.

A Return to Normalcy

All of the U.S. justifications for remolding the meaning of interde-pendence for Central America had one common similarity. All, when the verbiage was stripped away, postulated the need for U.S. guidance and leadership to fully achieve the benefits of interdependence. Interde-pendent economic, political, and military systems were needed by all free world nations. The Central Americans, perhaps, did not quite understand that now, nor were they completely prepared to reap all of the rewards of those systems. In the long run, however, they would come to appreciate their necessity and, with U.S. help, could more fruitfully enjoy their advantages.

When Dulles spoke in 1954 of the need for "a return to normalcy," he did not mean a return to gunboat diplomacy, or to the rather hazy guide-lines of the Good Neighbor, or, most significantly, an abandonment of the theory of interdependence. Faced, for the last decade, with unstable and uncontrollable political developments, economic nationalism (often with an anti-American viewpoint), and a disconcerting disinterest in the Cold War among the republics of Central America, what U.S. policymakers wanted was an acceptance of U.S. guidelines for the development of an interdependent hemispheric (and, by extension, world) system. As we have seen, despite the supposedly collaborationist nature of interdependence, U.S. policymakers had plenty of justifications for pursuing a more unilateral implementation of the programs and systems needed.

Those justifications helped U.S. officials to overlook the apparent contradiction with the very goals interdependence set out to accomplish. While the United States prospered, the Central American nations suffered through underdevelopment, repressive militaries, and vicious dictators.

The United States, of course, cannot bear sole (or perhaps even most) of the responsibility for the political, social, and economic makeup of Central America. It did not create repressive militaries, dictatorships, or underdevelopment in the nations of that area. Indeed, coming out of World War II, it did—sincerely, I believe—attempt to reconstruct the world in such a fashion as to eliminate those burdens bearing down on many underdeveloped nations. Interdependence was the policy it chose to pursue; it promised not only the relief of suffering in other areas of the world, but also great—and necessary—benefits for the United States. The failure of Washington to do much to help the Central Americans achieve the fruits of interdependence was not due to its obsession with anti-communism at the cost of all else; or its inability to stretch its already thinly stretched resources to the relatively unimportant Central American region; or the fact that the goals announced by U.S. policymakers were ridiculously unattainable. It failed because interdependence, at least as they defined it, could never achieve its idealistic goals in Central America. It failed because, despite the internationalistic rhetoric they used, most U.S. officials could never wholeheartedly support an interdependence that threatened what they perceived as definite nationalistic interests of the United States. It failed, in essence, because interdependence—guided and defined, as it necessarily had to be, by the United States—could never quite surmount the fact that there were inescapable contradictions between what the United States needed and what Central America needed. As they struggled against those contradictions during the postwar period, U.S. policymakers discovered that the chains of interdependence, designed to link nations in a mutually beneficial fashion, could also bind and hobble them in their search for a better world.

Notes

1. Memcon, 18 Aug. 1954, RG 59, Records of OMAA, Costa Rica and Nicaragua, Box 3, 1954–Relations with U.S. file, NA.

2. "Latin America—as a Demonstration Area of U.S. Foreign Policy in Action," contained in "Psychological Aspects of United States Strategy: Source Book of Individual Papers," Nov. 1955, Documents of the NSC: Third Suppl., reel 3.

3. Lieuwen, *Arms and Politics*, 202; "U.S. Economic Assistance Programs Administered by the Agency for International Development and Predecessor Agencies, April 3, 1948–June 30, 1971," 29 Feb. 1972, Huntington Papers, Box 5, AID: U.S. Economic Assistance Programs, 1948–1971 file, HSTL.

4. Millikan and Rostow, "Proposal for a New United States Foreign Economic Policy," n.d., enclosed in Jackson to Dodge, 24 Nov. 1954, Records of CFEP, Chairman, Dodge Series: Subject Subseries, Box 2, Economic Policy (2) file, DDEL.

Bibliography

PRIMARY SOURCES

Manuscript Collections

Archives of the Council on Foreign Relations, New York, New York
  Records of Groups, 1945–1954
Dwight D. Eisenhower Library, Abilene, Kansas
  Dwight D. Eisenhower, Papers as President (Ann Whitman File)
  Dwight D. Eisenhower, Records as President, White House Central
    Files, 1953–1961
  Papers of John Foster Dulles
  Records of the President's Citizen Advisors on the Mutual
    Security Program (Fairless Committee), 1956–1957
  Records of the President's Commission on Foreign Economic
    Policy (Randall Commission)
  Records of the President's Commission to Study the U.S.
    Military Assistance Program
  Records of the U.S. Council on Foreign Economic Policy,
    Office of the Chairman
  White House Office, Papers of the National Security Council
    Staff, 1948–1961
Edward Ginn Library, The Fletcher School of Law and Diplomacy,
    Tufts University, Medford, Massachusetts
  Diplomatic Papers of John Moors Cabot (microfilm)
Seeley G. Mudd Manuscript Library, Department of Rare Books
    and Special Collections, Princeton University Libraries, Princeton,
    New Jersey
  Papers of John Foster Dulles
  Papers of Whiting Willauer
Harry S. Truman Library, Independence, Missouri
  Papers of Stanley Andrews
  Papers of Thomas C. Blaisdell, Jr.
  Papers of Benjamin Hardy

Papers of Albert Huntington
Papers of Edward G. Miller
Papers of Richard C. Patterson, Jr.
Papers of Harry S. Truman, Papers as President of the United
    States, White House Central Files, 1945–1953
Records of the President's Materials Policy Commission

Oral Histories

Dwight D. Eisenhower Library, Abilene, Kansas
  Robert R. Bowie
  Ellis Briggs
  Arthur Burnes
  Milton Eisenhower
  Dennis FitzGerald
  John Stambaugh
Harry S. Truman Library, Independence, Missouri
  Stanley Andrews
  George Elsey
  Lincoln Gordon
  John Ohly

Government Documents

National Security Council
  Documents of the National Security Council: First and Third
    Supplements (Microfilm) (University Publications of America,
    Bethesda, Maryland)
National Archives, Washington, DC
  Record Group 43. Records of United States Participation in
      International Conferences, Commissions, and Expositions
      Records of the Organization of American States, 1949–1960
  Record Group 59. General Records of the Department of State
    Decimal File, 1945–1954
    Office Files of the Assistant Secretary of State for Inter-
    American Affairs (Edward G. Miller), 1949–1953
    Records of the Assistant Secretary of State for Inter-
    American Affairs: Records of Henry F. Holland

Records of the Deputy Assistant Secretaries of State for Inter-American Affairs, Subject File, 1945–1956

Records of the Office of American Republic Affairs, 1918–1947

Records of the Office of Intelligence Research

Records of the Office of Middle American Affairs, 1951–1956: Miscellaneous Records

Records of the Office of Middle American Affairs: Records Relating to Costa Rica and Nicaragua, 1951–1955

Records of the Office of Middle American Affairs: Records Relating to El Salvador and Guatemala, 1952–1954

Records of the Office of Middle American Affairs: Subject File, 1947–1956

Records of the Office of Regional American Affairs, Bureau of Inter-American Affairs (Mutual Security Program Budget Files), 1951–1955

Records of the Policy Planning Staff, 1947–1953

Record Group 84. Records of the Foreign Service Posts of the Department of State

Record Group 151. Records of the Bureau of Foreign and Domestic Commerce

Record Group 218. Records of the Joint Chiefs of Staff

Geographic File, 1951–1953

Central Decimal File, 1951–1953

Record Group 330. Records of the Office of the Secretary of Defense

Assistant Secretary of Defense (International Security Affairs), Office of Military Aid Programs: Operations Division: Control Branch, Subject File, 1950–1953

Record Group 353. Records of the Department of State: Interdepartmental and Intradepartmental Committees

Inter-American Economic Affairs Committee, 1945–1950

Records of Interdepartmental and Intradepartmental Committees, 1943–1951

U.S. Department of Commerce. *Annual Report of the Secretary of Commerce*, 1946–1955. Washington, DC: Government Printing Office, 1946–1955.

————. *Factors Limiting U.S. Investment Abroad: Part 1—Survey of Factors in Foreign Countries*. Washington, DC: Government Printing Office, 1953.

U.S. Department of State. *Foreign Relations of the United States*, 1945–1954. Washington, DC: Government Printing Office, 1967–1983.

BOOKS AND ARTICLES

Abel, Christopher, and Colin M. Lewis, eds. *Latin America, Economic Imperialism and the State: The Political Economy of the External Connection from Independence to the Present*. London: The Athlone Press, 1985.

Acker, Alison. *Honduras: The Making of a Banana Republic*. Boston: South End Press, 1988.

Albert, Bill. *South America and the First World War: The Impact of the War on Brazil, Argentina, Peru and Chile*. Cambridge: Cambridge University Press, 1988.

Ameringer, Charles D. *The Democratic Left in Exile: The Antidictatorial Struggle in the Caribbean, 1945–1959*. Coral Gables, FL: University of Miami Press, 1974.

————. *Don Pepe: A Political Biography of José Figueres of Costa Rica*. Albuquerque: University of New Mexico Press, 1978.

Anderson, Thomas. *Matanza: El Salvador's Communist Revolt of 1932*. Lincoln: University of Nebraska Press, 1971.

Armstrong, Robert, and Janet Shenk. *El Salvador: The Face of Revolution*. Boston: South End Press, 1982.

Arnson, Cynthia. *El Salvador: A Revolution Confronts the United States*. Washington, D.C.: Institute for Policy Studies, 1982.

Aybar, José M. *The Guatemalan Agrarian Reform of 1952: An Abortive Challenge to United States Dominance and the Prelude to United States Intervention in 1954*. Ann Arbor, MI: University Microfilms International, 1978.

Baily, Samuel L. *The United States and the Development of South America, 1945–1975*. New York: New Viewpoints, 1976.

Baldwin, David A. *Economic Development and American Foreign Policy, 1943–1962*. Chicago: University of Chicago Press, 1966.

Baloyra, Enrique. *El Salvador in Transition.* Chapel Hill, NC: University of North Carolina Press, 1982.

Barber, Willard, and C. Neale Ronning. *International Security and Military Power: Counterinsurgency and Civic Action in Latin America.* Athens, OH: Ohio State University Press, 1966.

Becerra, Longino. "The Early History of the Labor Movement," in *Honduras: Portrait of a Captive Nation,* eds. Nancy Peckenham and Annie Street. New York: Praeger Publishers, 1985.

Bermann, Karl. *Under the Big Stick: Nicaragua and the United States Since 1848.* Boston: South End Press, 1986

Bingham, Jonathan B. *Shirt-Sleeve Diplomacy: Point 4 in Action.* New York: The John Day Company, 1953.

Black, George. *Garrison Guatemala.* New York: Monthly Review Press, 1984.

Blasier, Cole. *The Hovering Giant: U.S. Responses to Revolutionary Change in Latin America, 1910–1985.* Rev. ed. Pittsburgh: University of Pittsburgh Press, 1985.

Blum, Robert M. *Drawing the Line: The Origin of the American Containment Policy in East Asia.* New York: W.W. Norton, 1982.

Bulmer-Thomas, Victor. *The Political Economy of Central America Since 1920.* Cambridge: Cambridge University Press, 1987.

Calvert, Peter. *Guatemala: A Nation in Turmoil.* Boulder, CO: Westview Press, 1985.

Child, John. *Unequal Alliance: The Inter-American Military System, 1938–1978.* Boulder, CO: Westview Press, 1980.

Cook, Blanche Wiesen. *The Declassified Eisenhower: A Divided Legacy.* Garden City, NY: Doubleday, 1981.

Crawley, Eduardo. *Dictators Never Die: A Portrait of Nicaragua and the Somozas.* New York: St. Martin's Press, 1979.

Daniels, Walter M., ed. *The Point Four Program.* New York: The H.W. Wilson Company, 1951.

Diederich, Bernard. *Somoza and the Legacy of U.S. Involvement in Central America.* New York: E.P. Dutton, 1981.

Duignan, Peter, and L. H. Gann, *The United States and Africa: A History.* New York: Cambridge University Press, 1984.

Dunkerley, James. *The Long War: Dictatorship and Revolution in El Salvador*. London: Verso, 1985.

Erb, Claude C. "Prelude to Point Four: The Institute of Inter-American Affairs." *Diplomatic History* 9 (1985):249–69.

Etchison, Don L. *The United States and Militarism in Central America*. New York: Praeger Publishers, 1975.

Feinberg, Richard, and Robert A. Pastor. "Far From Hopeless: An Economic Program for Post-War Central America," in *Central America: Anatomy of Conflict*, ed. Robert S. Leiken. New York: Pergamon Press, 1984.

Findling, John E. *Close Neighbors, Distant Friends: United States–Central American Relations*. New York: Greenwood Press, 1987.

Fitzgibbon, Russell H. "'Continuismo' in Central America," *The Inter-American Quarterly* 2 (July 1940): 56–74.

Gleijeses, Piero. *Shattered Hope: The Guatemalan Revolution and the United States, 1944–1954*. Princeton, NJ: Princeton University Press, 1991.

Glick, Philip. *The Administration of Technical Assistance: Growth in the Americas*. Chicago: University of Chicago Press, 1957.

Green, David. *The Containment of Latin America: A History of Myths and Realities of the Good Neighbor Policy*. Chicago: Quadrangle, 1971.

———. "The Cold War Comes to Latin America." In *Politics and Policies of the Truman Administration*, ed. Barton Bernstein. Chicago: Quadrangle Books, 1970:149–195.

Grieb, Kenneth. *Guatemalan Caudillo: The Regime of Jorge Ubico: Guatemala, 1931–1944*. Athens, OH: Ohio University Press, 1979.

———. "American Involvement in the Rise of Jorge Ubico." *Caribbean Studies* 10, no. 1 (April 1970):5–21.

Haines, Gerald K. *The Americanization of Brazil: A Study of U.S. Cold War Diplomacy in the Third World, 1945–1954*. Wilmington, DE: Scholarly Resources, Inc., 1989.

Handy, Jim. *Gift of the Devil: A History of Guatemala*. Boston: South End Press, 1984.

Hess, Gary R. *The U.S. Emergence as a Southeast Asian Power, 1940–1950*. New York: Columbia University Press, 1986.

Hogan, Michael. *The Marshall Plan: America, Britain and the Reconstruction of Western Europe, 1947–1952*. New York: Cambridge University Press, 1987.

Hovey, Harold A. *United States Military Assistance: A Study of Policies and Practices*. New York: Frederick A. Praeger, Publishers, 1966.

Immerman, Richard H. *The CIA in Guatemala: The Foreign Policy of Intervention*. Austin, TX: University of Texas Press, 1982.

Kamman, William. *A Search for Stability: United States Diplomacy Toward Nicaragua, 1925–1933*. Notre Dame, IN: University of Notre Dame Press, 1968.

Kaufman, Burton I. *Trade and Aid: Eisenhower's Foreign Economic Policy, 1953–1961*. Baltimore: The Johns Hopkins University Press, 1982.

Krenn, Michael L. *U.S. Policy Toward Economic Nationalism in Latin America, 1917–1929*. Wilmington, DE: Scholarly Resources, Inc., 1990.

———. "By the Numbers: The Use of Statistics in U.S. Policy Toward Latin America During the 1950s." *The SHAFR Newsletter* 21, No. 1 (March 1990):7–17.

LaFeber, Walter. *Inevitable Revolutions: The United States in Central America*. New York: W.W. Norton, 1984.

Leffler, Melvyn. *A Preponderance of Power: National Security, the Truman Administration, and the Cold War, 1945–1952*. Stanford: Stanford University Press, 1992.

Leonard, Thomas M. *Central America and the United States: The Search for Stability*. Athens, GA: The University of Georgia Press, 1991.

———. *The United States and Central America, 1944–1949*. University, AL: The University of Alabama Press, 1984.

Lewontin, Steve. "'A Blessed Peace': Honduras Under Carías," in *Honduras: Portrait of a Captive Nation*, eds. Nancy Peckenham and Annie Street. New York: Praeger Publishers, 1985.

Lieuwen, Edwin. *Arms and Politics in Latin America*. New York: Frederick A. Praeger, 1961.

Longley, Kyle. "Resistance and Accommodation: The United States
and the Nationalism of José Figueres, 1953–1957." *Diplomatic
History* 18, No. 1 (Winter 1994):1–28.

Louis, William Roger. *The British Empire in the Middle East,
1945–1951*. New York: Oxford University Press, 1984.

MacCameron, Robert. *Bananas, Labor, and Politics in Honduras:
1954–1963*. Syracuse, NY: Maxwell School of Citizenship
and Public Affairs, Syracuse University, 1983.

Marks, Frederick, III. "The CIA and Castillo Armas in Guatemala,
1954: New Clues to an Old Puzzle." *Diplomatic History* 14
(1990):67–86.

Martz, John D. *Central America: The Crisis and the Challenge*.
Chapel Hill, NC: University of North Carolina Press, 1959.

McCamant, John. *Development Assistance in Latin America*. New
York: Frederick A. Praeger, 1968.

McCormick, Thomas. *America's Half-Century: United States
Foreign Policy in the Cold War*. Baltimore: The Johns Hopkins
University Press, 1989.

Millett, Richard. *Guardians of the Dynasty*. New York: Orbis
Books, 1977.

Montgomery, Tommie C. "El Salvador: The Roots of Revolution,"
in *Central America: Crisis and Adaptation*, eds. Steve C.
Ropp and James A. Morris. Albuquerque: University of New
Mexico Press, 1984.

Morris, James A. *Honduras: Caudillo Politics and Military
Rulers*. Boulder, CO: Westview, 1984.

Morris, James A., and Steve C. Ropp, "Corporatism and Dependent
Development." *Latin American Research Review* 12, No. 2
(Summer 1977):31–42.

National Planning Association. *Technical Cooperation in Latin
America: Recommendations for the Future*. Washington, DC:
National Planning Association, 1956.

Noer, Thomas J. *Cold War and Black Liberation: The United
States and White Rule in Africa, 1948–1968*. Columbia, MO:
University of Missouri Press, 1985.

North, Liisa. *Bitter Grounds: Roots of Revolt in El Salvador*.
Westport, CT: Lawrence Hill & Co., 1985.

Pach, Chester J., Jr. "The Containment of U.S. Military Aid to Latin America, 1944–49." *Diplomatic History* 6 (1982):225–43.

——. *Arming the Free World: The Origins of the United Military Assistance Program, 1945–1950.* Chapel Hill: The University of North Carolina Press, 1991.

Painter, David S. *Oil and the American Century: The Political Economy of U.S. Foreign Oil Policy, 1941–1954.* Baltimore: Johns Hopkins University Press, 1986.

Park, James William. *Latin American Underdevelopment: A History of Perspectives in the United States, 1870–1965.* Baton Rouge: Louisiana State University Press, 1995.

Parkinson, F. *Latin America, the Cold War, and the World Powers, 1945–1973.* Beverly Hills, CA: Sage Publishers, 1974.

Parkman, Patricia. *Nonviolent Insurrection in El Salvador: The Fall of Maximiliano Hernández Martínez.* Tucson: University of Arizona Press, 1988.

Pastor, Robert A. *Condemned to Repetition: The United States and Nicaragua.* Princeton, NJ: Princeton University Press, 1987.

Paterson, Thomas G. *Meeting the Communist Threat: Truman to Reagan.* New York: Oxford University Press, 1988.

——. "Foreign Aid Under Wraps: The Point Four Program." *Wisconsin Magazine of History* 56 (Winter 1972–1973):119–26.

Pérez, Louis A., Jr. "International Dimensions of Inter-American Relations, 1944–1960." Inter-*American Economic Affairs* 27:1 (1973):47–68.

Perez-Brignoli, Hector. *A Brief History of Central America.* Trans. by Ricardo B. Sawrey A. and Susana Stettri de Sawrey. Berkeley: University of California Press, 1989.

Rabe, Stephen G. "Inter-American Military Cooperation, 1944–1951." *World Affairs* 137 (Fall 1974): 132–49.

——. "The Elusive Conference: United States Relations with Latin America, 1945–1952," *Diplomatic History* 2 (1978):279–94.

——. "Eisenhower and Latin America: Arms and Dictators," *Peace and Change* 11 (Spring 1985): 49–61.

——. *Eisenhower and Latin America: The Foreign Policy of Anticommunism.* Chapel Hill, NC: University of North Carolina Press, 1988.

——. "The Clues Didn't Check Out: Commentary on 'The CIA and Castillo Armas.'" *Diplomatic History* 14 (1990):87–95.

Randall, Stephen J. *Colombia and the United States: Hegemony and Interdependence.* Athens, GA: University of Georgia Press, 1992.

Ropp, Steve C. "The Honduran Army in the Sociopolitical Evolution of the Honduran State," *The Americas* 30, No. 4 (April 1974):504–528.

Rotter, Andrew J. *The Path to Vietnam: Origins of the American Commitment to Southeast Asia.* Ithaca, NY: Cornell University Press, 1987.

Schaller, Michael. *The American Occupation of Japan: The Origins of the Cold War in Asia.* New York: Oxford University Press, 1985.

Schlesinger, Stephen, and Stephen Kinzer. *Bitter Fruit: The Untold Story of the American Coup in Guatemala.* Garden City, NY: Anchor Books, 1983.

Schmitter, Philippe C. *Autonomy or Dependence as Regional Integration Outcomes: Central America.* Berkeley, CA: Institute of International Studies, 1972.

Schnabel, James F. *The History of the Joint Chiefs of Staff: The Joint Chiefs of Staff and National Policy, Vol. I, 1945–1947.* Washington, DC: Historical Division, Joint Secretariat, Joint Chiefs of Staff, 1979.

Schulz, Donald, and Deborah Sundloff Schulz, eds. *The United States, Honduras, and the Crisis in Central America.* Boulder, CO: Westview Press, 1994.

Smith, Gaddis. *The Last Years of the Monroe Doctrine, 1945–1993.* New York: Hill and Wang, 1994.

Steward, Dick. *Money, Marines, and Mission: Recent U.S.–Latin American Policy.* Lanham, MD: University Press of America, 1980.

Stiller, Jesse H. *George Messersmith: Diplomat of Democracy.* Chapel Hill, NC: The University of North Carolina Press, 1987.

Tancer, Shoshana. *Economic Nationalism in Latin America: The Quest for Economic Independence.* New York: Praeger Publishers, 1976.

Trask, Roger. "George F. Kennan's Report on Latin America (1950)." *Diplomatic History* 2 (1978):307–311.

——. "The Impact of the Cold War on United States–Latin American Relations, 1945–49." *Diplomatic History* 1 (1977):271–84.

Walter, Knut. *The Regime of Anastasio Somoza, 1936–1956.* Chapel Hill, NC: The University of North Carolina Press, 1993.

Watson, Robert J. *The History of the Joint Chiefs of Staff: The Joint Chiefs of Staff and National Policy, Vol. V: 1953–1954.* Washington, DC: Historical Division, Joint Secretariat, Joint Chiefs of Staff, 1986.

Wood, Bryce. *The Dismantling of the Good Neighbor Policy.* Austin, TX: University of Texas Press, 1985.

Index

Michael L. Krenn is an Associate Professor of History and Associate Chair of the Department of History at the University of Miami, where he has taught since 1985. He received his Ph.D. from Rutgers University in 1985, studying under the guidance of Lloyd C. Gardner. His first book, *U.S. Policy Toward Economic Nationalism in Latin America, 1917–1929*, was published in 1990. His articles have appeared in *Diplomatic History*, *The SHAFR Newsletter*, *SECOLAS Annals*, *Radical History Review*, and *Nature, Society and Thought*. He is currently working on a study of African-Americans and the Department of State, 1945–1969.